6,95
3/24

D0558566

SERGIUS BOLSHAKOFF

RUSSIAN   MYSTICS

RUSSIAN MYSTICS

by

SERGIUS BOLSHAKOFF

Introduction
by

THOMAS MERTON

Cistercian Publications
Kalamazoo, Michigan
1980

© Cistercian Publications, Inc. 1976

Cistercian Publications, Inc.
WMU Station
Kalamazoo, Michigan 49008

ISBN (case) 0 87907 826 X
ISBN (paper) 0 87907 926 6

Available in Britain and Europe
from A. R. Mowbray & Co Ltd.
St Thomas House Becket Street
Oxford OX1 1 SJ

Library of Congress Catalogue Card Number: 76-15485

Printed in the United States of America

The Editors of Cistercian Publications
dedicate this edition
to
Father Panteleimon
and his disciples at the Skete of the Holy Transfiguration
who are implanting in America today in living reality
all that Sergius Bolshakoff
has sought to bring to the West.

CONTENTS

PREFACE

THE AUTHOR OF THIS UNUSUAL BOOK has given it much too modest a title. It is in fact not only an introduction to the lives, the spirituality and the writings of great mystics, many of whom are unknown in the West, but it is also at the same time a clear and practical outline of Russian monastic history. The journey which the reader now begins is not without excitement, for it takes him into new territory, the silence of the great Russian forests which Konstantin Paustovsky has described with such mastery in his autobiography.

Russian mysticism is predominantly monastic (though one may in passing regret that we do not meet in these pages such modern non-monastic mystics as Fr Yelchaninov). It therefore thrives in solitude and renunciation of the world. Yet anyone who has even the most superficial acquaintance with Russian Christendom is aware that the monasteries of Russia, even more than those of the West, exercised a crucially important influence on society, whether as centers of spiritual life and transformation to which pilgrims flocked from everywhere, or as bases for missionary expansion or, finally, as powerful social forces sometimes manipulated—or suppressed—for political advantage. Such struggles as those between St Nilus of Sora and St Joseph of Volokolamsk (barely suggested here) speak eloquently of the age-old conflict, within monasticism itself, between the charismatic drive to solitary contemplation plus charismatic pastoral action, and the institutional drive to fit the monastic community into a structure of organized socio-religious power, as a center of liturgy and education and as a nursery of bishops.

Other conflicts, such as that between Eastern Orthodox spirituality and Westernizing influences, play an important part in the lives of the monks and mystics of Russia. Many readers will be surprised to learn what a great part Western theological attitudes and devotions played in the formation of St Tikhon. The seminary which Tikhon attended was organized on the Jesuit pattern and yet he was not influenced by post-Tridentine Catholic thought. Dr Bolshakoff identifies him rather with German pietism. In any case, we must not be too quick to assume that St Tikhon's spirituality is purely and ideally "Russian." Yet paradoxically this combination of Western and Eastern holiness is a peculiarly Russian phenomenon. St Tikhon was perhaps the greatest mystic of the age of rationalist enlightenment.

Russian mysticism is to be traced largely to the greatest monastic center of Orthodox mysticism, Mount Athos. Ever since the eleventh century the Russian monastic movement had been nourished by direct contact with the "Holy Mountain"—interrupted only by the Tartar invasions of the Middle Ages. Liturgy, asceticism and mysticism in Russia owed their development in great part not to literary documents but to the living experience of pilgrim monks who spent a certain time at Athos, either in the "Rossikon" (the Russian monastery of St Panteleimon) or in various sketes (groups of small cottages around a monastery) and cells, before returning to found new monasteries or renew the life of old ones in their country. Periods when, for one reason or another, communication with Athos has diminished, have also been periods of monastic decline in Russia.

One of the characteristic fruits of Russian monachism on Athos is the "Prayer of Jesus," the constant repetition of a short formula in conjunction with rhythmic breathing and with deep faith in the supernatural power of the Holy Name. This was a Russian development of the Greek Hesychast way of prayer taught by St Gregory Palamas. The "Prayer of

Jesus" became the normal way of contemplative prayer in
Russian monasticism but, more important still, it was adopted on all sides by devout lay-people especially among the
masses of the poor peasantry.

Until recently, Western theologians were highly suspicious
of Athonite "Hesychasm" and regarded it as perilous, even
heretical. Deeper study and a wider acquaintance with non-
Western forms of spirituality have made Hesychasm seem a
little less outlandish. It is now no longer necessary to repeat
the outraged platitudes of those who thought that the Hesychasts were practising self-hypnosis, or who believed that, at
best, the monks of Athos were engaged in a kind of Western
Yoga.

The "Prayer of Jesus," made known to Western readers by
the "Tale of the Pilgrim," surely one of the great classics of
the literature of prayer, is now practised not only by charac-
ters in Salinger's novels, but even at times by some Western
monks. Needless to say that a way of prayer for which, in its
land of origin, the direction of a "staretz" was mandatory, is
not safely to be followed by us in the West without profes-
sional direction.

The mystical Russian "pilgrim" received from his staretz an
anthology of Patristic quotations on prayer: the famous
Philokalia. One of the most interesting chapters of Dr
Bolshakoff's book deals with Paisius Velichkovsky
(1722-1794) who, after living for some time in a skete on
Mount Athos during a period of monastic decline, translated
the *Philokalia* into Slavonic and introduced it to Russia. It
was then done into Russian by another mystic, Bishop
Theophane the Recluse.

Paisius and his disciples also translated other works of the
Fathers and in addition to this exercised a direct and living
influence on Russian monachism through the numerous pilgrims who constantly visited the monasteries reformed by
him in Moldavia and Walachia. Here the faithful from all
parts of Russia encountered not only a pure and austere
monastic discipline but also the spiritual direction of special-
ists in asceticism and Hesychast prayer, who came to be
known as *Startzy.* The translations of the *Philokalia,* the

monastic reform of Paisius, and especially *Starchestvo*, the direction of the Startzy, set in motion the great development that was to make the nineteenth century the golden age of Russian mysticism. This was also the time when the Rossikon on Mount Athos reached its peak in numbers, fervor and prosperity.

One of the best known (or least unknown) of the Russian mystics is St Seraphim of Sarov who lived the life of a desert Father in the forests at the beginning of the nineteenth century. He affords a striking contrast to other post-medieval saints and ascetics who have tried to imitate the Desert Fathers. In many of these, together with a sincere ascetic and monastic purpose and devotion to authentic ideals, we seem to encounter a spirit of willfulness that is often violent and artificial even to the point of obsession. As a result we find a negative, gloomy and tense spirituality in which one is not sure whether the dominant note is hatred of wickedness or love of good—and hatred of wickedness can so easily include hatred of human beings who are perhaps less wicked than they seem. The study of ascetic tradition and the passion for austerity do not suffice by themselves to make monastic saints, although it must be admitted that a specious "humanism" which turns its back on all austerity and solitude is hardly more effective in this regard!

Whether or not Seraphim had studied ancient monastic tradition, it is certain that he was a living and spontaneous exemplar of the most authentic monastic ideal. His solitary life in the forest was extremely austere and yet his spirituality was marked by pure joy. Though he gave himself unsparingly to each ascetic exploit (*podvig*) he remained simple, child-like, meek, astonishingly open to life and to other men, gentle and profoundly compassionate.

He is without doubt the greatest mystic of the Russian Church, and the Hesychast tradition is evident in his mysticism of light. Yet Hesychasm is, so to speak, absorbed in the Evangelical and Patristic purity of his experience of the great Christian mystery, the presence of the Spirit given by God through the Risen Christ to his Body, the Church. Seraphim's simplicity reminds us in may ways of St Francis of Assisi though his life was more like that of St Anthony of the Desert. But like every other great contemplative saint, Seraphim had his eyes wide open to the truth of the Gospel, and could not understand how the rest of men could be content with an "enlightenment" that was in reality nothing but ignorance and spiritual blindness. The only contemporary figure in the West who speaks so eloquently and with such ingenuous amazement of the divine light shining in darkness, is the English poet, William Blake. But there is in Seraphim none of Blake's gnosticism: only the pure and traditional theology of the Church.

Seraphim of Sarov is then the most perfect example of that mysticism of light which is characteristic of the Orthodox Church: completely positive and yet compatible with, indeed based on, the apophatic (negative) theology of Pseudo Dionysius and St Maximus the Confessor. It is perhaps this which distinguishes Russian mysticism in its pure state. Not an intellectualist and negative ascent to the Invisible above all that is visible, but more paradoxically an apprehension of the invisible as visible in so far as all creation is suddenly experienced as trasfigured in a light for which there is no accounting in terms of any philosophy, a light which is given directly by God, procedes from God, and in a sense *is* the Divine Light. Yet this experience is not a substantial vision of God because in Oriental theology the light experienced by the mystic is a divine "energy," distinct from God's nature but which can be apprehended in contact with the *Person* of the Holy Spirit, by mystical love and grace.

Thus it is easy to see that though there are on record some instances of a negative mysticism comparable to the Dark Night in St John of the Cross (and the author mentions several here) yet they are not characteristic of Russian mystical theology, which is a theology not of suffering but of transfiguration.

Nevertheless, this theology of resurrection and joy is firmly based on repentance and on tears, and one does not easily find in it the impertinences of a devout sentimentality which simply assumes that "everything is bound to turn out all right." The reality of redemption and transfiguration depends on the most basic experience of the evil of sin.

Not all the Russian mystics were able to experience this evil as totally consumed in the flames of redemptive Love. Bishop Ignatius Brianchaninov, an aristocrat and an army engineer converted to the monastic life, looked out upon the world with profound pessimism. The world of matter was not, for him, transfigured by the divine light: it was purely and simply the subject of corruption. For him (as for so many others in the nineteenth century) science and religion were in conflict, and to know Christ one had to reject all earthly knowledge as false and totally misleading. And yet, as Dr Bolshakoff points out, science does nevertheless contribute something of positive value to the meditations of Bishop Brianchaninov. However, we observe with regret in Brianchaninov a tendency to impose a kind of unnatural constraint upon the body and the mind, and we are not surprised when he informs us that he considers visions of devils rather a usual thing in the monastic life. His pessimism and suspicion toward women as such blend with the rest of his dark view of things. Yet, even where his negative attitude repels us, we must admit he often displays remarkable psychological insight. All in all Brianchaninov is too rigid, too suspicious of the light, too closed to ordinary human experience to impress us as St Seraphim does. And yet it would seem that the negativism of Brianchaninov had a deeper influence on nineteenth-century Russian monasticism than the marvelous Gospel optimism of St Seraphim. Dr Bolshakoff gives us rather copious quotations from Brianchaninov and they will help us to understand the conservative reaction of Leontiev and of the monks of Optino against Dostoievski's idealized and forward-looking portrait of Staretz Zosima.

This portrait was supposed to have been based on the living figure of Staretz Ambrose of Optino, but the monks in general rejected its optimism, its "humanism," as untrue to the genuine monastic tradition of Russia. Perhaps the generality of monks were more disposed to look at life through the embittered and blazing eyes of the fanatical ascetic, Ferrapont, in whom Dostoievski himself evidently intended to attack the kind of negativism typified by the old school, the critics and opponents of the Startzy.

It is curious that the Russian revolution was preceded not by a century of monastic decadence and torpor, but by a monastic Golden Age. But if the term "Golden Age" is to mean anything, it must mean a time of vitality. Vitality means variety and this, in turn, may imply conflict. Even in the serene pages of this book which views its subject in its overall unity, we detect the interplay of various conflicting forces in Russian monasticism. There is darkness and light, world-denial and loving affirmation of human values, a general hardening of resistance to forces of atheist humanism and revolution and yet an anguished concern at the sinful oppression of the poor. We cannot with justice dismiss the whole Russian monastic movement as negative, pessimistic, world-hating. Nor can we identify its deep and traditional contemplative aspirations with mere political or cultural conservatism. There was an unquestionably prophetic spirit at work in the movement, and St Seraphim is only one among many examples that prove this. There was also a profound concern for "the world" and for humanity, a wonderful, unequalled compassion that reached out to all mankind and indeed to all living creatures, to embrace them in God's love and in merciful concern. It cannot be doubted that the great Startzy, in their humane and tender simplicity, were sometimes completely identified with the humble and the poor. It would be ludicrous to class them as obscurantists and reactionaries.

On the other hand, there was a less prophetic, but none the less amazing spirit of ascetic fervor, of discipline, of order, which, while it was undeniably one of the things that made the age "Golden," still had rather more human and even political implications. And here monasticism was, indeed, more deeply involved in social structures and national aspirations, even where it most forcefully asserted its hatred of "the world." Here, too, contempt for the world and pessimistic rigorism were in fact inseparable from social and political conservatism. The ascetic who renounced the city of man in order to lament his sins in the *Poustyna* (desert) may well have been giving his support to a condition of social inertia by implicitly affirming that all concern with improvement was futile and even sinful. We may cite as an example Constantin Leontiev, Dostoievsky's adversary and critic, who entered a monastery, gloried in extreme austerity, and doubtless expressed monastic views that were those of most monks of the time.

Leontiev actually stated that the Orthodoxy on Mount Athos depended on the peaceful and harmonious interaction of Turkish political power, Russian wealth and Greek ecclesiastical authority. Most of his compatriots, monks included, were probably too nationalistic to follow this "realist" view all the way.[1] They were Panslavist and therefore anti-Greek as well as anti-Western. But the point is that their monastic fervor formed part of a complex Russian nationalist mystique and contributed much energy to it. The average good monk, who was not raised by sanctity above this level, tended to identify himself and his religious ideal with this mystique of Russia. It would be interesting to compare this with the ideas of such lay theologians as Soloviev who was very open to Rome and the West, but space does not permit us to do so here.

This is a book that becomes more absorbing as it progresses, and the most interesting pages are those which deal with the Startzy of the last hundred and fifty years. Their doctrine is rich in monastic wisdom, as well as in ordinary religious psychology and plain good sense. It is interesting to see that they were concerned with many traditional monastic problems which are being rather warmly discussed in Western monasteries today. The answers of the Startzy can be of special value to Western monks who are interested in discovering the deepest meaning of their monastic vocation, and ways to live that vocation more perfectly.

1. See Igor Smolitsch, "Le Mont Athos et la Russie" in *Le Millénaire du Mont Athos,* Chevetogne (Belgium), 1963, p. 299. Smolitsch calls this opinion of Leontiev a "somewhat unusual estimate."

The reason for this is perhaps simpler than one might expect. It is not so much that the Startzy were exceptionally austere men, or that they had acquired great learning, but that they had surrendered themselves completely to the demands of the Gospel and to evangelical charity, totally forgetting themselves in obedience to the Spirit of God so that they lived as perfect Christians, notable above all for their humility, their meekness, their openness to all men, their apparently inexhaustible capacity for patient and compassionate love. The purpose of Starchestve is then not so much to make use of daily spiritual direction in order to inculcate a special method of prayer, but rather to keep the heart of the disciple open to love, to prevent it from hardening in self-centered concern (whether moral, spiritual or ascetical). All the worst sins are denials and rejections of love, refusals to love. The chief aim of the Staretz is first to teach his disciple not to sin against love, then to enourage and assist his growth in love until he becomes a saint. This total surrender to the power of love was the sole basis of their spiritual authority, and on this basis the Startzy demanded complete and unquestioning obedience. They could do so because they themselves never resisted the claims and demands of charity.

One cannot refrain from observing, in this connection, how much Pope John XXIII displayed this same charismatic and evangelical openness. His life as pope is filled with incidents in which this great warm-hearted man unquestioningly obeyed the Spirit of Goodness that was in him, and met with consternation when he expected others to obey the same Spirit with equal readiness! So many Christians exalt the demands and rigors of law because, in reality, law is less demanding than pure charity. The law after all has reasonable and safe limits!

The mention of Pope John naturally suggests a conclusion to this introduction. Pope John's love for the Church of the Orient, of the Balkans, Greece and Russia, is well known. His idea of calling the Second Vatican Council was prompted in large part by this love of our separated Orthodox brothers. Knowledge of the spirit and teaching of the Russian mystics can be of great help to us in carrying on the work of mutual understanding which Pope John has bequeathed to us. This is therefore a very timely book for an age of ecumenism and of renewal. Full of interesting historical material and of spiritual wisdom, written for the ordinary reader, it provides a much needed popular introduction to a subject of great interest and importance to all Christians.

Thomas Merton*

*Reprinted with the permission of Farrar, Straus & Giroux, Inc. from *Mystics and Zen Masters* by Thomas Merton, Copyright 1961, 1962, 1964, 1965, 1966, 1967 by the Abbey of Gethsemani.

INTRODUCTION

THE RUSSIAN MYSTICS are still very little known in the West. Yet they are numerous, profound and interesting. Professor Vladimir Lossky stressed the importance of the mystics in his remarkable book: *Essai sur la Théologie mystique de l'Eglise d'Orient*.

In that book Professor Lossky shows that, as far as the Orthodox Church is concerned, no split has developed as in the West to separate theology and mysticism, and indeed in the East there is no theology without mysticism. He states: "Eastern tradition never differentiated clearly between mysticism and theology, between personal experience of divine mysteries and the dogma approved by the Church. Words pronounced a century ago by a great Orthodox theologian, Metropolitan Philarete of Moscow, express this perfectly. He said: 'No mystery of Divine Wisdom, even the most secret, must appear to us strange or altogether transcendent, but in true humility we must adapt our mind to the contemplation of Divine Things.' "[1]

This means that a dogma defining revealed truth which appears as a mystery to our way of understanding, must be lived by us. But we must not try to adapt the mystery to our level of understanding. On the contrary, we should ourselves undergo a profound change, being transformed from within, in order to be capable of mystical experience.

1. *Sermons and Speeches of Metropolitan Philaret* (in Russian), vol. 2, p. 87.

Far from opposing each other, theology and mysticism assist and complete each other. The first is impossible without the second and vice versa. There is no Christian mysticism without theology. Still less is there true theology without mysticism. For that very reason the tradition of the Eastern Church has reserved the title of "Theologian" to three sacred authors: St John, the most mystical of the four Evangelists, St Gregory Nazianzen, author of contemplative poems, and St Symeon, called the New Theologian, minstrel of union with God. Mysticism therefore, must be, considered as a perfection, the crown of all theology, a theology par excellence.

If mysticism is the crown of theology, true theology, then obviously monks, and particularly contemplative monks, should be the greatest theologians. So it was in history. Most of the Fathers and Doctors of the Church in the East were monks. Something similar may be noticed also in the West. The greatest periods of theological activity in the East nearly always coincided with the flowering of monasticism. This was so during the Christological, iconoclastic and Hesychastic controversies. Once theology and mysticism start to drift apart the former tends invariably to become a "theology of concepts," an abstract science, a mere religious philosophy. Those who teach theology cease to live up to it as the mystics did. In order to return to the great age of theology, dogma must be brought back to life and mystically experienced.

What is true generally is equally true for the Russian Church. There, too, the periods of the greatest glory have coincided with the ages of the prosperity of monasteries and of numerous mystics. Russian contemplatives have as their patriarch St Anthony of Kiev (983-1073). According to tradition he was professed in Esphigmenou Monastery on Mount Athos. With St Theodosius (1035-1074), St Anthony founded in 1062 the first large Russian monastery, which is still in existence, the celebrated Pechersky Monastery in Kiev. The first Russian bishops, missionaries and sacred writers came from that monastery.

The foundation of the Russian Church in the tenth century coincided with the golden age of the Byzantine Empire, when it reached its zenith under Basil II. Bolgarokrotonos, brother-in-law of St Vladimir, Grand Prince of Russia, and of Othon II, Holy Roman Emperor. The son of the latter, Othon III, was a friend of St Nilus, founder of Grottaferrata Abbey near Rome. Grottaferrata was founded in the same century as Pechersky Monastery.

St Anthony brought Athonite spirituality and customs to Russia. Since early times the Russians have possessed a large collection of Slavonic translations of patristic writings. Even before the Mongol invasion of 1236 the Russians read St Athanasius the Great, St Gregory Nazianzen, St Gregory of Nyssa, St Gregory the Great, St Basil the Great, St Ephrem the Syrian, St John Climacus, St John Chrysostom, St John Damascene, St Maximus, St Hippolytus of Rome, as well as several Palestinian and Egyptian mystics. Although the Russians were in continuous contact with Constantinople and Mount Athos in the age when St Symeon the New Theologian and St Athanasius of Mount Athos flourished, they were still too new in Christianity to produce mystics. Nevertheless, they produced many good and saintly monks and ecclesiastical writers.

The thirteenth century was marked by the Mongol invasion of Russia and the foundation of the Latin Empire in Constantinople. Many Russian monasteries were destroyed by the Mongols and communication with the Byzantine Empire became restricted. This could not but have repercussions on the prosperity and development of the Russian monasteries. However, this painful period did not last long. In the fourteenth century, with the appearance of St Sergius of Radonesh (1314-92), Russian monasticism revived. The great Monastery of the Holy Trinity, founded by St Sergius in 1354, quickly became the largest, wealthiest and most influential Russian monastery. It still exists and has over a hundred monks. The abbot is the Patriarch of Moscow. The monastery also houses the Moscow Theological Academy and Seminary. Enormous crowds from all over the Soviet Union and many pilgrims from abroad come even today to this monastery, which is a splendid city in itself. They pray there and consult the monks on spiritual problems.

St Sergius personally founded nine monasteries, while his

disciples founded twelve more. Besides these, a number of monasteries was founded by friends of St Sergius. At that time the number of monasteries in Russia was already considerable. Although many of these were quite small, not a few numbered from one to three hundred monks. The fourteenth century was the age of the Hesychast movement in the Byzantine Empire. This movement was started by St Gregory the Sinaite, who was successively a monk of Mount Sinai and Mount Athos. He died in 1346 and left a long treatise of one hundred and fifty chapters on contemplative prayer. Gregory Palamas, another Athonite monk, afterwards abbot of Esphigmenou and Archbishop of Thessalonica, who died in 1360, composed several treatises which define Orthodox mystical theology. His writings and teaching were made known in Russia by several Russian primates: Theognost, St Alexius, Cyprian and Photius.

Besides the primates, other Greeks, such as the Athonite monk Dionisios, later Archbishop of Rostov and Lasar of Murmansk and Sergius of Murom, two monks, brought the same ideas to Russia. Epiphanius the Wise, a disciple of St Sergius of Radonesh, and St Arsenius, abbot of Konevetz, both visited Mount Athos at the peak of the Hesychast movement. St Nilus of Sora (1433-1508), who visited Mount Athos in the fifteenth century, was the first, and perhaps the greatest Russian mystic. As a nobleman he studied Byzantine mystics in Slavonic translation at St Cyril's Monastery on the White Lake. In 1465 he went to the East returning home in 1478. On his return St Nilus founded his own Skete[2] on the Athonite model, and wrote his celebrated *Tradition of Sketic Life*. This remarkable short treatise is a masterly summary of Orthodox mystical and ascetical teaching. It precedes the *Philokalia*, a larger summary, by nearly 350 years.

According to St Nilus the outward forms of monastic life, although important, are secondary. The chief work of the monk is spiritual: the cultivation of the Prayer of Jesus, read-

2. Groups of monks living in cottages around a central church and dependent upon a parent monastery.

ing the Holy Scriptures and the Fathers and keeping death in mind. Without this one cannot attain union with God. The teaching of St Nilus is based on St Anthony the Great, St Basil the Great, St Ephrem, St Isaac the Syrian, St Macarius the Great, St John Climacus and St Symeon the New Theologian. St Nilus did not approve of monastic wealth and the interference of monks in the affairs of the state. He also disapproved of ritualism and formalism in religion, as well as blind attachment to conventions and outworn traditions.

The supporters of the opposite view, led by St Joseph of Volokolamsk (1440-1515), entered quickly into conflict with the disciples of St Nilus. The Josephians stood for monastic estates, which they considered essential for the wellbeing of the Church, and for the strictest ritual observance. The struggle between the two parties ended in victory for the Josephians, and led to the further growth of monastic land-owing, rigid ritualism, intolerance toward all foreigners, including Orthodox, and an unreasonable worship of the past. Among many people who suffered in this struggle was a brilliant Greek scholar and humanist, Michael Trivolis, known in Russia as St Maximus the Greek (1480-1556). Maximus had studied in Italy and had been a novice in the convent of Savonarola in Florence. He afterwards became a monk of Vatopedi on Mount Athos. He was sent to Moscow as a scholar to reorganize the Grand Ducal library. The victory of the Josephians was an unhappy event for Russia and produced in the seventeenth century the Great Russian Schism. The Josephians were opposed to the liturgical reforms of Patriarch Nikon (1652-1667). Unable to undo these reforms the conservatives preferred to leave the Russian Church rather than submit. Professor Fedotov, in his book *Saints of Ancient Russia,*[3] stressed the fact that while in the sixteenth century thirty saints were canonized, only fifteen were canonized in the following century. No one was canonized in the last quarter of that century. Still 220 new monasteries were founded in the seventeenth century.

3. G. Fedotov, *Saints of Ancient Russia* (in Russian) (Paris, 1931), pp. 201-202.

Church wealth unavoidably excited the jealousy of the state. Already in the seventeenth century the first attempts were made to limit monastic wealth. Peter the Great, who reformed the Russian state in the first quarter of the eighteenth century, met stiff resistance among the conservatives, particularly the clergy and the monks. In order to overcome this resistance he abolished the office of the Patriarch and replaced him by a board of ecclesiastics nominated by himself and called the Holy Synod. Death prevented him from carrying out drastic plans for the suppression and confiscation of monasteries.

In 1763 Catherine II confiscated the landed estates of the Church which by this time included one-fourth of the entire Russian territory. Certain monasteries were fabulously wealthy. The Laura[4] of the Holy Trinity, near Moscow, founded by St Sergius of Radonesh in 1354, possessed 100,000 serfs. Catherine II closed down 568 monasteries out of 953 and greatly reduced the membership of those that remained. The decree forbade the profession of new monks and nuns without special permission from the capital in every case. It seemed that Russian monasteries were condemned to disappear. Yet this did not happen. In spite of their critical situation, the Russian monks produced in the first half of the eighteenth century two outstanding Russian mystics, both bishops, St Demetrius of Rostov (1651-1709) and St Tikhon Zadonsky (1724-1783). The first wrote a voluminous collection of the *Lives of Saints* as well as many ascetical and mystical treatises, while the second published a fine book entitled *True Christianity* and some shorter works. Although strictly Orthodox, neither bishop belonged to the traditional Hesychast school. St Demetrius was deeply influenced by the Latins in his outlook, while St Tikhon was well read in Protestant spiritual writers, including Anglicans and German pietists. After St Tikhon, Zadonsk Monastery

---

4. A community of monks living in separate cells around a central church.

produced another mystic, George the Recluse (1789-1836).

The new revival of monasticism and the golden age of Russian mysticism is connected with Mount Athos. Paisius Velichkovsky (1722-1794), a native of Poltava in the Ukraine, lived in the difficult period of Russian monastic history. Realizing early that there was not much chance of becoming a monk in Russia, Paisius left Russia in 1744 for Rumania where he made his profession. In 1747 he retired to Mount Athos where he founded the Russian Skete of St Elias which is still in existence. The ever recurring wars between Russia and Turkey prevented Paisius from remaining on Mount Athos. In 1754 he returned to Rumania (Principality of Moldavia), where in 1774 he became abbot of five hundred monks at Neamtu, a monastery still flourishing today.

While living in Neamtu, Paisius translated into Slavonic several patristic treatises, including the *Philokalia* which had just been published by Metropolitan Macarius of Corinth and St Nicodemus the Hagiorite. The *Philokalia* is a collection of patristic and Hesychast writings concerning interior prayer and the monastic life. It was printed in Venice in 1782. It is divided into two parts. The first includes the writings of Anthony the Great, Isaiah, Evagrius, Cassian, Mark, Hesychius, John Damascene, Philemon, Theognost, Philotheus of Sinai, Elias and Theophane. The second part contains treatises of Peter of Damascus, Simeon Metaphrastes, Symeon the New Theologian, Nicetas Stethatos, Theoleptus, Nicephorus, Gregory of Sinai, Gregory Palamas, Callixtus and Ignatius Xanthopulos, Callixtus the Patriarch, Callixtus Angelikudes, Callixtus Cataphygiotes, Symeon of Thessalonica, Mark of Ephesus and Maximus Kapsokalyvitis. Paisius translated only twenty-five treatises out of thirty-six. He named his translation *Dobrotolyubie* or *Love of Beauty*.

Gabriel Petrov (1730-1801), Metropolitan of St Petersburg, printed the *Dobrotolyubie* in 1793. This edition was quickly sold and rapidly spread through Russia. Among Paisius' monks in Rumania and Mount Athos there were many Russians. Some of them returned home and settled in various monasteries. They brought the Hesychast spirituality to Russia. The nineteenth century witnessed the Golden Age of Russian mysticism which, in modern times, can only be compared to the Golden Age of the Spanish mystics in the sixteenth century. This Golden Age coincided with the renewed monastic expansion in Russia. Over 300 new monasteries were founded in the nineteenth century, nearly 200 of them during the reign of Alexander III which lasted barely thirteen years. By 1900 there were in Russia 800 monasteries, of which 300 were for women. There were 17,000 professed monks and nuns and 30,000 novices. In 1914 there were in Russia 11,845 professed monks and 9,485 novices, while the number of nuns reached 17,283 with 56,016 novices. Several monasteries numbered over 1,000 members. A good many monasteries were running schools, hospitals, homes for the aged and printing presses. They attracted vast crowds of pilgrims.

Many mystics lived in Russia in the nineteenth century. They can be divided into several groups. The first includes two bishops, Ignatius Brianchaninov (1807-1867) and Theophane Govorov (1815-1894). Bishop Brianchaninov was a nobleman and an army officer before he became a monk. He left six volumes of ascetical and mystical writings which were widely read by Russians in search of perfection. Trained by the monks of Optino, Ignatius became abbot of St Sergius' Monastery near St Petersburg in 1834. In 1857 he was consecrated Bishop of Caucasus but within four years he resigned and retired to Nikolo-Babaev Monastery in order to live a strictly contemplative life.

Bishop Theophane, after a brilliant scholastic career as professor and rector of various seminaries, went to the Holy Land, Syria, Egypt and Constantinople in 1847 for scholarly research. He also visited Rome and had an audience with Pius IX. Returning to Russia in 1855 as rector of St Petersburg Academy, Theophane was consecrated bishop of Tambov in 1859. Transferred to Vladimir in 1863, he resigned three years later and retired to the Monastery of Vysh. During his twenty-eight years as a recluse, Theophane published several books on the spiritual life. In his principal mystical work, *The Way of Salvation,* Theophane summed up his teaching. The goal of human life is union with God. The way to this goal is faith and life according to Christ's commandments. We are saved by the grace of the Holy Spirit which is ours without cost because of our redemption by Christ. The Church is our guide. We attain to interior purification by ascetical exercises and become Christlike. There are three stages in the interior life: beginning, growth and perfection. The description of this process by Theophane is a masterpiece, hardly equalled in mystical literature.

In 1877 Theophane published the first Russian edition, in five volumes, of *Dobrotolyubie,* which he had translated from Greek. The Russian edition is longer than the Slavonic. It was printed at the Russian Monastery of St Panteleimon on Mount Athos and has been reprinted three times. Theophane published also *The Ancient Monastic Rules of Pachomius the Great, Basil the Great, John Cassian and Benedict.* He also published *The Spiritual Combat* by Lorenzo Scupoli (1529-1610), an Italian mystical writer of the Counterreformation period. But he made a great many changes in his translation of Scupoli. The writings of Theophane made a deep impression on the Russian monks, clergy and laity who were attracted to the contemplative life.

The second and most remarkable group of Russian mystics of this period was centered around the renowned Monastery of Optino. Founded in the sixteenth century, Optino became prominent only in the nineteenth when it produced its three great Startzy, or spiritual directors, Fathers Leonid Nagolkin (1769-1841), Macarius Ivanov (1783-1860) and Ambrose Grenkov (1812-1891). Several other great contemplatives were connected with Optino, including the two brothers Putilov; Moses was abbot of Optino (1962) and Anthony, abbot of Maloyaroslavetz. The Staretz Basil Kishkin and the anonymous author of the celebrated Russian mystical classic *Tales of the Russian Pilgrim* belong to the same circle. Macarius Ivanov, Ambrose Grenkov and Anthony Putilov left very illuminating letters of direction.

Father Macarius published several of the Slavonic translations made by Paisius Velichkovsky. In this work he was
assisted by the Russian philosopher Ivan Kyreevsky (1806-
1856) and some of the monks. Altogether sixteen titles were published. They include Barsanuphius the Great,
John, Symeon the New Theologian, Theodore Studite, Maximus the Confessor, Isaac the Syrian, Thalassius, Dorotheus,
Mark, Orisius and Isaiah. Most of these books were published
in Slavonic, but some in Russian. They greatly influenced the
revival of mystical life in Russia. The Startzy of Optino directed several eminent Russians, authors, ministers and statesmen, like N. Gogol, S. Shevirev, M. Pogodin, L. Kavelin, A.
Norov, A. Muraviev, T. Filipov, C. Leontiev and C. Zeder-
golm. Four great Russian writers and thinkers, T. Dostoevsky, L. Tolstoy, V. Soloviev and B. Rozanov visited the Staretz Ambrose. Dostoevsky tried to picture him as the Staretz
Zosima in *Brothers Karamazov* and Vladimir Sloviev did the
same for his Staretz John in *Three Conversations*. The Monastery of Optino was closed by the Soviet government in 1923
and its last Staretz, Father Nectarius, died in 1928.

The third group of the Russian mystics centers around the
great Sarov Monastery, founded about 1700. Its greatest
representative was Seraphim Moshnin (1759-1833), canonized by the Russian Church in 1904. He is the most popular
saint of modern Russia as well as its most profound mystic.
St Seraphim himself left *Instructions,* while his sayings are
recorded by his friends and disciples. His *Talks with Motovilov* on the purpose of Christian life is a classic of Russian
mysticism. During this conversation the phenomenon of the
transfiguration of St Seraphim occured. It is fully described
by Motovilov. According to St Seraphim the goal of Christian
life is the acquisition of the grace of the Holy Spirit. This
grace was given to Adam but was lost by him through his sin.
Christ redeemed us and gave us back this grace. We all receive
it when we are baptized and confirmed but lose it afterwards
by our sins. We can regain the lost grace by penance, Holy
Communion, true faith and Christlike living. When this is
done, we become temples of the Holy Spirit. Those who

attain the highest degree of this sanctification are transfigured as Christ was on the Mount Thabor.

To the same group belong Father Mark the Hermit, Nazarius, abbot of Valaam (1735-1809), Staretz Theodore Ushakov, abbot of Sanaksar, and others. Some writings by Nazarius and Theodore remain. Abbot Nazarius introduced into Valaam many patristic and mystical writings. This monastery later produced several first class mystics, particularly Abbot Damaskin (1795-1881), Abbot Khariton and Father Michael the Recluse. Abbot Damaskin and Khariton left some writings. I have described my conversations with Father Michael in many articles and in a book *Father Michael, Recluse of Uusi Valamo.*[5]

The fourth group of the Russian mystics is made up of the solitaries of the Roslavl Forests. About thirty contemplatives developed in these forests. In addition to the brothers Putilov, mentioned above, the group includes Father Adrian, abbot of Konevetz, Father Zosima Verkhovsky (1767-1833) and Staretz Vasilisk. The latter two contemplatives spent many years as solitaries in Siberia and left remarkable writings. Staretz Daniel of Achinsk (1784-1843) was another remarkable Siberian mystic, although he is not connected with Father Zosima and Staretz Vasilisk.

A fifth group of Russian mystics gravitated around Kiev. Its central figure was the Metropolitan of Kiev, Philarete Amfiteatrov, who did much to revive the Monastery of Optino as Bishop of Kaluga. To this group belongs Father Parthenius of Kiev, and Archimandrite Lawrence, Superior of Iversky Monastery in Novgorod.

The sixth group of Russian mystics is connected with Mount Athos. It has several remarkable men, Father John of Modavia, Abbot Parthenius of Guslitsi, Father Arsenius, Father Jerome Solomentsev (1803-1885), Father Hilarion of the Caucasus, Staretz Siluan and the still living Father Ilian. All these mystics belong to the pure Hesychast tradition and some of them have left treatises of a great depth.

5. Oxford, 1956.

While in the Latin Church, particularly in the modern period, there were a great many women mystics such as St Theresa of Avila, St Thérèse of Lisieux and St Margaret Mary of Paray-le-Monial, there were few in the Russian Church. Still there were some, like Abbess Mary of Makhrishky, Princess Serafima Odoevsky, who lived in the fifteenth century and Taisia Solopov, abbess of Leushin at the end of the Imperial period, and others. Abbess Taisia left memoirs of great value.

In the present book only the Russian mystics who belonged to the Orthodox Church and were either religious or closely connected with the monasteries are studied. There were in Russia also a number of mystics among the diocesan clergy, like the celebrated Father John of Kronstadt of whom we will say something, and among the laity. This book would become too long and unwieldly if all were included. For the same reason nothing is said about the Russian mystics who belonged to various non-conformist sects.

RUSSIAN MONASTICISM TO THE END OF THE FIFTEENTH CENTURY

T HE RUSSIAN NATION came into being in the ninth century. At that period several scattered Slavonic tribes occupied what is now Western Russia, living along the Volkhov and the Dnieper and their tributaries. These tribes, partly hunters, partly agriculturists, were nature-worshippers in their religion. They lived in small isolated communities under a patriarchal regime. The great plain was politically unorganized although the civilized and powerful states of Byzantine, the Volga Bulgarians and the Khazars lay on its borders.

Scandinavian adventurers, traders and robbers, known to the Slavs as Varyags, travelling along the Volkhov and the Dnieper to Constantinople, explored this Slavonic country and gradually subjected it to their overlordship, founding an enormous but loosely organized state. Tradition dates it from 862, when a Scandinavian chieftain, named Rurik settled in Aldeigjuborg on the lake of Ladoga. Rurik, who died in 879, is recognized as the first Russian sovereign. He and his son Igor were pagans like the majority of their Norse soldiers. Nevertheless, Christianity had already found converts among these turbulent and cruel warriors and in Kiev, the capital of the Russian state, a Christian church and community existed long before St Vladimir (972-1015), who is regarded as the Apostle of Russia.

Christianity came to the Varyags both from the Latin West and from the Byzantine East. The Latin prelates appeared in

1

Scandinavia in 823, when Archbishop Ebbo of Rheims, visited Denmark hoping to evangelize this country. In 826 King Harald of Jutland was baptized with his family. St Anscar, a Benedictine monk from Corbie Abbey in Picardy, dedicated his life to the conversion of Scandinavia. In 826 he visited Denmark, and in 829 and 831 Sweden. By that time he had been consecrated bishop. In 834 the Pope made him Archbishop of Hamburg and Papal Legate in the North. In 853 Anscar again visited Sweden, in 859 he gave Sweden its first bishop, a Danish monk named Rimbert. St Anscar died in 865.

Although the Varyags were overwhelmingly pagan, they knew something of the Latins. Baron Michael von Taube in his book on early Russian Christianity thinks that Askold, Varyag Prince of Kiev, was baptized in 862 and probably by a Latin priest because he assumed the name of Nicholas after his contemporary, Pope Nicholas I.[1]

On the other side some Varyags settled in colonies in Crimea. There they mixed with those Goths who remained there after their cousins moved to the West. There, too, they entered into contact with the Byzantines. The Crimean Goths had been Christians for some time. They possessed the Scriptures and the liturgical books in their own language. The Varyags probably received the Christian faith from them.

In any case the celebrated Patriarch Photius of Constantinople announced in 867 in his Encyclical to the Eastern Patriarchs that the Russians had decided to become Christians and had requested him to send them a bishop.[2] Scholars still cannot agree where this bishop was sent and who he was. According to Russian tradition the name of this bishop was Michael. While some scholars believe that he was sent to the Azov-Crimean Russians to revive the ancient See of Tamatarkha, others suppose he went to Kiev at the request of Askold.

Meanwhile a pagan reaction led to the assassination of Askold in 882 and to the occupation of Kiev by Oleg, who succeeded Rurik in the North. The pagan reaction did not

---

1. Michael von Taube, *Rome et la Russie avant l'invasion des Tatares* (Paris, 1947), pp. 128-129.
2. E. Golubinsky, *Istoriya Russkoi Tserkvi*, 2 vols. (Moscow, 1900-1901), 1:51.

succeed in wiping out Christianity in Kiev. It survived so well that in the reign of Igor (913-945) the Christian Varyags already possessed in Kiev a collegiate church of St Elias, undoubtedly a daughter church of the similar Varyag church in Constantinople, where many Scandinavians served in the Imperial guard. The Christians were so numerous among the Russians of Kiev that in the treaty of Igor with the Eastern Empire in 944, they took the oath to observe the treaty together with their heathen cousins. They even promised to watch after its observance by the heathen.

Olga, who succeeded her husband, Igor, as Regent for her small son, Svyatoslav, became Christian herself in 954, taking the name of Helen. In 957 she visited Constantinople, where she was well received by the Emperor Constantin Porphyrogeneiis, who described her visit in the well known work $E\kappa\theta\epsilon o\iota\varsigma$ $\tau\eta\varsigma$ $\beta\alpha\sigma\iota\lambda\epsilon\tilde{\iota}o\upsilon$ $\tau\acute{\alpha}\xi\epsilon\omega\varsigma$[3] In 959 Olga sent an embassy to the Holy Roman Emperor, Otto the Great. According to Western chroniclers, she requested Otto to send a bishop with priests to Kiev. A Benedictine monk, St Adalbert, of St Maximin's Abbey in Trier, was sent to Kiev in 961 but the very next year he came back, prevented from settling in Kiev by pagan opposition.[4] He became afterwards the first Archbishop of Magdeburg.

Svyatoslav (942-972), son of Igor and Olga, was the last typical Viking who ruled in Kiev, although he already adopted a Slavonic name. Many of his entourage also began to adopt Slavonic names and to worship Slavonic gods. The Scandinavians and the Slavs began to fuse, forming one Russian nation. Although many attempts have been made to explain who the original Russians were, the most satisfying is the following. They were almost certainly Swedes, predominantly natives of Rosgalen, in the present province of Uppland.[5] Danes and Norwegians joined in from time to time. All Scandinavians who raided the Eastern European plains were called Russians by the Slavs and the Finns alike.

3. PG 112:1108.
4. Pertz, *Monumenta Germaniae Historica*, 1, 624.
5. K. Tiander, *Frankfurter Zeitung*, May 24, 1927.

Svyatoslav, a true Viking adventurer, had no sympathy with Christianity. He believed it effeminate and unworthy of a soldier. He spent his short life in wars with the Khazars, the Bulgarians and the Byzantines. He occupied Bulgaria and liked that country so much that he wanted to transfer his capital there. The Byzantine Emperor, John Zimisces, however, forced Svyatoslav out of Bulgaria. However, Svyatoslav's stay in Bulgaria greatly influenced the fortunes of Christianity among the Eastern Slavs. Under Svyatoslav many Christian Bulgarians came to Kiev as prisoners of war or allies. They helped to spread Slavonic Christianity in the capital.

The conversion of Bulgaria was the work of Clementi, Naum and Angelyar, disciples of St Cyril and St Methodius, Apostles of the Slavs. It took place in the ninth century. Boris, ruler of Bulgaria, could not make up his mind for a long time what form of Christianity to adopt, Latin or Byzantine. Both Pope Nicholas I and Photius, Patriarch of Constantinople, were eager to win Bulgaria over. Their rivalry produced the first dangerous rift between Eastern and Western Christendom. Finally, Bulgaria went over to the Byzantines. Very likely the fact that the Byzantines agreed to allow the Bulgarians to use their native language in the liturgy decided the choice. The rise of Bulgaria under the Tsar Symeon resulted in the independence of the Bulgarian Church in 927. The Byzantines conceded to the Bulgarians the right to elect their own Patriarch and to manage their own affairs. A few decades later the Bulgarian Church numbered thirty dioceses and was very flourishing.[6] At the same time not only the Holy Scriptures and liturgical services but many patristic writings and other texts were translated into Macedonian Slavonic which was then easily understood by all the Slavs.

The sudden death of Svyatoslav led to an internal struggle among his sons for the succession. His third son, St Vladimir, finally came out on top. This able statesman quickly realized that his enormous but loosely connected state, formed by an uneasy alliance of Scandinavian adventurers, Slavonic traders

6. Makarij Moskovskij, *Istoria Russkoi Cerkvi* (Moscow, 1889), p. 129.

and agriculturists, with a liberal admixture of Finnish hunters, would not survive for long unless it were unified by a common religion and culture. St Vladimir selected for such a religion and culture that of Byzantium.

The Byzantine Empire of the tenth century, renewed by great Emperors of the Macedonian dynasty, was a brilliant state. Its civil service, army and schools surpassed anything in the West. The arts and sciences flourished according to the standards of the period. The Byzantine Church was famous for the beauty of its worship, the learning of its theologians and the deep spirituality of its mystics.

Vladimir, it seems, was baptized in 987 in Vassiliev, near Kiev, while the population of the capital was baptized later, either in 988 or in 990. Very little is known about the first two Russian Primates, Leon and John I. In some documents they are occasionally called Archbishops and not Metropolitans. It seems they were Bulgarians, subjects of the Bulgarian Patriarch or perhaps even quite independent like the Archbishops of Georgia (in the Caucasus) and of Cyprus. These Bulgarians brought with them Slavonic-speaking clergy and Slavonic Scriptures, liturgical books and other literature.

In 1018 the first Bulgarian Empire was destroyed by the Byzantines and Bulgarian autonomy came to the end. The suppression of the Bulgarian Patriarchate resulted in the Hellenization of the Russian Primatial See. In 1037 a Greek prelate, Theophemtos, came to Kiev, and the Russian Church became an ecclesiastical province of the Patriarchal See of Constantinople, which it remained for several centuries. The Greek Primates, displeased by the fact that the Bulgarians had first organized the Russian Church, destroyed all relevant documents, and so the first fifty years of the existence of Russian Christianity are shrouded in impenetrable mystery.[7]

St Vladimir built two more churches in Kiev and introduced tithes, which were unknown in Byzantium, thus showing that there was a strong Latin influence in Kiev as well. Vladi-

7. S. Bolshakoff, *The Foreign Missions of the Russian Orthodox Church* (London: SPCK, 1943), p. 17.

mir also built churches and schools in several other Russian cities. Christianity rapidly spread in Southern Russia where it met no resistance. Progress was more difficult in Northern Russia, especially in Novgorod, but the resistance was quickly overcome. The See of Novgorod was founded by St Vladimir, and its second bishop. Russian by birth, St Luke Zhidyata, appointed in 1034, became the first Russian bishop and writer. All the Slavonic tribes of Russia were baptized under St Vladimir according to the Russian Church historian, Professor E. Golubinsky. His successors baptized the Finnish tribes which dwelt in the north-east.

Under Yaroslav the Wise (1019-1054), still a Scandinavian by race, Kiev reached its zenith. Yaroslav was a powerful prince. Kings Henry I of France, Andrew I of Hungary and Harold the Strict of Norway were his sons-in-law. Yaroslav was connected with the Imperial Houses of the Byzantine and Holy Roman Empires, the Polish Royal House and the Saxon dynasty of England.[8] During his reign Kiev became a flourishing metropolis with many fine buildings. According to Ditmar, Kiev possessed in those times 400 churches and eight markets. The celebrated Cathedral of St Sophia in Kiev, still standing, was built in 1037.

At this time, monastic life was introduced into Russia by St Anthony of Kiev (983-1073). A native of Lubech in the Principality of Chernigov, Antipas (as he was then called) became interested in monastic life at an early age. In order to learn about it he went abroad. According to tradition he was professed in the Monastery of Esphigmenou on Mount Athos and changed his name to Anthony. Russian monasticism is closely connected with Mount Athos from its very beginning.

The thousandth anniversary of Athos was celebrated in 1963. But actually hermits first settled there in the eighth century. St Peter of Athos, who died in 734, is the best known among them. The hermits gradually formed monastic settlements or lauras. Euthemius of Thessalonica was in 862

---

8. B. Leib in his *Rome, Kiev et Byzance à la fin du XIème siècle* (Paris, 1924) devotes the sixth chapter to the study of the relations of the Russian princes with the royal houses of the East and West.

head of such a laura. The first cenobitic monastery was established by John Kolob (869-873). In the tenth century St
Athanasius of Athos, founder of the Great Laura, provided
the monastic republic with its first constitution or *typikon*
which was confirmed by the Emperor John Zimisces, apparently in 972. Men in search of solitude began to flock to
Athos from all the provinces of the Byzantine Empire and
even from Armenia and Italy. In 985 Vatopedi Monastery
was founded. Between 980 and 984 the Georgians from the
Caucasus founded Iveron Monastery. Dochiariou appeared in
1030, Esphigmenou in 1045 and Kostamohitou in 1050.
Soon there were 180 monasteries. Some of them were very
populous. The Great Laura alone numbered 700 monks.[9]

Returning to Russia, Anthony settled in a cave near Kiev.
There he soon acquired a brilliant pupil, Hilarion, who became
in 1051 Primate of Russia. The second pupil of St Anthony
was St Theodosius (1035-1074). A native of Vassiliev, Theodosius, was brought up in Kursk and joined St Anthony quite
young. In 1062 they founded the celebrated Kievo-Pechers-
kaya Lavra which still exists in spite of wars, invasions and
revolutions. In 1067 Theodosius became abbot and introduced in his monastery the Rule of St Theodore the Studite
which was followed afterwards by many other monasteries.

The first Russian monks were simple folk who tried to
achieve eternal salvation by mortifications, humility, long
services and good deeds. Among the first Russian monks were
Moses the Hungarian, servant of Prince Boris, Grand Prince
Svyatopolk, and two Knights, Ephrem and Barlaam. Gradually the community increased to one hundred monks. The Rule
was observed very strictly. The porter did not allow even the
Grand Prince to enter the monastery when he came at an im-
proper time. Humility and obedience were the virtues held
most in esteem. Food was very simple. St Theodosius taught his
monks to trust in Divine Providence and not to worry about

9. For further study see Emmanuel Armand de Mendiera, *La Presqu'île des
Caloyers: Le Mont Athos* (Bruges: Desclée de Brouwer, 1955); Chrysostomus
Dahm and Ludger Bernhard, *Athos: Mountain of Light,* trans. Aileen O'Brien
(Offenburg, Baden: Burda, 1959).

possessions. Those who trust in Providence, he taught, are never deceived. Theodosius reserved ten percent of the monastic income for the poor, and built a hospice for the poor and the sick. Every Saturday he sent bread to the prisons. Theodosius worked hard and dressed poorly. He ate only dry bread. His soup was without oil. He slept sitting. He was a very humble abbot. Once his servant told him, when they were returning from work' "You are a monk and a parasite, while I am always working. You get on the horse and let me ride in the wagon." The Abbot agreed.[10]

St Theodosius was much respected by Grand Prince Isyaslav and others. In his time a well-known Scandinavian knight, Simon, who belonged to the Latin rite, entered the monastery as novice and later was professed. In that period there were in Kiev churches of the Byzantine and Latin rite alike. Under Abbot Stephen the abbey church was built. Its frescoes were executed by master painters from Constantinople. It was consecrated in 1089.

Among the best known disciples of St Theodosius were St Isaiah, Bishop of Rostov; Stephen, Bishop of Volhynia; Jeremiah the Non-Possessor; Gregory the Physician, who treated people gratis and was murdered by Prince Rostislav and Agapitus the Recluse. After the death of St Theodosius many more monks became known for their holy living, particularly Eusthatius, Pimen the Sick, St Kuksha the Missionary, Alipius the ikon painter, Nikon and Policarp. Theophilus the Recluse did not see the sun for twelve years. He lamented his sins day and night. John the Longsuffering ate only every other week. He wore heavy chains for thirty years. Nicetas became Bishop of Novgorod, while Prokhor, Theodore and Basil were killed by Prince Mstislav because they condemned his evil deeds.

Kievo-Pechersky Monastery produced several early Russian writers. James described the baptism of St Vladimir while another monk, Nestor, described the martyrdom of his sons,

10. P. Znamenskij, *Učebnoe rukovodstvo po istorii russkoj Cerkvi* (St Petersburg, 1904), p. 63.

Princes Boris and Gleb. Metropolitan Hilarion left a remarkable dogmatic work on grace. Abbot Sylvester wrote the first Russian chronicle. Simon, Bishop of Vladimir, and the monk, Polycarp, composed the renowned *Pechersky Paterik*, describing the lives of many saintly monks of Kiev.

The monks of Kiev admired most of all meekness and humility. This is particularly stressed in the life of St Boris and St Gleb by Nestor. These two princes, sons of St Vladimir, being informed by their friends that their brother, Grand Prince Svyatopolk, intended to murder them, refused to believe such a calumny. When it became clear that this was so, they neither resisted nor ran away but met their death as true Christians. For his crime Svyatopolk paid dearly. Another brother, Yaroslav the Wise, came from Novgorod and defeated Svyatopolk, who fled abroad. The *Paterik* is loud in praise of those monks who excel in humility and meekness. The monks of Kiev were severe ascetics and good Christians but they were not mystics—or at any rate they have left no mystical treatises or descriptions of their mystical experiences. Pechersky Monastery was the religious centre of Kievan Russia. [11] Many abbots and fifty bishops came out of Pechersky Monastery.

Monasticism spread rapidly over Russia. On the eve of the Mongol invasion in 1237 Kiev alone numbered twelve monasteries, Novgorod twenty in the city itself and ten in its dominions, Polotsk three, Rostov two, Suzdal four, and Smolensk five. As in Western Europe the monasteries became in Russia the homes of spiritual life and culture. Most of the books of ancient Russia came out of the monasteries. At an age when the Latin West almost entirely lacked theological literature in the vernacular, the Russians possessed a large number of translations from Greek, including most of the Bible, all their liturgical books and several dogmatic, mystical and ascetical treatises of Greek, Latin and Syriac Fathers, particularly St Athanasius the Great, St Gregory Nazianzen, St Gregory of

---

11. For details see L. Goetz, *Das Kiever Höhlenkloster als Kulturzentrum vormongolischen Zeit* (Passau, 1904).

Nyssa, St Gregory the Great, St Basil the Great, St Ephrem
the Syrian, St John Climacus, St John Damascene, St John
Chrysostom and St Maximus. [12] Kievan Russia was in regular
relations with the Byzantine Empire and translations were
mostly made there by Southern Slavs and then taken to
Russia.

The founder of Russian monasticism, St Anthony of Kiev,
visited Mount Athos twice. Ephrem the Eunuch brought to
St Theodosius the Studite Rule written in Constantinople.
Anthony (Dobrynya Andreikovich), Archbishop of Novgorod, visited Constantinople in the thirteenth century, before
it was looted by the Crusaders, and described his journey.
Dositheus, Abbot of Kievo-Pechersky Monastery, visited
Mount Athos in the thirteenth century. He described his journey and Athonite life. The mystical Prayer of Jesus was then
much in evidence. The Holy Land was visited by Barlaam of
St Demetrius Monastery in 1060, by Abbot Daniel (who described his journey) in 1115 and by St Euphrosine, Abbess of
Polotsk, who died on her pilgrimage in 1173.

Kiev was a true center of monastic life before the Mongol
invasion. It had 118 canonized monks. However, there were
several monastic saints elsewhere. Of those at Novgorod, St
Anthony the Roman (d. 1147) and St Barlaam of Khutyn are
the best known. The first was, according to tradition, a
Benedictine monk from Italy. He came to Novgorod and,
changing his rite, became founder of the large monastery
called after him. St Barlaam of Khutyn, who lived a little
later, was a friend of Anthony, the Archbishop of Novgorod
who visited Constantinople just before it was sacked by the
Crusaders. St Barlaam also founded a large monastery. St
Gerasim of Vologda (d. 1178) and St Abraham of Smolensk
also belong to the same period. Smolensk was a cultural
center. It possessed a school founded by Prince Roman. According to the chronicles, the second Russian-born Primate,
Clement Smolyatich, a native of Smolensk, read Homer,
Aristotle and Plato.

---

12. S. Bolshakoff, "Influence of Patristic Studies on Modern Russian Mystics,"
Studia Patristica, 2 vols. (Berlin, 1957), 2:457.

St Cyril, Bishop of Turov, another monastic saint of Western Russia (1130-1180), wrote a remarkable instruction to a monk. He said: "You are like a candle. You are free only till you reach the door of the church. Once you are inside, take no thought for what will happen to you or how you will be transformed. You are like clothes. You are free till you are taken and put on. After that do not reflect whether you will be torn to pieces. You are free only before entering the monastery. When professed, surrender yourself altogether to obedience; do not hide within yourself the smallest self-will in order not to lose your soul. When you are a monk try to find a man who has the spirit of Christ. This man must be resplendent with virtues. He must witness his saintliness by his very living and possess above everything else love for the Lord. He must be obedient to the abbot and meek with the brethren. Finally he ought to understand the Scriptures and be able to lead those who wish to ascend to heaven to God. Surrender yourself to such a man and renounce your self-will."[13] The entire system of Starchestvo is already here.

The Mongolian invasion of Russia ended the Kievian period of Russian history. Temuchin, later known as Jenghiz Khan, was born in Mongolia in 1162. He was the son of Yesukai, a Mongolian chieftain. By 1206 he unified the majority of the Mongolian tribes and began his incredible conquests. Destroying the Khanate of Naimans and the Kintatar Empire in Northern China, Jehghiz subjugated Turkestan and invaded Afghanistan and India. In 1222 his troops defeated the Russians and their allies on the river Kalka. Jenghiz died in 1227, dividing his vast Empire among his four sons and making one of them the overlord of the others, with the obligation to reside in Karakorum in Mongolia. Ogodai, the heir of Jenghiz, decided to begin a period of new conquests in 1235. In 1237 the Mongols entered Russia and in 1240 sacked and destroyed its capital, Kiev. Kievo-Pechersky Monastery, mother-house of Russian monasticism, shared the fate of the capital.

13. J. M. Koncevič, *Stjažanie Ducha Svjatago v Putjach Drevnej Rusi* (Paris, 1952), p. 93.

The Mongolian invasion left Russia in a terrible condition.
Except the great Northern Republics of Nobgorod and Pskov,
secure behind their impenetrable forests, all the Russian principalities suffered greatly. Both of the Russian capitals, Kiev
and Vladimir, and many other cities and villages were burned
to the ground and utterly destroyed. Many people were killed
by the Mongols or died from hunger and epidemics. Southern
Russia became depopulated while the population in the
North increased by the migration from the devastated area. A
large number of parish churches and monasteries disappeared
during the invasion. In 1243 Batu Khan, conqueror of Russia,
summoned the Russian princes to his capital at Serai on the
Lower Volga. The Russian princes became the vassals of the
Great Khan and were obliged to pay him a fixed tribute, assist him in his wars and accept his confirmation of
their authority over their districts. The Grand Prince became
the supervisor of the Russian princes on behalf of the Khan
and was responsible for their good behavior. The Mongols
never appointed their own governors over the Russians and
did not interfere with them except for exacting a fixed
tribute.

In 1267, Kublai Khan, the last Great Khan, left Karakorum
for Peking and proclaimed himself Emperor of China. The
Mongolian Empire ceased to exist and descendants of Bathu
Khan in Serai became independent rulers. In 1313 Uzbek
Khan abandoned the *Yasa,* the Mongolian Sacred Book, and
became Moslem. As Moslems, the Khans of the Golden Horde
forsook the perfect religious toleration of their heathen for-
bears but they never attempted to convert the Russians into
"Raya" in the way the Christians in Turkey were converted.

Up to the year 1240 seventeen of the twenty-three Russian
Primates were Greeks, three were Bulgarians and only three
were Russians. After the Mongolian invasion Russian-born
Primates became the rule and foreigners the exception. Cyril
III was the first Russian Primate under the Mongolian rule. In
1279 he obtained from the Khan Mangu-Temir an 'Iarlik' or
Imperial decree which guaranteed all the ancient privileges of

the Russian Church and conferred many new ones. It was forbidden to confiscate Church property in any form, to levy any taxation upon it or to exact any tribute whatsoever from the clergy, who along with their serfs were exempt from compulsory state service. Any Mongol found guilty of transgressing against the "Iarlik" was liable to torture and to capital punishment. The Khans made the Russian bishops of Serai their privy councillors and often employed them as ambassadors.

One year after Usbek Khan turned Moslem one of the greatest monastic figures of Russian history, St Sergius of Radonesh (1314-1392), was born. He was the second son of the Rostov nobles, Cyril and Maria. They moved nearer to Moscow, to Radonesh. Bartholemew (secular name of Sergius) was a very religious boy and was inclined to monastic life. When his parents died Bartholomew accompanied his eldest brother, Stephen, to a nearby forest to live as a hermit. Stephen was unable to bear the hardships of a life in the vast and empty northern forest and went to Bogoyavlensky Monastery in Moscow leaving his brother alone in the forest. The latter remained as a solitary for two years. When he was discovered by the neighboring peasants, they started to visit him seeking prayers and direction. A few expressed their wish to remain with him in the forest. Thus Sergius began to receive disciples. Gradually he received twelve novices. In 1354 Sergius was ordained and formed a monastic community under the Studite Rule and he became abbot. The peculiarity of St Sergius Monastery was a manifestation of conscience by disciples to the abbot during Matins when the fourth part of the Canon was sung.

Life in St Sergius Monastery was very austere. Food was poor and scarce. There was often nothing to eat for two or three days at a time. Instead of wax candles, wooden torches were used for lighting. Vestments were of colored linen and the sacred vessels of wood. Patriarch Philotheus of Constantinople and the Russian Primate, St Alexis, sent their blessing to St Sergius. The austerities prescribed by St Sergius could

not please everybody. Some monks rebelled against the abbot
and he retired to Kirzhach where he founded another monastery. He was soon asked to return to his original monastery.
St Alexius, Russian Primate, who was Regent for the young
Grand Prince, employed St Sergius' services as a peacemaker,
sending him to Nizhni Novgorod to pacify local princes. He
also wanted to make St Sergius his successor in the Primacy
but the latter declined the honor. Demetrius, Grand Prince of
Russia, greatly respected St Sergius and went to ask his prayers and blessing in 1380 when he went to meet the Khan
Mamai, who was attacking Russia. On the field of Kulikovo
the Russians routed the army of the Khan, inflicting the first
defeat on the Khans of the Golden Horde.

St Sergius was the most respected Russian abbot of his age.
Not only laymen, from peasants to princes, and clergy of all
ranks but also monks from various monasteries came to visit
and consult him. Among these monks Sergius of Nurom, an
Athonite Hesychast, Euthemius of Suzdal, Demetrius of
Priluki and Stephen of Makrischi are the best known. Epiphanius the Wise, a disciple of St Sergius, left the story of his
life. The saint had many visions. One of them was prophetic.
The saint saw many flying birds. A voice said: "Sergius, the
Lord has accepted your prayer. Your disciples who come
after you will be as many as the multitude of these birds." St
Sergius also saw the phenomenon of the forest illuminated
during the night, as Anthony, abbot of Maloyaroslavetz,
would see it several centuries later. Among the personal
friends of St Sergius, St Cyril of the White Lake, St Sylvester
and St Paul of Obnora are the most notable.

St Nikon succeeded St Sergius as abbot of his monastery.
The monastery soon became wealthy on account of the great
benefactions showered upon it by the Russians, sovereigns,
nobles and simple people. The Russian Tsars used to make
pilgrimages to it and to pray there before their coronation.
The Russian Patriarchs did likewise before their enthrone-
ment. Great wealth created difficulties for the abbey but it
never suffered decline. Indeed it is today the most flourishing
Russian monastery in the Soviet Union, attracting tremen-

dous crowds of pilgrims. St Sergius himself founded nine monasteries and his immediate disciples, twelve. Altogether fifty monasteries were founded from St Sergius' monastery, which was dedicated to the Most Holy Trinity. These fifty monasteries founded forty others in their turn. One hundred canonized monks came from St Sergius, foundations. From 1300, in the course of 150 years, 180 new monasteries were founded.

Besides St Sergius many other bishops and abbots founded monasteries. St Alexis, the Russian Primate and a contemporary of St Sergius, founded five monasteries. Some other monastic founders are Methodius Pesnoshsky (d. 1392), Abraham of Galich (d. 1375), Sylvester of Obnora (d. 1379), Sabbas of Storozhev (d. 1407), Sergius of Obnora (d. 1412) and James Zhelesnoborsky (d. 1442). There were eleven monasteries of Tver and four in Nizhni Novgorod. Grand Princess Eudoxia, widow of Demetrius Donskoy, founded in 1387 the Convent of Ascension in Moscow, where she became a nun and was buried. All the Russian Grand Princesses and Tsarinas till the eighteenth century were buried in that convent. It was a custom in Moscow for Russian sovereigns and their wives to make monastic profession on their death bed or earlier. This custom was abandoned with the accession of the House of the Romanovs in 1613.

A large number of monasteries were founded in the fifteenth century. Besides the founders listed above, there were several others, even more remarkable. Archbishop Moses of Novgorod founded five monasteries. Paphnutius of Borovsk founded a large monastery in 1444 which trained in due course the celebrated Russian monastic reformer, St Joseph of Volokolamsk. St Sabatins (d. 1439) founded, together with St Zosima, the celebrated Solovetsky Monastery on the White Sea. The Great Valaam Monastery on the Lake of Ladoga became prominent in the fifteenth century. Four monasteries, founded by St Stephen of Perm (1345-1396), the first Russian missionary to the Ural Finns, became centers of missionary activity in the fifteenth century.

Although fifteenth-century Russia was rich in monasteries,

they were mostly small. Communities of two to six monks were numerous, while those with 100 to 300 monks rather rare. The smaller monasteries were usually affiliated to the larger ones. Some monasteries were called patriarchal, or stavropigiac, others, metropolitan and princely according to their founder. In such monasteries administration and economy depended much on the patron. The best monasteries were cenobitic but these were a minority. The majority of Russian monasteries were idiorrhythmic; that is to say, each monk had his own rule and means of living. They came together only for services. Most of the northern monasteries were idiorrhythmic. The cenobitic monasteries observed various rules approved by the councils, bearing the name of St Basil the Great, St Ephrem the Syrian, St John Climacus or St Theodore Studite. Great estates involved the monks in distracting cares and worldly interests. One of the Russian Primates, Metropolitan Cyprian, believed that the possession of great estates was bad for monasteries. It would be better, he thought, to rent the lands to laymen. The great estates came to monks in a variety of ways—by gifts, by purchase and by colonization. Royal charters granted all kinds of privileges to monasteries. The monks were freed from taxation of any kind. The abbot was judge not only over his monks but also over the inhabitants of the monastic estates, except in cases of murder. When people of other estates were involved, the abbot sat with the lay judge appointed by the prince.

The Russian monasteries in the North were centers of colonization. Many peasants from poor or overpopulated districts moved into vast new estates of the distant monasteries where they expected a better living. Gradually villages began to ring monasteries and then towns. The townships of Ustyug, Varnavin, Kalyazin, Kirilov, Zagorsk, Pecheri and others came into existence in this way. Many people settled on the monastic estates for security's sake. They were sure that they would not be abandoned to die of sickness and hunger in hard times. Some Russian monasteries were renowned for charitable aid. Kirilov Monastery used to feed 600 people daily during famines while Paphnutiev fed up to 1,000. Moreover, the monasteries used to have hospitals, homes for the aged and guest houses. They were, in short, the welfare centers of the age. They were, of course, cultural centers as well. They possessed libraries, where manuscripts were copied and circulated. People went to monasteries to be educated. Schools were rare and were maintained mostly by monasteries. Those who wanted to learn reading and writing, arts and crafts went to the monasteries as well. The Russian monasteries were not only schools, universities and welfare centers, but also strongholds, offering refuge in times of trouble. They were also often missionary centers from which Christianity was spread among the heathens.

However great the merits of the Russian monasteries in the field of culture and welfare, the monks never forgot that their main purpose was to cultivate the religious life. As soon as people began to invade monasteries and settle around them, the best of the monks, who cared only for union with God in prayer and contemplation, moved out to distant and inaccessible spots, to the impenetrable northern forests, to islands in remote lakes or in the Arctic Ocean, to marshes, mountains and tundras. The saintliest Russian monks were always afraid that close contact with secular society would make them worldly and prevent them from living in union with God.

CHAPTER II

ST NILUS OF SORA

S T NILUS OF SORA, the first great Russian mystic, who
has left us remarkable treatises and letters, was born in
1433. Although nothing certain is known about the
place of his birth or of his social origin, it is thought that he
was born in Moscow and belonged to the renowned noble
family of Maikov.[1] According to tradition he was calligrapher
and copied books. As a young man he came to the celebrated
Kirillo-Belozersky Monastery, where he made his profession.

Belozersky Monastery played an important part in the history of Russian monasticism. Its founder, Cyril, was born in
Moscow in 1337. Brought up by a relative, a nobleman at the
court of Demetrius Donskoy, Grand Prince of Moscow, Cyril
early became a monk in Simonon Monastery in Moscow
where he was pupil of Staretz Michael, afterwards Bishop of
Smolensk. St Sergius of Radonezh met Cyril in Simonov
Monastery, liked him and arranged his ordination to priesthood. When the abbot of Simonov was consecrated Archbishop of Rostov, Cyril succeeded him. However, he did not
remain abbot for long. He loved solitude and did not feel
happy in the capital. Resigning his abbacy, Cyril retired to
the more isolated Old Simonov.

Once, when he was singing an acathyst, he heard a voice
which told him: "Cyril, go away from this place to the White
Lake where I have prepared a place for you to save your

1. Archimandrite Justin, *Prepodobnyi i Bogonosnyi otec năs Nil, podvižnik
Sorskij Ustav ego o skitskoj žizni* (Moscow, 1902[4]), p. 7.

18

soul." Obedient to the voice, Cyril went to the White Lake, lost in the mighty northern forests. With Cyril also went another Simonov monk, Pherapont, a native of the White Lake district. This took place in 1397. Cyril found a mountain, Maura, from the top of which a great panorama of the forest could be seen. Cyril, then already sixty years old, settled as a hermit on the mountain. On every side there were forests and lakes, but no villages. It was a perfect solitude. At first only one peasant, Isaiah, knew the whereabouts of Cyril. Afterwards two other peasants, Avksentius Voron and Matthew Kikos, helped St Cyril to build a hut. Two Simonov monks from Moscow, Zebedeus and Dionisius, followed by another monk, Nathaniel, joined Cyril and built a church dedicated to the Assumption of our Lady. A new monastery came into being. The monks observed very strict poverty. Everything was possessed in common. Donations from benefactors were refused. The monks lived by their own labor. St Cyril died in 1427.[2]

Innocent, Christopher and Cassian succeeded St Cyril as abbots of the new monastery. Under their rule the monks started to gather and to copy manuscripts for their library. One manuscript, that of St Maximus the Confessor, was translated from the Greek on Mount Athos in 1425 and brought to the abbey the same year.

Unfortunately, the monks failed to persevere in their austerity. After the death of St Cyril they accepted vast estates from Prince Andrew of Mozhaisk, son of Demetrius Donskoy, Grand Prince of Moscow. This donation led to dissensions in the community. The more austere among them condemned the possession of the vast estates as unsuitable to the monks and contradictory to the vow of poverty.

St Nilus entered Kirillo-Belozersky Monastery just at this time. Abbot Cassian entrusted the formation of St Nilus to Father Martinian, a disciple of St Cyril and Pherapont, partisans of non-possession. In Belozersky Monastery Nilus made friends with Father Paisius Yaroslav, a nobleman, who was professed in the celebrated Spaso-Kamenny Monastery, where the Atho-

2. V. P. Sevyrev, *Poezdka v Kirillo-Belozerskij monastyr* (Moscow, 1850) gives a good summary of the history of the monastery and of the life of its founder.

nite Greek monk, Dionisius of Constantinople was the first abbot. Paisius returned in 1469 to Spaso-Kamenny Monastery, and then became abbot of the greatest Russian monastery, Holy Trinity, founded by St Sergius of Radonezh. Paisius was offered the Russian Primacy but declined this honor. A leader of the Non-Possessors, Paisius greatly influenced St Nilus causing him to become an ardent opponent of monastic estates.

St Nilus wanted to visit the Orthodox East and to study monastic life there. In 1465 he was able to carry out his plan. He left for the East with a delegation that was returning to Constantinople from Moscow. Nilus was accompanied on his journey by his pupil, Father Innocent, who had formerly been a nobleman, John Okhlebinin. St Nilus spent thirteen years in the East, in Constantinople, the Holy Land and Mount Athos. It was hardly twelve years after the fall of the Byzantine Empire and Byzantine memories were still fresh in the Monastic Republic of Mount Athos even though the monks had acknowledged the lordship of the Sultan some years previously. Hesychast ideas were still very much alive in the Monastic Republic.[3]

The Hesychast movement was started by Gregory Palamas, whom the Orthodox Church venerates as a great saint. Born of a noble family in Constantinople in 1297 or 1299, Gregory was well educated and as a very young man learned the Prayer of Jesus. When he was twenty, Gregory went to Mount Athos with his two brothers. Later he persuaded his mother and sister to become nuns. On Mount Athos Gregory became first a pupil of the monk Nicodemus and then joined Nicephoros, with whom he stayed eight years. He then entered the Laura of St Athanasius and subsequently the Skete of Berrhoae. In a cave near that Skete, Gregory spent ten years, enjoying revelations and illuminations. But the hardships of his life in the cave nearly killed him and he had to return to his Skete. After ordination Gregory was made abbot of

3. The best biography of St Nilus is to be found in N. Kalestinov, *Veliky Staretz* (St Petersburg, 1907).

Esphigmenou. An illness required that he go to Thessalonica. This visit was to be a turning point in his life.[4]

While in Thessalonica Gregory was approached by local monks with a request for help in their controversy with Barlaam of Calabria. This Italian Greek, native of Seminara, was a renowned scholar. He had taught Greek to Petrarch and to the teachers of Boccaccio. He popularized the Greek classics in the West. In 1328, in the reign of the Emperor Andronicus the Younger, Barlaam settled in Thessalonica. Barlaam was much respected by the Emperor and his powerful minister, Kantakusen. At first he was a staunch Byzantine, and an opponent of the Filioque and of Papal supremacy. He served as imperial ambassador to the Pope. However, Barlaam gradually changed his position. He began to accuse the Eastern clergy of ignorance and the Athonite and Thessalonican monks of heresy.

Barlaam visited the Hesychast monastery in Thessalonica. Their contemplative, retired life and austerities astonished him. He was even more astonished, indeed scandalized, by his conversation with Simeon, a monk of Keroserou Monastery. The latter described to Barlaam some psychophysical methods of disposing the mind for contemplation. Simeon recommended sitting in a dark room with the head lowered and the chin pressed against the breast. The nostrils should be narrowed. Breathing was to be slow and controlled, and the eyes, both of mind and body, were to be fixed on a physical center, in an effort to concentrate all prayer in the heart, the seat of spiritual life. Though at first nothing would be "seen", this technique would lead to a perception of divine light around the heart.

Barlaam was horrified to hear such words and immediately

---

4. The study of the Hesychast movement in this chapter is chiefly based on the book of Bishop Alexis, Rector of Kazan Theological Academy, *Vizantijskie cerkovnye Mistiki 14-vo veka, Prepod Grigorij Palama, Nikolai Kavasila, i Prepod Grigoij Sinait* (Kazan, 1906). The later works of Archbishop Basil Krivoshein, *The Ascetic and Theological Teaching of Gregory Palamas* (London, 1954), and Cyprian Kern, *Antropologiya sv. Grigoriya Palamui* (Paris, 1950) were consulted.

attacked the Hesychasts, calling them Messalians and "navel gazers." Palamas agreed to defend the Hesychasts. He sent to Barlaam a delegation of a few monks and requested Barlaam to leave the monks in peace and desist from his attacks on the Hesychast way of prayer. Palamas found nothing strange in the divine light. The apostles had seen this uncreated light with their physical eyes on Mount Thabor.

But Palamas' intervention did not disarm Barlaam. On the contrary, the latter, hearing that the light of Thabor was called "uncreated," accused Palamas of introducing division into God, making a distinction between the divine substance as a supreme God and the divine energies as lower gods. These men can see and sense while the divine essence is above understanding. A vehement controversy resulted.[5]

In order to restore peace, the Patriarch of Constantinople, John Calecas, convened a Council on June 2, 1341 to discuss the light of Thabor and the Prayer of Jesus. The Council approved the Palamites. Barlaam left Thessalonica for Italy leaving behind his friend and supporter Akindin, who agitated for a new Council. This met on August 6, 1341 and discussed the uncreated divine "energies" and the distinction between "energies" and "substance" in God. The Council again approved the Palamites and condemned Barlaam and Akindin, who were excommunicated. Meanwhile the Emperor Andronicus the Younger died and the struggle between Anne Paleologa, her son, John, and Kantakusen began. The Patriarch sided with the Barlaamites and recalled Palamas in 1343 to Constantinople where he was imprisoned, being accused of Polytheism by Calecas and the Antiochian Patriarch Ignatius. In 1345 a new Council excommunicated Palamas and again imprisoned him. However, the Empress Anne freed Palamas. Still another Council convened in 1347, suspended the excommunication of Palamas and deposed the Patriarch Calecas. In the same year Kantakusen became Emperor and the Patriarch Isidore consecrated Gregory Palamas Archbishop of Thessalonica. Because of his friend-

---

5. A good background for this controversy can be found in F. Uspensky, *Očerki po istorii vizantijskoj obrazovannosti v XIV-om veke* (Odessa, 1892).

ship with Kantakusen, Palamas was not received in Thessalonica and was forced to retire to the island of Lemos. Palamas attended the Council of Constantinople in 1351, where the Barlaamites, led by Nicephore Gregora, were finally condemned. In 1354 Palamas again visited and remained prisoner for one year. Returning finally to his See he ruled there till his death on November 14, 1360.

Gregory Palamas left many writings some of which are still unpublished. He writes clearly and well. He very frequently quotes Holy Scripture and the Fathers, especially Macarius of Egypt, Maximus the Confessor, Gregory of Nyssa, Gregory the Theologian, Basil the Great, John Chrysostom and John Damascene. Palamas is at one and the same time an exegete, theologian and controversialist. His knowledge is encyclopedic. This great mystic was also a philosopher, a Platonist, and not unacquainted with Aristotle.

It is not easy to summarize the doctrine of Palamas. According to him the substance of nature of God, being above everything, can neither be named nor understood nor seen. God surpasses all things and every kind of knowledge, dwelling far above the highest spirits. He is, forever and for all, incomprehensible and indescribable. He cannot be named by any word in this world or the next. God cannot be expressed in any image. He cannot be understood either by the senses nor by reason. He only can be thought of as something perfect, incomprehensible, the sum of all negations and the supreme abstraction of every being and name.[6] Yet God is and is called the cause of everything existing.[7] Everything participates in God and by this participation it exists. This participation does not touch the essence of God but his actions or energies. We may say that God is the Being of beings, the Form of all forms as an architype, the Wisdom of the wise and generally all in all. But no creature has relations or communion with the Sublime Nature. The only way one comes to God is through his self-revelation in his actions or energies.[8]

6. PG 150:938
7. PG 150:1175.
8. Ibid.

Palamas generalizes divine actions in the word "grace." The Divine Nature, remaining unattainable and incommunicable, influences us and the world through these actions or energies. Supreme and transcendent Goodness is the source of goodness. God is the perfect Mind and the perfect Goodness from which, as from a source, came forth the Word and the Holy Spirit. The nature of God and his energies are called Godhead, although they are different and have nothing in common except being called Godhead. The substance of God is called Godhead properly, but not his actions. The divine substance is simple but his energies are distinct. The power and the energy are common to all three Persons of God. They are outside the divine nature and are manifested many times and in many ways because God is almighty. Through the divine energies many unite with God and in a variety of ways participate in him. The energies (or the grace of the Spirit) differ from divine Substance yet they are not detached from it. They attract those who are worthy to communion with the Holy Spirit. According to Palamas it is impossible to consider grace as created. Grace is not referred to as a creature. The divine energies are neither the *hypostases* nor the substance nor the nature of God, yet they are uncreated and eternal because they are divine power, existing in God before the creation of the world. Therefore they are the source and the cause of everything created and everything capable of deification.[9]

Creatures can participate in divine actions naturally and freely. In the latter case, only reasonable creatures. They can approach or withdraw from God, be happy or otherwise. All reasonable creatures can learn from creation the power and goodness of God which are manifest in nature. But only the saints, in the proper sense of this word, see them and participate in them, becoming full of this indescribable light and radiant with its effulgence.[10] Man is created in the image of God, but he turned evil and corrupted in himself the image of

9. Alexis Molčanov, *Vizantijskie cerkovnye mistiki 14-veke* (Kazan, 1906), p. 21.
10. Ibid., p. 22.

God. As a result there came death of soul and body and separation from God. The Incarnation restored man. The beginning of renewal for the individual soul is in baptism, through the forgiveness of sins. Its continuation is through holy living. The first stage is penance, followed by the denial of everything earthly for love of heavenly things. Penance is the beginning of salvation. It consists in humility, contrition, interior sorrow of heart, meekness and charity. Fasting and abstinence aid spiritual progress. It is impossible to be freed from the domination of evil without a contrite heart. The latter cannot be obtained without abstinence in sleep, food and pleasure. All these means destroy the external man and revive the internal. Fleshly passions are extinguished by the crucifixion of the body with prayer.

He who wants to attain holiness must remain in his cell, suffer and pray. The cell is a safe haven. Prayer precedes all the virtues. By prayer the mind ascends to God. It is hard to lead a life of prayer and few men attain to perpetual prayer. Concentration and self-knowledge help in the attainment of this. Solitude and reclusion help much to attain peace of soul. The body is the temple of the Holy Spirit. It is not evil, but evil inhabits it. This indwelling evil must be expelled by the mind acting as "bishop", overseer. By purifying the body with abstinence and by hating our faults we can acquire virtues and stand before God with pure hearts. We shall see then in ourselves the grace promised to those pure of heart. We must confine the mind within the limits of our body, in the heart, to prevent our thoughts from wandering at random. We must watch over our body because the enemy seduces us through it. Therefore we begin with penance, fasting and abstinence and rise to prayer and self-knowledge. Freed from vain thoughts and rejecting everything created for love of God, the soul becomes impassible and silent. Only then can the soul stand before God and rejoice in heavenly rest because nothing external solicits its attention. Divine grace which dwells within the soul transforms it into a better state, and illuminates it with indescribable light, perfecting the interior man. When day begins and the sun rises in our hearts, then the true man goes to a true work and guided by inner light ascends or is taken to the eternal mountains. In this light he contemplates heavenly things. [11] Those who have attained purity of mind see during prayer the light of the Holy Trinity. Their bodies become capable of receiving the incomprehensible, godlike life. They are strong, indifferent to evil, able to understand the mysteries of nature. They can perform miracles and prophesy. They are full of wisdom. Like Maximus, Gregory compares the union of a soul with God to a marriage.

Hesychast ideology as well as the study of the Prayer of Jesus on Mount Athos considerably influenced St Nilus. The Prayer of Jesus was revived on Mount Athos by St Gregory the Sinaite, a contemporary of Gregory Palamas. This Prayer, which is based on the prayer of the blind man in the Gospel, is: "Lord Jesus Christ, Son of God, have mercy upon me, a sinner." It is an ejaculatory prayer and is prescribed to be said by all Eastern monks. This prayer is known from the earliest days of monasticism. St John Climacus knew of it. In due course several methods of reciting this prayer were elaborated.

Gregory the Sinaite was born in Asia Minor. Together with his father and brothers he was captured by the Moslems but was eventually ransomed. It seems that this misadventure impressed the Sinaite. He retired to Cyprus and finally to Mount Sinai, where he was professed. He went afterwards to Mount Athos. He found the monks there pious and observant but ignorant in mystical matters. They did not even know the meaning of solitude and contemplation. However, he found in the Skete of Magula three monks, Isaiah, Cornelius and Macarius, who were familiar with the Prayer of Jesus. The Sinaite started to teach monks the Prayer of Jesus. Later he built three monasteries in Macedonia. He visited cities and provinces leading souls to the higher forms of the Prayer of Jesus. The Sinaite left several treatises. [12]

11. Ibid., pp. 44-45.

12. Some of the writings of St Gregory of Sinai, or the Sinaite, can be found in the celebrated collection of mystical writings entitled the *Philokalia,* first pub-

The doctrine of St Gregory may be summed up in this way. Orthodoxy is the correct teaching about Trinity and Duality. Trinity is a simple unmixed unity. The one God in three Persons has three separate Hypostases. God is known and understood in everything through three Hypotases. God keeps and maintains everything by the Son and the Spirit. None of them is named or thought to be outside or separate. Man was created in the image of God not only in his soul but in his body as well, which in its physical structure shows forth the Holy Trinity. The human soul is similar to the Trinity because mind, word and spirit do not exist one without the other, always one in the other and yet by themselves. After the fall the fallen mind is led about as a prisoner and cannot resist evil if it will not return to God, will not live in him and be united with him by praying unceasingly and confessing its thoughts. In order to be wise one must attain to purity and impassibility. The wisdom of this world is not enough. Wordly wisdom corrupts the mind because it produces a multitude of evil thoughts. Man must preserve his heart from evil and from useless thoughts by the action of the Holy Spirit. The heart, freed of unsuitable thoughts, is a temple of the Holy Spirit. It possesses a pure, unique gnosis (knowledge) that is the intuition of truth by grace. Living, active faith is necessary for salvation. The latter begins with obedience and fasting and continuous memory of God. All baptized in Christ must pass through his life. His conception is for us a pledge of the Holy Spirit, his birth, our share in spiritual joy; his baptism is for us the purifying power of the fire of the Holy Spirit, his transfiguration the source of our contemplation; his crucifixion, our death to everything; his burial, the treasuring in our heart of the divine love; his resurrection the lifegiving awakening of our soul; his ascension our rising above the limits of senses, the rapture of mind toward God.

---

lished in Venice in the eighteenth century; trans. (partial) E. Kadloubovsky and G. E. H. Palmer, *Early Fathers from the Philokalia: Together with Some Writings of St Abba Dorotheus, St Isaac of Syria and St Gregory Palamas* (London: Faber and Faber, 1954).

Gregory of Sinai gives the following method for practicing the Prayer of Jesus. In the morning sit down on a low seat and force your mind to descend from the head to the heart. Keep it there and call unceasingly, mentally and from the depth of your soul: "Lord, Jesus Christ, have mercy on me." When you become weary of this, turn your mind to the second half of the prayer: "Jesus, Son of God, have mercy on me." After repeating this appeal many times, go back to the first half. When disturbing thoughts assail you, do not pay attention to them. Ignore even good thoughts, but continue to keep your mind recollected crying out to Jesus Christ. Soon you will be able to expel these thoughts and their inspirers, the devils, castigating and burning them with the divine name. The worst passions are fornication and pride. Prayer gradually gives us full control over all the passions. [13]

Gradually the mind becomes a stranger to everything material. It is now full of light, ineffably united with God in one spirit. The beginning of this prayer is the purifying action of the Holy Spirit; the middle of it is the illuminating power of the Spirit and contemplation; the end is the rapture of the mind in God. Although virtues and prayer are necessary for union with God, yet they are merely the body and bones. We need living soul, grace. Actual grace is the power of the fire of the Divine Spirit acting in the heart and filling the latter with gladness and joy, raising the soul to heavenly things, warming and illuminating it, stopping sinful thoughts and killing every impure movement of flesh. As we ascend still further, true knowledge and spiritual worship become possible. After that one enters into rest, admiration, ecstasy and love, One becomes as it were bodiless and incorruptible with flesh full of light, as though full of fire.

It is easy to understand why St Nilus was impressed by this teaching!

St Nilus returned to Russia in 1478. The new abbot, Niphont, was a partisan of monastic landowning. Perhaps due to him the monastery was taken from the jurisdiction of

13. Molčanov, *Vizantijskie*, p. 80.

Vassian, Archbishop of Rostov, by the Primate, Gerontius, and transferred to the patronage of Prince Michael of Vereia on the ground that St Cyril put his monastery under the patronage of Prince Andrew, father of Prince Michael. The Archbishop of Rostov complained to the Grand Prince, John, and the latter ordered Prince Michael to restore the monastery to the Archbishop and convened a Council to discuss similar happenings. Nilus arrived just at this time. At once he joined the Non-Possessors. [14] Niphont refused to accept St Nilus back into the community. However, the Primate, reconciled with the Grand Prince, deposed Abbot Niphont and sent him to Simonov Monastery as a penitent. St Nilus was offered the Abbey of Kirillov but declined. He went to live as a solitary on the river Sorka. There he was occasionally visited by the new abbot of Kirillov, Gurius Tushin, and a holy monk, Germanus.

Nilus was joined soon by Dionisius of the House of the Princes of Zvenigorod. Dionisius was professed in Volokolamsk, where in the bakery he did the work of two men. He used to sing seventy-seven psalms and made 3,000 metanias (prostrations) daily. Nilus and Dionisius together built a small church. The next recruit was Nilus Polev, from the family of the Princes of Smolensk. Paisius Yaroslav visited St Nilus in 1485. The Russian Primate Gerontius quarrelled with the Grand Prince and retired. The latter offered the Russian Primacy to Paisius but he declined. Meanwhile the Russian Church became troubled by the heresy of the Judaizers. Paisius and Nilus were called upon to defend Orthodoxy.

The Judaizing heresy originated in Novgord. In 1470 Michael Olelkovich, Prince of Kiev, visited Novgorod. A Jewish doctor, Skharia, came in his suite. Skharia met the Novgorodian priests, Dionisius and Alexis, and seduced them from Orthodoxy. Skharia persuaded the priests that Christianity is wrong. According to Skharia God is one and there

---

14. The Non-Possessors opposed monastic landowning. A. Pavlov gives the history of monastic landowning in Russia in *Istoričeskij očerk sekuljarizacii cerkovnych zemel' v Rossii* (Moscow, 1871).

are not three Persons in him. The Messiah had not yet come. Christ was a mere man. In order to be saved one must become a Jew. After Skharia, two other Jews visited Novgorod, Joseph Shmoilo-Skaryavei and Moses Hanush. These Jews persuaded both priests to accept Judaism but did not allow them to be circumcised fearing notoriety and scandal. The new converts were to remain outwardly Christians. Soon another priest, Maximus, and his son, John were converted, and finally Gabriel, the Dean of St Sophia's, the great Cathedral of Novgorod, embraced the heresy. In 1480 Ivan III visited Novgorod and was charmed by Alexius and Dionisius. He called them to Moscow and appointed them Deans of the Cathedrals of the Assumption and the Archangel. In Moscow the heretics succeeded in convincing the Chancellor of the Grand Prince, the learned Kuritsin, Archimandrite Zosima of Simonov Monastery, and even Princess Helen, daughter-in-law of the Grand Prince. [15]

In 1480, Gennadius, Archbishop of Novgorod, accidentally discovered the existence of a secret heretical society in his archdiocese. At once the Archbishop began his struggle with the heretics. It was long and difficult because the heretics possessed influential protectors. Indeed in 1489, when the Russian Primate died, the powerful Chancellor succeeded in raising the heretic Zosima to the Russian Primacy. Nevertheless, under the pressure of the disturbed Orthodox the Grand Prince convened a Church Council on October 17, 1490. Besides the bishops, several abbots and priests attended, including Paisius and St Nilus. Several Judaizers were present. While the Archbishop of Rostov and other prelates demanded the heretics be burned, Paisius and St Nilus stood for kindness. Heresy developed, they said, because of the ignorance of the clergy and the superstition of the people. The Council excommunicated the heretics and ordered them to be imprisoned in various monasteries for life. At this point the celebrated abbot of Volokolamsk, Joseph Sanin, inter-

---

15. I devoted a chapter to the Judaizers in *Russian Nonconformity* (Philadelphia: Westminster, 1950).

vened. Sanin had been born of a noble family in 1440. He became a monk at twenty in Borovsk Monastery, where he was elected abbot in 1477. Joseph's austerity displeased the monks and he resigned and founded the celebrated Volokolamsk Monastery in 1479. The Rule of Volokolamsk stressed obedience to the abbot and covered the smallest details of monastic life with innumerable rules, such as dictating where one might sit and walk and so on. The rule divided the monks into three groups according to their occupation, clothing and food. About the contemplative life little was said. Volokolamsk was a disciplined and well-managed monastery with admirably ordered services. It was famous for its charity and its learning. St Joseph was himself an encyclopedic scholar and very intelligent but he lacked a critical spirit and systematic training. Against the Judaizers he composed a book, *The Enlightener, PROS VETITEL* which is well written and shows his very wide range of reading.

Volokolamsk was in the archdiocese of Gennadius of Novgorod and St Joseph became his friend and helper. Together they forced the Primate Zosima, a secret Judaizer, to retire on May 17, 1494. The Judaizers, however, still had powerful protectors at the Court, including Princess Helen and Chancellor Kuritsin. In 1499 the situation changed; Princes Helen lost her influence which passed to Sophia Paleologa, second wife of Ivan III, niece of the last two Byzantine Emperors, and her son Basil III, who succeeded to Ivan III in due course. [16] Sophia Paleologa was the daughter of Thomas, Despot of Morea. After the fall of Byzantium, she was taken to Rome where she became the ward of the Pope and a pupil of the celebrated humanist, Cardinal Bessarion, Metropolitan of Nikea and abbot of Grottaferrata. The Pope married her to Ivan III, who adopted subsequently the Byzantine coat of arms and court ceremonial. In the same year Prince Basil Patrikeev, who opposed new changes, was expelled from Moscow to Kirillov-Belozersky Monastery and forced to become a monk there. He was given the name of

16. The history of the marriage of Sophia Paleologa to Ivan III was studied by F. Pierling: *La Russie et le Saint Siège*.

Vassian. He soon became a friend of St Nilus and like him a resolute opponent of monastic landowning. [17]

A new Council to discuss church affairs was convened in Moscow in 1503. Both St Nilus and Paisius Yaroslavov were invited. The new Primate, Simon, the Grand Prince and his heir, Basil, Gennadius, archbishop of Novgorod, six bishops and numerous lower clergy attended. The Council prohibited the payment of fees to bishops for ordinations, closed double monasteries and forbade widowed priests to serve in parishes. When the Grand Prince wanted to dissolve the Council after its program was completed, St Nilus, Paisius Yaroslavov, Vassian Patrikeev and the Belosersky monks requested the Grand Prince to issue a decree prohibiting monastic landowning and to confiscate monastic estates. The Archbishop of Novgorod protested. The Grand Prince, although very happy to dispossess monasteries, was afraid to antagonize the powerful clergy. He suggested asking the advice of St Joseph of Volokolamsk. The latter championed monastic landowning. Vast estates, he asserted, enable monasteries to help parish churches, to maintain hospitals and schools and provide suitable conditions for great noblemen to enter the monastic order to become bishops. St Nilus opposed Joseph's ideal of monastic life. In his view, purely contemplative monks must live by their own work and not depend on a multitude of hired laborers and servants. The views of St Joseph prevailed. St Nilus retired to his monastery, where he died on May 7, 1508. He requested in his will that his body be thrown to wild beasts to be devoured, or, if this were not acceptable, to be buried without ceremonies.

St Nilus left two letters to Cassian, a former Byzantine Prince, who died as a monk in Russia; one letter to his friend and companion in travels, Innocent, who founded his own monastery and two letters to unknown monks. But his greatest work is *The Tradition of Sketic Life*[18]

---

17. A. C. Arkhangelsky, *Nil Sorskij i Vassijan Patrikeev, ich literaturnye trudy i idei v drevnej Rusi* 2 vols. (St Petersburg, 1882), is still the best study of the writings of St Nilus and Vassian.

18. I have used the edition of the *Tradition* published by Archmandrite Justin, *Prepodobnij i Bogonosnij Otec naš Nil, Podvižnik Sorsky i Ustav ego o Skitskoj žizni* (Moscow, 1902).

The Tradition consists of a foreword and eleven chapters. In the foreword St Nilus discusses the external behavior of monks. He stresses obedience to the abbot. Those who are rebellious should be expelled. The sketic monks must live by their own work, by various arts and crafts. They should not possess vast estates. If work fails, the monks may accept charity but within limits. St Nilus forbade his monks to engage in external works of charity. The sketic monks are to be poor. They can receive pilgrims for a short time and also give spiritual advice but no more. Food and drink must be of the simplest. Neither women nor young men must be allowed to visit the skete nor even female animals be kept.

The skete of St Nilus was organized according to his *Tradition*. There was one priest, one deacon and twelve monks. Everyone lived in his own cell, a little hut, which was to be about a stone's throw from the others and the church. The sketic monks went to their church in the middle of their laura only on Saturdays, Sundays and feasts. Otherwise, everyone prayed and worked in his own cell. The night vigil lasted, as on Mount Athos, the entire night. After each Kafisma[19] there were three or four readings from the Fathers. During the Liturgy the monks sang only the Trisagion, Alleluja, Cherubikon and hymn to Our Lady. Everything else was read. On Saturdays there was a service of the dead.

The text of the *Tradition* is divided into eleven chapters. The first chapter deals with the nature of the spiritual struggle, the second discusses resistance to unsuitable thoughts and the third shows how to fortify oneself in this struggle. The fourth chapter describes the struggle. The fifth chapter describes the eight passions and the sixth, how to resist them. The seventh chapter stresses the memory of death and judgment. The last chapters tell of tears, compunction, death to the world and of the gradualness of the entire process of spiritual progress. St Nilus was very well read. He knew well the Bible and the Fathers, particularly St Anthony the Great, St Basil the Great, St Ephrem and St Isaac the Syrian, Macarius the Great, Barsanuphius, John Climacus, Abbot

19. *Kafisma (cathisma):* a portion of the Psalter.

Dorotheus, Maximus the Confessor, Hesychius, Symeon the New Theologian, Peter Damascene, Gregory, Nilus and Philotheus of Sinai.[20]

In the first chapter St Nilus shows that victory and defeat in our struggle with the passions and vices depend on how we react to the various thoughts coming to us. At first, a thought comes to us as a pure appearance. This appearance is neutral and sinless because it does not depend on us. Then we begin to discuss this thought. This may already be sinful if the thought is evil. We must resist the evil suggestion by opposing it with good thoughts. The next stage is consent, when we accept the evil suggestion voluntarily. If a fully experienced monk yields to an evil thought, it is sinful; but in the case of newcomers, if they repent immediately, it is pardonable. This is the first form of consent. The second form occurs when man not only willingly accepts evil suggestions, but is ready to perform them, only stopping because he is prevented by circumstances. This is very sinful. The next stage is capture. In this case a person continually thinks of his evil desires and is enslaved by them. He still may return to virtue but not easily. Capture comes from dissipation and useless and vain conversations. There are many degrees of it. Suggestions may come during prayer or at other times. Unsuitable thoughts during prayer are particularly evil. The last stage is passion when a man willingly and continually surrenders himself to evil suggestions and they become his second nature. All passions, unless purged by corresponding penance, lead to torments in the next world.

The second chapter describes how to resist evil suggestions. Two methods are recommended: the rejection of the suggestion as soon as it appears and unceasing prayer. During prayer, according to St Nilus of Sinai, the mind must be deaf and dumb and the heart free of

20. In a letter to Innocent, St Nilus says; "Living alone I am occupied with the study of spiritual writings. I study first the commandments of the Lord and commentaries on them. I do the same with the apostolic traditions, and with the lives and instruction of the holy fathers. I meditate over all that and what I find according to my judgment God-pleasing and useful for my soul, that I copy down. My life, in short, is in this." — Justin, *Prepodobnij*, p. 10.

all thoughts, even good ones, as Hesychius of Jerusalem said, because after good thoughts come the bad. St Nilus recommends then the Prayer of Jesus as St Gregory of Sinai described it. St Nilus advises continual repetition of this prayer, keeping the mind "within the heart" and breathing slowly. [21] If thoughts come one must not be depressed but continue his excercise and disregard them. If thoughts persist one must rise up and pray against them. If this is still not enough, then the prayer must be said vocally, patiently and for a long time. Gradually the thoughts will disappear and calm will return. To pray without wandering thoughts is an achievement and demands time. But grace is given to the persevering and prayer becomes pleasant. When this is attained one must be still more faithful to it. Prayer, chanting of the sacred hymns and psalms, reading the lives of the Fathers may alternate, with prayer predominating. The summit of the spiritual life is silence, unceasing prayer and contemplation. A time comes when indescribable joy seizes one and takes one beyond prayer. "Then the soul has no more prayer and not only loses its movement but itself is led by some other power. The soul is mysteriously captured and finds itself in the uncomprehensible which it knows not. This is called rightly contemplation and a form of prayer but it is not prayer itself. In this case the mind is already above prayer, which is left aside for the better. A person is then in rapture and wholly without desire. This phenomenon is called prayer only because it proceeds from prayer. This indescribable gift, which no one can name, is given to the saints. The soul forgets itself and this passing world and no longer desires anything. It is illuminated with an unspeakable joy, the heart overflows with sweetness. The very body of man forgets not only all the passions but even its very life. It thinks that this must surely be the kingdom of God." [22]

St Nilus quotes St Symeon the New Theologian: "O, wonder, what word can describe this because it is truly awful and above every word! I see a light which the world does not

21. Ibid., p. 32.
22. Ibid., p. 39.

possess. Sitting in the cell I see within me the Creator of the world and talk with him and love him and am nourished only by the Knowledge of God. United to him, I ascend to heaven. But where is the body? I know not. . . . " [23] What was possible to the saints is possible to those who pray unceasingly. Night is the best time for prayer. Nocturnal prayer rapidly leads to perfection.

When a person is tired of this prayer of Jesus, he may turn to psalms or to reading or even to work.

The third and fourth chapters continue describing the struggle against interior temptation. The chief virtue is courage, to persevere and never give up prayer. One must always be vigilant and meditate on his own frailty. We must live according to the Holy Scriptures, live in God. In the morning we must glorify God in vocal prayer and confess our faults and only after that should we begin mental prayer, psalms, reading or work. If we meet someone we must avoid empty talk, controversies and judgments. While eating and drinking we must remember God. Even sleeping we must rest in God, going to bed with suitable meditations. Healthy people should exercise the body with work, fasting and vigils.[24]

The long fifth chapter is devoted to the description of eight passions: gluttony, impurity, meanness, anger, sadness, acedia, vanity and pride. St Nilus advices the monk to eat little and not to break his fast before three PM. Food must be simple and according to age, health and occupation. Against temptations of impurity, St Nilus recommends meditation and prayer, and particularly, the immediate rejection of unsuitable thoughts. Avarice is the result of weak faith and foolishness. The victory over it is attained when one has nothing and does not want possessions. After mentioning anger and sadness, St Nilus describes acedia. The struggle with the last is very difficult and the best antidote is patience and perseverance. The study of vanity and pride completes the chapter. The following chapter shows how to over-

23. Ibid.
24. Ibid., p. 48.

come all these passions and suggests prayer and meditation
on the Bible.

In the seventh chapter St Nilus recommends the memory of
death and quotes many Fathers to this effect. In the eighth
chapter the Saint speaks of tears. Remembering our life and
the future torments, we must weep much. Blessed are those
who have the grace of tears which warm the heart. St Nilus
recommends the writings of St Symeon the New Theologian
to those who are anxious to gain the gift of tears. These can
be gained especially by meditation, prayer and reading. We
must cultivate every exercise which brings us to tears. The
ninth chapter stresses the need of vigilance in those who have
attained the grace of tears and pure, undistracted prayer. The
tenth chapter stresses the need to die to the world. He who is
preoccupied with anxieties and deeds of the world cannot
reach perfection. The Saint quotes St John Climacus: "Life
in solitude is the giving up of worries about things not only
unsuitable but good in themselves as well." "Under the latter
things," the Saint says, "Climacus does not mean the external
occupations common nowadays, like the administration of
villages, management of many estates, etc., which unite
monks to the world. Such things have no place in a monk's
life. For him they are not good. The Holy Father indicated
those which are good and useful for the salvation of souls,
like sermons, discussions and meetings, properly timed and
ordered, with spiritual fathers and brothers." But even these
can become occasions for disputation, judging of others and
the like. St Symeon the New Theologian says that for a spiritual man life must be solitary, free of anxiety and dead to
everything. Only after emphasizing this does Symeon teach
one how to pray and to watch after thoughts. Nilus praises
greatly the wonderful Syrian mystic, St Isaac, who strongly
condemned those who want to live in solitude and yet are
unable to break off with the world. [25]

In the last chapter St Nilus stresses the need of discretion.
Everything should be done in its own time and in its own

25. Ibid., pp. 97ff.

way. Those who want to become solitaries must first be trained how to live in monasteries. Only then may they go to live
in small communities with a few brethren. Finally, after that
experience they may dare to live alone. Different people have
different vocations. St Nilus prefers living in a small skete
with a few brethren. People subject to vanity, a high opinion
of themselves, cunning, and the like, should never go into
solitude but those who struggle with the flesh may prudently
do so. St Isaac the Syrian greatly praised St Arsenius the
Great as a perfect solitary, yet he had disciples. The same was
true of St Nilus of Sinai and Daniel of Skete. Mentioning his
journey in the East, the Saint stresses that he saw the same
type of life among those who love solitude on Mount Athos,
near Constantinople and other places. If for the perfect it is
good to live in twos or threes, for the humbler people the
community life is best.[26]

The *Tradition* ends with a short conclusion in which St
Nilus states that he advances nothing new but merely propounds the doctrine of the Fathers. This is so. The *Tradition*
is in a sense a short *Philokalia* or collection of maxims from the
ancient Fathers, commented upon by St Nilus. It preceded
the *Philokalia* of Metropolitan Macarius of Corinth and St
Nicodemus Hagiorite by nearly four centuries.

The *Tradition* of St Nilus was copied in many monasteries
and afterwards printed in Slavonic and Russian. Generations
of Russian monks were brought up on it. In his outlook St
Nilus is a typical Athonite of his age. In many respects he was
very different from the Russian monks who were his contemporaries. St Joseph of Volokolamsk, a very good monk too,
was also a statesman and a Russian nationalist, while St Nilus
was a contemplative, scholar and a stranger to political struggles. The disciples of St Nilus, inheriting his spirit, soon entered into a conflict with the majority of the Russian monks
who found the ideology of St Joseph more congenial and
easier to understand.

26. Ibid., pp. 100-101.

CHAPTER III

RUSSIAN MONASTICISM IN THE SIXTEENTH, SEVENTEENTH, AND EIGHTEENTH CENTURIES

SOON AFTER THE DEATH OF ST NILUS the struggle between his disciples and those of St Joseph of Volokolamsk began. The kindness of the Trans-Volga Elders, as the disciples and friends of St Nilus were called, toward the Judaizers and their opposition to the death penalty were construed as sympathy toward the heretics. Moreover, many Elders stood for the old political regime of the autonomous principalities and city-states against the new autocratic, centralized monarchy. They also opposed monastic landowning and domination of the Church by the state. All this created for them a multitude of powerful enemies. The first to suffer was Vassian Patrikeev, who was imprisoned after many trials for his supposed deviations from Orthodoxy. The real reason for his imprisonment was his opposition to monastic landowning which was now championed by a new Russian Primate, Metropolitan Daniel, a former monk of Volokolamsk.[1] Many other people suffered with Vassian, including the remarkable Greek humanist Michael Trivilis, known in Russia as Maximus the Greek.

Michael Trivolis was born of a great Byzantine aristocratic family in Arta in Epirus in 1470, only a few years after the fall of the Empire.[2] He received his education in Venice and

1. There is a good study of Daniel: V. Zmakin, *Mitropolit Daniil i ego sočinenija* (Moscow, 1881).
2. The most exhaustive work on Maximus the Greek is G. Papamichael, *Maximos Graikos: 'O protos fotiotés tan Roson En Athenai* (Athens, 1951). V. Ikonnikov's *Maksim Grek* (Kiev, 1915) remains the classic. E. Denisoff, *Maxime le Grec et l'Occident* (Paris-Louvain, 1943) is interesting.

in the Italian universities of Ferrara and Padua. He collaborated with Aldo Manuci in the publication of Greek philosophers. Trivolis was much impressed by Savanarola and entered his convent. After the burning of his master in 1498, Trivolis returned to Greece and entered Vatopedi Monastery on Mount Athos in 1507, taking the name of Maximus. In 1515 he arrived in Moscow, invited by the Grand Prince Basil III, son of Ivan III and Sophia Paleologa, to put his library in order and to supervise the correction of the Russian liturgical books. Many errors due to ignorant copyists had crept into these books. The opposition of Maximus to monastic landowning and his relations with Vassian Patrikeev made Maximus objectionable to the Josephites, disciples of St Joseph of Volokolamsk. The latter accused Maximus of deliberately corrupting the liturgical books by wrong translations. Maximus condemned Russian superstitions and nationalist pride. He also asked how the Russian Church became independent from her Mother Church of Constantinople and who gave her this independence. Such questions offended the Russians. The theory of the Third Rome was already in elaboration. According to this theory the first Rome fell because of heresy and the second, Constantinople, was subjected to Moslem conquest because the Greeks betrayed Orthodoxy in Florence. The Russians now formed the only independent Orthodox nation. All other Orthodox kingdoms and principalities have melted into the Russian state or will do so. Moscow is the Third Rome and there will be no fourth. The Russian Sovereign is the heir to the Byzantine Basileus with all his rights and duties. This theory was propounded by a monk, Philotheus, of Eleazarov Monastery in Pskov in his letters to the Pskov Chancellor Misiur Munekhin and to Basil III.[3]

When Maximus opposed the divorce of Basil III from his wife, Solomonia Saburov, because the latter was barren, all the past indiscretions of Maximus were remembered and he was condemned as a heretic. He spent many years in prison in

---

3. A bibliography on the history of Novgorod and Pskov is given in my book, *Russian Non-Conformity*.

various monasteries. Toward the end of his life Maximus was released but not allowed to return to Mount Athos. Maximus wrote several treatises, dogmatic, historical, philosophical, controversial and grammatical. He wrote a remarkable instruction for Ivan the Terrible, the first Russian sovereign to be imperially crowned. Maximus influenced many prominent Russians who played an important part in the reign of Ivan IV, particularly the Russian Primate Macarius, Archpriest Sylvester, Alexis Adashev, Archbishop Germanus of Kazan and Ivan IV himself. The influence of Maximus could be observed also in the decrees of the Russian Council of the Hundred Chapters, the Codex of Ivan IV and the works of Metropolitan Macarius.

Maximus was a scholar but not a mystic. Yet he saved something from the inheritance of St Nilus which was compromised by the heretical teaching of one Trans-Volga Elder, Vassian Kosoy, who developed rationalist and judaizing theories and fled to Poland.[4] Arthemius, Abbot of the celebrated Trinity Monastery, near Moscow, was likewise, but unjustly, accused of heterodoxy and also fled to Poland where he did much for Orthodoxy.

To this period belongs also the Abbess Mary, of Mikhalitsky Monastery in Novgorod.[5] She was a younger contemporary of St Nilus and belonged to the same social class. Her ideology is similar to that of St Nilus. Her most interesting notes of "Zapiski" are the first memoirs by a woman in Russian literature. Princess Serafima Odoevsky, her name by birth, was the daughter of Prince Michael Odoevsky. The Prince had migrated in the second half of the fifteenth cen-

4. One of the Trans-Volga Elders who was a good theologian, Zinovij Otenskij, wrote two remarkable treatises against Kosoy: *Istiny Pokazanie* and *Mnogoslovnoe poslanie na zlamudrie Kosogo.*

5. Mary Odoevsky described her life in a ms which was printed, as far as it survived, by Rul-Ignatiev in the supplement to nos. 41, 42 and 47 of *Novgotodskiya Gubernskiya Vedomosti* (1849). S. R. Mintzlov, unable to find the ms, found a copy of *Vedomosti* and reprinted the memoirs in fifty copies: *Zapiski Igumenii Marii, Urozhdennoy Knyachnui Odoevskoy* (Novgorodskiya Gubernskiya Tipografya, 1912). *Zapiski* is very rare. The copy which I consulted is in the library of the Pontifical Oriental Institute in Rome.

tury from Toropetz to Novgorod, the capital of the great
Russian city-state and a member of the Hanseatic League.
Novgorod was never invaded by the Mongols. Its enormous
territories occupied all the Russian North. A turbulent aristocratic Republic, with a good deal of democratic representa-
tion, Novgorod was wealthy and progressive because of its
continuous contacts with the West. The Western merchants
lived in Novgorod, and there were Latin churches in this city.
In their work of unifying Russia the Grand Princes of
Moscow were bound to interfere with Novgorod and to incor-
porate the Northern Republic in their state. This happened in
the reign of Ivan III when Princess Serafima resided in Novgorod.[6]

The *Memoirs* of the abbess are an interesting human and
historical document but they are also important for the study
of Russian mysticism. The Memoirs give a remarkable picture
of aristocratic life in Novgorod on the eve of its loss of independence. Serafima was well educated by her father in an
age when the education of girls was considered superfluous.
She was educated together with her brother and a boy, Nazarius, an orphan son of a gentleman killed in war. When Nazarius was thirteen years old he was sent to Riga to be trained
by wealthy German merchants for a career. When Nazarius
returned he was appointed secretary to the Veche, the Novgorodian Parliament. He soon became quite prominent. Nazarius and the young Princess fell in love. Prince Michael could
not approve the marriage of his daughter to a mere nobleman. He forbade Nazarius to visit his palace. Nazarius submitted but said: "I came here as a slave. I leave as a foe and I
shall return as master." Meanwhile the Prince decided to
marry his daughter to Demetrius, the only son and heir of
Basil Maximov, an immensely rich Novgorodian nobleman
and commander-in-chief. Demetrius was merely thirteen
years old but cruel and abnormal. Nazarius went to Moscow,
where Ivan III received him well and granted him several
estates.

6. See note 3 above.

In 1478 the Grand Prince declared war on Novgorod and Nazarius Podvoysky was appointed general. He rode with his cavalry to the country house where the Princess stayed and said to her: "Come with me to church to be married at once." The proud girl answered that she would not marry a Novgorodian traitor who came to take her by force. Nazarius was ashamed. Returning to Moscow he resigned his office and declared himself for Novgorod. The irritated Grand Prince ordered the confiscation of all his properties and threw him in prison. The Princess, having lost Nazarius, was afraid to marry Demetrius Maximov. All these disasters made her very ill. She then made a vow to enter a monastery if she recovered. When she did recover the Prince was very unwilling to allow his only daughter to become a nun but nevertheless he brought her to Mikhalitsky Convent, where the abess gladly received such a great and wealthy aristocrat. Serafima was only a short time in the convent when the body of Nazarius, who died in prison in Moscow, was brought to the convent for burial. This convinced Serafima that she should remain in the convent and pray for his soul as he died without the last sacraments.

The conquest of Novgorod by Ivan III ruined the family of Maximov. The former fiancé of the Princess, Demetrius Maximov, was imprisoned for life. Serafima's father went to serve Ivan III and was richly rewarded. He wanted to transfer his daughter to a convent in Moscow but did not succeed. Professed in Mikhalitsky Convent under the name of Mary, Princess Odoevsky became its abbess in 1515, seven years after the death of St Nilus.

The abbess was venerated as a saint after her death. A chapel built over her grave was restored in 1904 when the abbess' body was found incorrupt. She was buried as a nun but covered with a red princely mantle.

The abbess wrote her *Memoirs* in her old age. She says: "I write this, starting from my childhood, in memory of my sister and of my spiritual father, Archimandrite Macarius. I ask forgiveness from my spiritual children. If I have omitted anything, I ask them not to blame me, neither now nor in the

future when my writings will be found. I ask the same of my
relations, the Princes Odoevsky if they are still in this world.
I beg my relations and you sisters of the Convent of the
Nativity of Our Lady the Theotokos to remember what I say.
May my sisters remember me as long as the world exists. Do
not let the monastery go to ruin for the sake of men. The
time of my departure from this corruptible world is near. I
rejoice like a bird which has escaped from the net of the
hunter and flies to eternal beauty. I remember many fiendish
temptations and bitter struggles but I have stood firm refus-
ing to become the prey of the enemy and destroyer of mankind, the devil, but rather I have hope to attain eternal beatitude."[7]

Mary's meditations after taking the veil are written in the
superb and colorful Russian of the fifteenth century: "The
life of this world is as far from the ascetical or monastic life
as East is from West. What does it avail a man to gain the
whole world and forfeit his soul by separation from God?
Shall I prefer the corruptible to the incorruptible? No, this
must be not so. This is the net of the devil, the ancient
enemy, the destroyer of men. All we, as men, die and princes
fall. We study the Scriptures but take no notice of them and
do what we should not do. How I, myself a sinner, was
troubled in my first year in the monastery! I was sad even to
death, tempted by wicked and vile thoughts. I remembered
my life in the world and the wealth of my father. I longed for
the pleasures of this world, jewels, dresses and worldly songs.
I prayed often for long periods with tears in order to overcome the tempest. I confessed all to the abbess and she told
me to pray to St Phomaide, the martyr."[8]

When Mary was professed the Prince came to visit his
daughter as a nun and, seeing her, wept bitterly but Mary said
to her father: "This is no time for tears but for gladness and
joy. I was dead and now I am alive."[9]

Like St Nilus, Mary was a student of the Bible and of the

7. *Zapiski,* p. 44.
8. Ibid., p. 31.
9. Ibid., p. 45.

Fathers: "I began to read with application the God-inspired books and thus to meditate on the things of God. I then started to copy books and chronicles. The abbess prized my work but some sisters blamed me because they were illiterate. I give glory to the Lord God in thanksgiving for my father because he had me educated in the liberal arts. Many people blamed my father for having his daughter taught to read, as this was thought useless for a girl. But my father took no notice of such foolish ideas."[10] It would take too much space to describe the visions of Mary. They are interesting and often astonishing. In many ways Princess Odoevsky reminds us of St Nilus, all the more so because she is unique. Three centuries were to pass by before another Abbess like her appeared in Russia.

After the defeat of the Trans-Volga Elders Russian monasticism turned to active, missionary work and took on a ritualistic character. The contemplatives became fewer and fewer while the number of missionaires grew space. St Stephen of Perm begins the long line of Russian missionaries. [11] Son of a sexton from Ustyug, Stephen entered the Monastery of St Gregory in Rostov in 1365. He studied Greek for thirteen years in order to translate the scripture into Zuiryan. The Zuiryans, a Finnish Ural tribe, who inhabit the Komi Autonomous Republic in the Soviet Union, were then heathen. St Stephen invented an alphabet for them and after ordination went to preach the Gospel to them. He built the first church in Ust-Vuim.

After a long struggle with pagan clergy St Stephen succeeded in evangelizing Little Perm, Vuichegda and Vuim. He was made bishop in 1383 and died in 1396. He was a friend of St Sergius of Radonezh. The successor of St Stephen, Isaac, and Gerasim converted Great Perm. In 1442 Gerasim was murdered by a Vogul. In 1454 Bishop Pitirim died a prisoner of the Voguls, another Finnish tribe. Finally in 1462

10. Ibid., p. 33.
11. Details may be found in my book, *The Foreign Missions of the Russian Orthodox Church.*

the Prince of Perm and his people were baptized. In this way the present Udmurt Soviet Republic was evangelized.

In 1472 Perm was conquered by Ivan III and evangelization of the Ural Finns made considerable progress. Yet Metropolitan Simon still complained in 1501 about the persistence of paganism. Many people still worshipped idols. After the conquest of Perm the great Stroganov family settled in the territory and founded the Peskorsky and Solikamsky Monasteries. St Triphon of Vyatka, monk of Peskorsky Monastery, went farther to the East and founded a new monastery at the river of Chusuvaya, where he remained nine years. He went then to Vyatka and founded there in 1580 Assumption Monastery. He died in 1612.

The Russian missions were invariably started by monks. The founders moved into the pagan territory and founded a monastery which served them as a missionary center. As soon as possible they translated the Scriptures and liturgical books into the native language, ordained native priests and moved on farther, leaving behind them the monasteries as permanent spiritual centers. In this way nearly all the tribes of European Russia were evangelized and converted.

In the North, the celebrated Solovetjky Monastery on an archipelago in the White Sea was a great missionary center. It was founded in the beginning of the fifteenth century by St Sabbatius (d. 1435), a monk from Kirillov Monastery. The well-known champion of Orthodoxy against the Judaizers, Archbishop Gennadius of Novgorod (1484-1504), was his disciple. Theodoret, a monk of Solovetzky, founded in Lapland Kolsky Monastery to evangelize the Lapons. He was successful, baptizing 2,000 Lapons in a single day. Theodoret was a highly cultured man. Ivan the Terrible sent him to Constantinople to obtain from the Patriarch the acknowledgment of his title of Tsar. St Triphon of Pechenga, (1495-1583) another Solovetzky monk, founded the Lapons' Pechenga Monastery.

The reign of Ivan the Terrible, particularly its first half, was magnificent. The Tatar Moslem Kingdoms of Kazan and

Astrakhan were conquered. This was followed by the conquest of Western Siberia. Kazan was captured in 1552. A
monastery, Sylantov, was founded at once in the Moslem
city. A number of Tatars were baptized, including Kings
Ediger and Utelish Girey. In 1555 the archdiocese of Kazan
was created. The abbot of Selizharov, Gurius Rugotin, was
the first archbishop. A native of Voronezh he had served
Prince Penkov. Just as the Patriarch Joseph, the son of Jacob,
was slandered by the wife of Potiphar, so Guirus was slandered by the princess, and suffered unjust punishment. He
became a monk of Volokolamsk and later abbot of Selizharov. He baptized several thousand Moslems during the nine
years he was archbishop of Kazan. He died December 4, 1569
and was later canonized.

Barsonuphius and Germanus were the closest assistants to
Gurius. The first was prisoner of the Tatars for three years
and learned their language. As abbot of Pesnosh he founded
St Savior's Monastery in Kazan. Consecrated bishop of Tver
in 1567 he returned to Kazan and died there in 1567.
Germanus Polev, a monk of Volokolamsk, founded Svyazhsk
Monastery in Kazan. He succeeded Gurius as archbishop and
died in 1567. When Astrakhan was taken in 1567 its queen
and her son were baptized. The following year, a monk,
Abbot Cyril, was sent to preach the Gospel.

Besides missionary activities the monks were engaged in
works of charity on a grand scale. During a famine, Kirillov
Monastery alone provided food for 600 persons daily while
that of Borovsk fed 1,000 people daily. Most monasteries
possessed hospitals, institutions for old people and guesthouses. Nor did they forget spiritual food. The monks possessed libraries, where they copied books and sold them,
wrote sermons and instructions and painted ikons. People
used to go to monasteries to learn to read and write and to
study. Children were sent for the same purpose. Many
Russian monks were well read but they lacked critical acu-
men. Every written word they considered sacrosant. Obscure
treatises by unknown authors and legendary lives of saints
they respected as much as the Bible itself. Contemplation,
the Prayer of Jesus and serious meditation on the Scriptures

were replaced by extreme rigorism in the observance of
multitude of rites and by an astonishing severity in bodily
mortifications. Long vigils, endless services, countless prostrations, extraordinary penances and fasting were de rigeur for
every good monk, who, however, understood but little of the
Scriptures and the Fathers.

From the second half of the fifteenth century till the seventeenth century three hundred new monasteries were founded
and fifty saints, nearly all monks, were canonized. The better
known ones are Macarius of Kalyazin (d. 1483); Alexander of
Svirsk (d. 1533); Cornelius Komelsky (d. 1537); Daniel of
Pereyaslav (d. 1540); Zosima (d. 1478); Germanus (d. 1484)
and Philip (d. 1569) of Solovetzky; Anthony Siisky (d.
1556); Nilus Stolbensky (d. 1554) and Nicander of Pskov (d.
1581).

St Cornelius Komelsky was born in Rostov of the noble
family of Kryukov. Professed in Kirillov-Belozersky Monastery, Cornelius went first to Rostov, then to Novgorod, and
afterwards to the Sabbatian Desert in the Principality of
Tver, seeking all the time more remote habitations and
greater solitude. Finally he found a solitude according to his
heart in the virgin forests in Komelsk. Ordained by the
Russian Primate, Simon, Cornelius lived alone for nineteen
years. At the age of sixty he founded his own monastery for
which he composed a Rule based on the writings of St Nilus
of Sora, whose junior contemporary he was. He belonged to
St Nilus's school of thought. Having organized his monastery,
Cornelius left it with his pupil, Gennadius, and went to a still
more remote place, Sursk Lake. Basil III sent him back to
Komelsk at the request of his community. Cornelius was a
strict non-possessor and yet extremely charitable to the poor.
Although he believed that the sketic monks must not occupy
themselves in farming, he allowed them to have fields to
provide the poor with bread.

St Philip, the Russian Primate, is perhaps, the most venerated saint of the reign of Ivan the Terrible. The latter, a very
brilliant and learned man by the standards of his time, was
also a staunch churchman. In the beginning of his reign Ivan
did much for the Church. Later, however, his character dete-

riorated. The Tsar became exceedingly suspicious, seeing traitors everywhere. He started executions on a grand scale and became a cruel man committing untold atrocities.

St Philip was his most illustrious ecclesiastical victim. As a great nobleman, Theodore Kolhichev had retired from the court when he was thirty. In 1538 he entered the northernmost Russian monastery, Solovetzky. Professed with the name of Philip, he became abbot of Solovetzky in 1540. He ruled there for eighteen years and performed wonders, building churches, hospitals, lighthouses, workshops, planting gardens and preparing fields in the Arctic. In 1566 the Tsar invited him to Moscow to become Primate.

The Tsar quickly changed his attitude towards the new Primate when Philip reproached him for his evil conduct. He deposed him and had him murdered. Peredelkino-Koluichevo, the country seat of the great family of Koluichev, now fully restored, is a summer place of the Russian Patriarch.

Another monastic victim of the Tsar was St Cornelius of Pskov, evangelizer of the Eastern Estonians. He was abbot of Pskovo-Perchersky Monastery which still flourishes. The Tsar murdered him with his own hands in 1570.

A special type of Russian saint, the *Yurodivuie*, or fools for Christ's sake, were much in evidence in the reign of Ivan the Terrible. These men ridiculed the customs and manners of this world and left their fortune, home and family in order to live solely in the care of Divine Providence. Their life was one of extreme austerity and poverty in the midst of humiliations. In the West St Francis of Assisi and, still more, St Benedict Joseph Labre may be considered *Yurodivuie*. They are highly unconventional saints.

Byzantium knew two canonized *Yurodivuie,* St Simeon (sixth cent.) and St Andrew (tenth cent.). In Russia they were far more numerous. According to the study of Fedotov the Russians canonized four *Yurodivuie* in the fourteenth century, eleven in the fifteenth century, fourteen and seven in the sixteenth and seventeenth centuries respectively. [12] Among the *Yurodivuie* of the reign of Ivan IV, the most

12. G. P. Fedotov, *Svyatuie Drevney Rusi* (Paris, 1931).

remarkable are St Basil Blazhennui (d. 1552) in whose honor the celebrated church opposite the Kremlin in Moscow is named, Nicholas Salos (d. 1576), who met Ivan the Terrible at the gates of Pskov, when he had come to destroy the city, and ordered him to turn back, and John the Big Kolpak (d. 1859). Some of the *Yurodivuie* were, no doubt, mystics, but as they left no writings of their own, we can say nothing concerning this.

In the reign of the son of Ivan IV, Theodore, the Russian Primate received the title of the Patriarch of Moscow and all Russia. He was acknowledged as such by the Eastern Patriarchs with a seniority after that of Jerusalem. Theodore was the last sovereign of the House of Rurik. After his death Boris Godunov, his brother-in-law, a brilliant and cultured statesman, succeeded Theodore. However, many noblemen were against him and contrived to set up against him an adventurer known as the False Demetrius, who pretended to be the younger son of Ivan who died in mysterious circumstances.

A long civil war ensued in which the Poles and the Swedes intervened. Russia was in danger of disappearing as a great nation but, at last, with the advent of the new Imperial House of Romanov in 1613 the Poles and the Swedes were repulsed and the internal order reestablished.

The Russian Church demonstrated her patriotism by organizing for the defense of the country. The monks were again in the front ranks. Holy Trinity Monastery, near Moscow, immensely rich, contributed large funds. It was besieged for sixteen months by a Polish army of 30,000 men but could not be taken since it had been converted into a powerful fortress. Solovetzky Monastery also contributed large funds, while Priluki surrendered all of its wealth. Kirillov Monastery withstood a siege for five years.

The abbot of Holy Trinity Monastery, Dionisius, and one of its monks, Abraham Palitsin, wrote letters calling the Russians to defend their country. One of these letters produced, in 1611, the formation of a new Russian Army in Nizhni Novgorod and the subsequent liberation of Moscow from the

Poles, who shortly before that had captured the Russian Patriarch Hermogen and starved him to death. He was succeeded by the father of Michael Romanov, the new Tsar. Theodore Romanov, Metropolitan of Rostov, subsequently Patriarch Philaret, was originally a great Russian nobleman who had been forced into the monastic life by Tsar Boris Godhnov.

The Russian Church came out of this civil war with immense prestige. One third of the Russian territory belonged to the Church, chiefly to monasteries. This great wealth could not but excite the envy of the impoverished nation. On account of their victories the Russians became very proud and intolerant. This pride and intolerance were particularly strong among churchmen. Comparing their great empire with the state of other Orthodox who were subject either to the Moslem Turkish Sultans or to the Catholic Kings of Poland and Hungary, the Russian churchmen attributed their high estate to the fact that they preserved their Orthodoxy pure while others did not and were consequently punished by God. Yet the Russian liturgical books were full of errors made by ignorant scribes in the course of centuries. They needed corrections. The first effort to correct them, made in the reign of Michael Romanov, was abandoned because the Josephites considered such an attempt sacrilegious. In the reign of Tsar Alexis, Patriarch Nikon (Minin), a Volga Finn, a man of iron will, forced the correction of Russian liturgical books and rites, bringing them into line with those of the Greeks.

The conservatives, the Josephites, horrified by the reforms of Nikon, left the Russian Church in great numbers and formed the Great Russian Schism or "Raskol." [13] The latter seriously undermined the Russian Church and weakened her before the new, powerful, centralized state. Masses of ardent, fanatic churchmen, instead of supporting the Church, turned against her and established Russian Nonconformism which

13. The history of this schism, with relevant bibliography, can be found in my book, *Russian Nonconformity.*

was, perhaps, twenty-five million strong by the eve of the Revolution in 1917. The Russian Nonconformists quickly broke into a multitude of mutually opposed sects, unified only by their hatred of the Russian Orthodox Church. The decree of the Moscow Council of 1667 excommunicating the Raskolniks is the official beginning of Russian Nonconformism. In due course it produced its own mystics but we do not consider them in this study.

The Russian state quickly took advantage of the situation. Already in the reign of Ivan IV the first attempts to limit monastic landowning and to control monastic estates were successfully made. In 1573 it was forbidden to leave any more estates to monasteries. In 1580 the state tried to take back some estates in compensation for losses. In the reign of Alexis a special Ministry, Monastursky Prikaz, was established to control Church property. The Moscow Councils of 1666 and 1667 under the pressure of the state forbade any future monastic professions except under certain conditions. This was done, allegedly, to prevent people from evading military service and taxation by entering the cloister. No one could become a monk without the bishop's knowledge and only after a proper novitiate. Profession could be made only in monasteries. The novices were not allowed to donate estates to monasteries. In 1682 the foundation of new monasteries was prohibited.

Nevertheless, 220 new monasteries were founded in the seventeenth century and many new saints appeared. Some of them still continued the manner of life of St Nilus of Sora. St Martirius Zelenetsky (d. 1603) lived first in Velikiya Luki Monastery with Staretz Bogolep. They ate once a day. Besides the appointed services and prayers they recited the Prayer of Jesus a thousand times and said two hundred prayers to Our Lady daily and made six hundred Metanias. They worked during the night. St Martirius founded Zelenetsky Monastery in a remote marshy district. In 1582 there was an abbot and twelve monks. The converted Moslem King of Kasimov, Simeon, was their chief benefactor.

Diodore Yuriegorsky (d. 1633) was also a contemplative

and a Non-Possessor. Originally a monk of Solovetzky, Diodore retired to live in the forest. Gradually a few other hermits joined him. Kirik, Cellarer of Solovetzky, left his monastery to live with Diodore. This displeased the abbot who ordered the hermits to disperse and imprisoned Diodore. The latter escaped and settled near Keno Lake but peasants drove him away. Finally Diodore settled in Yurieva Gora, where he founded a monastery. Diodore is known for his visions and miracles.

St Eleazar of Anzer (d. 1656) was a writer and bibliophile. He was originally a monk of Solovetsky. In 1616 he retired to the island of Anzer in the White Sea to live as a hermit. Finally he founded a skete very much like that of St Nilus. The huts of the monks were, however, nearly a mile apart. The monks practised starchestvo, that is, the daily non-sacramental confession of deeds and thoughts to the spiritual director or staretz.

The spirit of these monks was severely ascetic. The essence of religious life was understood to be the strictest observance of rites and customs, together with austerities. St Galaktion of Vologda (d. 1612), in the world Prince Gabriel Belsky, after the hardest possible life chained himself to a wall and slept kneeling. He was murdered by Polish bandits.

St Irinarkh of Rostov (d. 1616) surpassed everyone else in mortifications. He walked always without shoes and wore chains and a hairshirt. The abbot was obliged to restrain his ardor for austerities. After his death a collection of iron and copper chains, belts and helmets was found in his cell. The celebrated *Yurodivuie,* John the Big Kolpak, himself an incredible ascetic, once said to Irinarkh: "God gives you a horse (body) which no man but you can ride and none can even sit on." Irinarkh was endowed with many spiritual gifts. Cases are recorded of his seeing things happen a hundred miles away.

The monks were still engaged in missions. After the conquest of Siberia the archdiocese of Tobolsk was founded with Cyprian as the first archbishop (1620-24). The first missionary monastery, however, was founded on the river Iset only in 1644 by Staretz Dalmat. In 1653 Kondsky Monastery was founded for the evangelization of the Ostyaks. From 1660 to 1672 monasteries were founded all over Siberia, in Yakutsk, Kirensk and Trkutsk. In 1671 Hermogen founded Alabasin Monastery on the Chinese frontier. The next step in the monastic advance was the foundation of Bei-Guan Monastery in Peking a few decades later. The mass baptism of the Moslem Tatar and pagan Mordvinians continued in European Russia. The Mordvinians of Ryazan and Tambov province, a future home of the greatest Russian mystics, were nearly all baptized. Misael, archbishop of Ryazan (1651-56), baptized personally crowds of Tatars and Mordvinians. He died a martyr. At this time we notice a significant phenomenon. With the growth of monastic wealth, the attitude of the peasants toward the monks changes. The monks are now considered exploiters and hated as slave-owners. The appearance of a hermit often suggested the possible foundation of a new monastery with the reduction to serfdom of the neighboring peasants. St Adrian of Andrhsov was murdered in 1549 by peasants suspicious of his intentions. Likewise Adrian of Poshekhon was murdered in 1550, Igapetus Markushevsky in 1572, Simon Volomsky in 1613 and Job Ushelsky in 1628, all of them for the same reason. Others, like St Nilus Stolbensky, Arsenius Komelsky and Diodore Yuriegorsky barely escaped violent death.

In Southern and Western Russia things went differently than in Great Russia. After the Mongolian invasion the Ukrainian and White Ruthenian lands were conquered or, rather, simply occupied, by the Poles, the Lithuanians and the Hungarians. They were, however, ecclesiastically, under the Russian Primate in Moscow. This lasted more or less till the aftermath of the Council of Florence. The Great Russian dioceses did not recognize the Union, while the Ukrainian and White Ruthenian bishops to some extent accepted it. The Pope appointed for them a separate Primate. These new Primates lived in Vilno and depended sometimes on the Popes and sometimes on the Patriarchs of Constantinople. In the sixteenth century the Kingdom of Poland and Grand

Duchy of Lithuania formed a single state. In the same century efforts were made in Poland to promote ecclesiastical union by making the Orthodox accept Roman Catholicism but leaving them their own rite and organization.[14] This was achieved in the Council of Brest at the end of the century. A great many Orthodox refused to recognize the acts of the Council. Civil wars led by the Ukrainian Cossacks followed. Finally, the Polish government was forced to recognize the existing fact and to allow a new Orthodox hierarchy to be established for those Ukrainians and White Ruthenians who rejected the Council of Brest. The most remarkable among the new Primates, who settled in Kiev, was Metropolitan Peter Mogila, son of the Rumanian Prince, Simeon Modila, a great aristocrat, scholar and statesman, who published in 1640 *Orthodox Confession of Faith*. This work was approved by the Council of Kiev in 1640, in Jassi in the following year and by the Eastern Patriarchs in 1643.[15] This confession is quite Orthodox but it is strongly influenced by the Post-Tridentine Catholic theology. In 1632 Mogila founded a college in Kiev on the Jesuit pattern. He also published corrected liturgical books and a Catechism. He died in 1647. Some years later a large part of the Ukraine including Kiev was united to Russia. In due course the Ukrainian dioceses were incorporated into the Russian Church. The Ukrainian and White Ruthenian monasteries, although numerous, were in poor condition for a long time. Under Peter Mogila they started to revive. The best known among the Ukrainian abbots was St Job Zhelezo, (d. 1651) founder of the great Pochaev Monastery, an Orthodox stronghold in the Western Ukraine.

The eighteenth century opened in Russia with the reign of Peter the Great. It was marked by numerous and radical reforms, victories and conquests. Peter the Great wanted to

14. There is an enormous literature on the relations between the Orthodox and the Catholics in Poland. See my book, *Russian Nonconformity* for an outline and bibliography.

15. I have analyzed this work in *The Doctrine of the Unity of the Church in the Works of Khomyakov and Moehler* (London: SPCK, 1946).

transform Muscovite Russia into a Western European State. The clergy, particularly the monks, were opposed to the Petrine reforms. They had to be curbed. The office of the Patriarch was suppressed. He was replaced by the Holy Synod, a board of bishops and other prelates appointed by the emperor and removed by him at will. Peter obtained from the Eastern Patriarch the approbation of his reform. The Monastuirsky Prikaz took over the control of church properties in order to finance Peter's wars and reforms from monastic estates. Peter disliked the monks whom he considered useless drones. At first he limited the number of monks and nuns in each monastery. No man could be professed before three years novitiate and only if there were vacancies. No man could be professed before thirty and no woman before fifty. In 1723 a new decree was published forbidding any profession even if there were vacancies. Such vacancies were to be reserved for veterans wounded in war. This decree, however, was afterward repealed. All Beltsi and Belitsi (the Orthodox equivalent of Western oblates) were expelled from the monasteries and convents. The foundation of new monasteries without a special permit from the Holy Synod and the emperor was forbidden. The order was given to unite smaller communities into single large houses, turning over the vacant churches to parishes. Many monasteries were suppressed. The monks were ordered to remain where they were and forbidden to wander about. Austere living was enjoined on them. Peter even thought of suppressing monasteries altogether.[16]

Instead, "The Proclamation on Monasticism" was published in 1724. The Proclamation ordered that uneducated monks must learn to be craftsmen and good agricultural workers while nuns were to work in handicrafts. The educated monks were to be trained for posts in special monastic schools. The monasteries were ordered to organize hospitals, orphanages, homes for the aged and invalids. Keeping recluses was forbid-

16. The reigns of Peter and Anne as far as the Church was concerned are described in A. Dobroklonsky, *Rukovodstvo po istorii russkoj Cerkvi* (Moscow, 1893) and P. Znamensky, *Učebnoe rukovodstvo po istorii russkoj Cerkvi* (St Petersburg, 1904). See also G. Florovsky, *Puti russkago bogoslovija* (Paris, 1937).

den. Finally, the monks were forbidden to have paper and ink without permission of the abbot, to prevent them from circulating letters against the emperor. Peter founded in 1712 in St Petersburg St Alexander Nevsky Monastery which was to be his model monastery. It was destined to train monks from various monasteries for bishoprics and abbacies. When Peter died these regulations were relaxed but in the reign of the Empress Anne (1730-1740) they were further strengthened. In 1732 the general reform of all monasteries was ordered. Many technical irregularities were discovered, including the profession of monks without the knowledge of the Synod. All these illegally professed monks were expelled from the monasteries. In 1734 a decree prohibited all monastic professions except for widowed clergy and veterans. When Anne's government met resistance to its decree among the clergy it imposed imprisonment, deportation and forced military service.

In 1740 the Synod reported to the empress that monasteries were being deserted and falling into ruins, and permissions for further professions were once again granted.

The Empress Elizabeth restored the confiscated monastic estates and facilitated new professions. When Catherine II, surnamed the Great, became empress, new anti-monastic laws appeared. The secularization of monastic estates took place in 1764. From 1700 till 1769, 175 monasteries out of 1,200 were closed and forty-seven were founded. In 1764 there were 1,072 monasteries, one-fourth of them nunneries. The empress confiscated nearly all monastic estates and limited, besides the number of monks or nuns allowed in each monastery in the future. The monasteries were divided into three classes in this respect. There were, however, some exceptions. To replace the income from the confiscated estates each monk or nun was to receive from the government a meagre annual allowance for subsistance. In Great Russia out of 953 monasteries more than a half were suppressed, 224 were allowed to continue on the state payroll (*Statny* monasteries) and 161 *Zastatny* monasteries continued under strict controls. In the Ukraine and white Ruthenia over forty monasteries were suppressed. The closed monasteries were turned into prisons, hospitals, mental homes and barracks. In 1762 there were 12,444 religious, while the new order "Shtatui" allowed only 5,105. The remainder had to disperse. Because the state paid very irregularly and miserably even the monasteries it supported, these began to decay through the lack of personnel. While there were 1,200 monasteries in 1700, only 452 remained by 1800.

The eighteenth century was a disastrous period for Russian monasticism yet it saw also the beginning of the new era, the sunrise of a new day, the Golden Age of Russian mysticism of the following century. The first forerunners appeared already in the reign of Peter the Great. St Demetrius of Rostov was one of them. Son of an Ukrainian officer from Poltava, born in 1651, Demetrius became a monk in Kirillov Monastery in Kiev in 1668. After being a preacher in Poland he became abbot of various Ukrainian monasteries. On his visit to Moscow in 1689 he came to the attention of Peter the Great. In 1701 the Tsar appointed him Metropolitan of Siberia. Demetrius was duly consecrated; however, on account of ill health he was allowed to remain in European Russia. He was appointed Metropolitan of Rostov, where he died on October 18, 1709.

St Demetrius left numerous writings, particularly his monumental Lives of the Saints. He also wrote against the Russian Raskolniks or Old Believers, those who left the Russian Church after the liturgical reforms of the Patriarch Nikon. St Demetrius was a saintly and scholarly man. Educated in Kiev, where the Latin seminaries and colleges were copied, St Demetrius, while remaining strictly Orthodox, was much influenced by Counter-Reformation Catholic devotions and mentality. He translated the *Anima Christi*. He wrote in his *Lamentations on the Burial of Christ* several expressions implying the cult of the Sacred Heart like: "His heart which was the source and the beginning of every love was wounded. . . , heart compassionate, charitable! How enflamed was the heart of Christ! It was enflamed by an immense love for man! In order to reduce this heat he received into his heart the cold iron! "[17] In one hymn to Our Lady St Demetrius wrote: "I venerate your Immaculate Conception and your Nativity from your holy progenitors, Joachim and Anne."[18]

He knew, however, the Prayer of Jesus and wrote about it quite clearly. Man, the saint wrote, is both exterior and interior, fleshly and spiritual. "There are also two prayers, exterior, visible, common, and interior, secret, lonely. For the second neither mouth nor books are needed." Man must hide himself in the inner chamber of the heart more than behind walls. Gathering there all his thoughts, he must offer his mind to God and pray to him secretly with all the warmth of spirit and living faith. At the same time one must take thought how to grow up into a perfect man.[19] In another place he says: "Man must unite with God, reject everything external, love God and pray frequently, plunging the mind in God. This arouses love. Prayer without attention is nothing. It is better to say a short prayer and to repeat it often. Prayer is the turning of the mind and heart to God. To pray is to stand in awareness before God, to see him constantly and to talk with him in hope and pious fear."[20]

Peter the Great having no confidence in Great Russian ecclesiastics, started to appoint the Ukrainians to all the Russian Sees. Many of these Ukrainians not only studied in the latinizing Kiev College but went to Catholic universities and even to Rome as well. In order to do this they temporarily became Eastern Catholics or even outright Latins. Returning home they returned to the Orthodox Church. Both of the principal ecclesiastical advisers to Peter the Great, the Metropolitan of Ryazan, Stephen Yavorsky, and the Archbishop of Pskov, Theophan Prokopovich, did this. While the first remained Latin in his mentality, the second, after his training in Rome, conceived a violent hatred of Catholicism and an ardent sympathy for the Protestants.

17. *Tvoreniya iže vo svjatych otca našego Sv. Dimitriya Rostovskago* (St Petersburg, 1912) 1:151.
18. Ibid., p. 178.
19. Ibid., p. 122.   20. Ibid., p. 126.

Peter the Great also liked the latter. Abandoning Stephen, he made Theophan his chief collaborator in ecclesiastical affairs. "The Ecclesiastical Regulations" which established the Synod, Peter's "Proclamation on Monasticism," and other documents were prepared by Theophan who became in the reign of the Empress Anne the actual Primate of Russia. He greatly weakened Russian monasteries and thereby prepared for the secularization of church estates later on. Theophan was, however, a first class scholar, statesman and cultured man. The first Russian mystic of the eighteenth century, St Tikhon of Zadonsk, came out of his diocese.

CHAPTER IV

ST TIKHON OF ZADONSK

ST TIKHON, in the world Timothy Sokolov, son of a psalmist,[1] Sabelius Sokolov, was born in 1724 in the village of Korotzk, Valdai district, in the province of Novgorod, which became some years later the archdiocese of Theophan Propkopovich.[2] The father of the saint died early and the family was left destitute. Remembering later his childhood, St Tikhov once said: "We were four brothers and two sisters. I do not remember my father. We were brought up by our mother. The eldest brother acted as psalmist, the middle brother went soldiering and two remained at home. We lived in extreme poverty. Once a well-to-do coachman who was childless, and liked me, said to mother: 'Give me Tima to bring him up and I shall make him my sole heir.' My mother liked the idea and was about to take me to the coachman but was stopped on the way by my eldest brother who said: 'If you take him to the coachman, he will remain a coachman all his life. I would rather go and beg than give my brother to the coachman. Let us try to educate him and he may become a sexton or a psalmist.' At home we had nothing to eat. I worked as a laborer for peasants in order to eat. At this time a seminary was opened in Novgorod and my mother succeeded in having me admitted. She died soon afterwards."[3]

1. A lector who reads the *cathisma* and the Epistles.
2. A Lebedev, *Svjatitelj Tichon Zadonsky i vesja Rossii Čudotvorec: Ego žizn, pisanija i proslavlenie* (St Petersburg, 1865) is still the best book on St Tikhon.
3. *Tvorenija iže vo svjatych otca našego Tichona Zadonskago,* 5 vols. (Moscow, 1898-1899[6], vol. 5, supplement, p. 4.

St Tikhon's years in the seminary were no less hard than his childhood years at home. He was poorly dressed, never took part in amusements but was engrossed in studies. Sons of the well-to-do parents often ridiculed him. They used to surround him and, waving rags like thuribles sang: "All praise to you! " "When I came to Novgorod as bishop," the saint remembered afterwards, "several of my former school fellows came to be blessed by me and I said to them: 'You, brethren, used to laugh at me when we were boys in the seminary, and you waved rags at me, but now you will cense me.' At this time some of them were deacons and priests. And they said to me: 'Forgive us, Excellency! ' and I said to them: 'I am only joking, brethren.' "[4]

When Tikhon entered the seminary in Novgorod on December 11, 1733, there were 1,000 pupils but only two teachers. Before Peter the Great, regular schools in Russia were very rare, particularly in the provinces. The emperor founded a great many schools for the gentry. He also obliged diocesan bishops to open major and minor seminaries for their dioceses. Sons of priests and deacons (in Russia these men married as elsewhere in the East) and also of psalmists and sextons were ordered to go to the new schools. However, there were only a very few teachers to staff these seminaries, mostly monks from the Ukraine. Such was the position in Novgorod. In 1740 St Tikhon was accepted by the seminary as a pupil along with 200 others. He received a scholarship. The Russian seminaries were organized on the Catholic, more exactly on the Jesuit, pattern, adopted in Kiev. The language of instruction was Latin.

For nearly 150 years all Russian bishops and priests were trained in the Latin language in the same manner as Catholic priests. Practically all the early teachers in Russian seminaries were Ukrainians from Kiev. For fifty years nearly all Russian episcopal sees as well as seminary posts, deaneries of cathedrals and the more important abbacies were occupied by Ukrainians.

4. Ibid.

In the time of St Tikhon the seminary occupied some buildings in the monastery of St Anthony the Roman (d. 1147). This Novgorodian saint was a Roman, perhaps a Benedictine, who left the West for Russia, where he settled in Novgorod and, adopting the Byzantine rite, founded a large monastery. In the seminary St Tikhon first studied humanities including four years of rhetoric and Greek. In 1746 he studied philosophy for two years and then began theology. At the same time he taught Greek in the seminary. In 1754 St Tikhon finished his fourteen year course. He remained in the seminary for five years more as tutor of rhetoric and philosophy and a prefect of the seminary. On August 27, 1758 Timothy Sokolovsky (his name in the seminary) was professed as a monk with the name of Tikhon. In due course he was ordained. On August 26, 1759 Tikhon was appointed archimandrite of Zheltikov Monastery in the diocese of Tiver and then archimandrite of Otroch Monastery, where Maximus the Greek was imprisoned two centuries before, and rector of Tver Seminary. Two years later Tikhon, aged 37, was ordained bishop.

Looking back, St Tikhon describes his appointment to the bishopric. In Tver on Easter Day, when Athanasius, Bishop of Tver, pontificated Tikhon was concelebrant at the Liturgy. When Tikhon, during the singing of Cherubikon, said to the bishop at the Prothese: "Remember me, Holy Lord," the latter, by mistake, instead of saying: "God remembers your archimandria," said, "God remembers your Episcopacy." Athanasius, realizing his error, smiled and said: "It seems that God wants you to be a bishop." On that very day in St Petersburg Metropolitan Demetrius Sechenov and Epiphanius, Bishop of Smolensk, were casting lots for a new bishop. There were seven candidates but Epiphanius suggested Tikhon as well. Metropolitan Demetrius said: "He is too young yet," but added: "However, let him be the eighth." The lots were thrown thrice and the same name "Tikhon" came up each time. The Metropolitan said: "This must be the will of God, but I wanted to send him to Holy Trinity Monastery.[5]

5. From the remembrances of B. Chebotarev, ibid, p. 5.

Tikhon was consecrated bishop of Keksholm and Ladoga in St Petersburg on May 13, 1761. Demetrius Sechenov, Metropolitan of Novgorod, the actual Russian Primate, entrusted Tikhon with the rule of his own archdiocese, being himself preoccupied in the Synod. A splendid reception was arranged for the bishop in Novgorod. Remembering it later, St Tikhon said: "My sister, a very poor widow, was in the crowd watching the ceremony. She had earned her living, when she lived in Valday, by washing floors for rich people. Later when I was appointed tutor in Novgorod Seminary, I had supported her. Now I sent a carriage to bring her to me the next morning. When she arrived, she was afraid to enter into my room. I opened the door and said to her: 'Welcome, Sister.' She entered and began to cry. I asked her: 'Why do you cry, sister?' 'I cry' she said, 'for great joy, brother. Do you remember in what poverty we were brought up by our mother? Now and then we lacked even daily food. But now you are appointed to a great office. Yesterday I was in the crowd and saw what a reception they gave you!' I said to her: 'Come often, sister, there is now a carriage for you to ride in. I have servants, horses and a carriage, and they are yours.' But she said: 'Thank you, brother, but I may tire you with my visits.' 'No,' I said, 'I shall never grow tired of your visits. I love you from my heart and revere you (because she was my eldest sister).' But after my arrival in Novgorod my sister lived only one month and died. I buried her myself. According to the Pontifical service, I kissed the holy ikons and went to the coffin. I opened the cover and blessed her body. It seemed to me that she smiled. God only knows if this was merely an illusion or what it was. I do not attempt to say. Driving to the funeral and during the entire Liturgy and burial I could hardly celebrate because of bitter tears. I was beside myself with compunction. She led such a good life.'"[6]

St Tikhon was hardly established in Novgorod when he was recalled to St Petersburg to administer the Russian Church in the absence of the Holy Synod, the members of which went

6. Ibid., p. 6.

to Moscow to take part in the coronation of the Empress Catherine II. In the mission entrusted to him Tikhon performed to the satisfaction of all concerned. The Synod decided then to translate him to the enormous diocese of Voronezh in South-Eastern Russia. This diocese required a first-class administrator. On February 3, 1763 Tikhon was made Bishop of Voronezh.

On his way to the South, Tikhon was ordered to take part in the tragic ceremony of the deposition of the Metropolitan of Rostov, Arsenius Matsievich, who vehemently protested against the secularization of church lands and severely reprimanded the empress for her dissolute life. The ceremony took place in Moscow and was a shattering experience for Tikhon. He became nervous and inclined to melancholy ever after.

Tikhon was not very happy in Voronezh. The diocese was enormous and new, on the border of European Russia. The population was scattered, primitive and given to all the kinds of vices found in frontier provinces. The clergy were uneducated and of low moral standard. The civil authorities were no better. Finally, the Cossacks were willful and rebellious to any discipline. Churchgoing was poor. A large number of Raskolniks, the Old Believers, and many sectarians lived in the diocese.

Tikhon applied himself to the work. He tried to improve the educational standard of the clergy and the moral standard of the laity. He was not unsuccessful and yet he was hardly four years and seven months in the diocese when he suddenly requested the Synod to relieve him of his duties and to allow him to retire to a monastery.

The Synod was astonished at the Bishop's request but complied with it. Tikhon retired first to Tolshev Monastery, but its marshy surroundings and the pro-Raskolnik sympathies of the monks were unsupportable to the retired bishop. He changed his residence, moving to the Monastery of Zadonsk, where he spent thirteen years in ever greater solitude. St Tikhon died on August 13, 1783, being fifty-nine years old.

The Zadonsk period of the life of Tikhon is the most important in his development as a mystic. In Zadonsk Tikhon wrote nearly all his books. His life in Zadonsk was described in detail by his two keleiniks or personal attendants, Basil Cheboratev and Ivan Efimov. We can study Tikhon's spiritual progress in Zadonsk with the help of the information they provide. Basil Cheboratev is particularly rich in details. The bishop took his meals in his cell. At dinner the Old Testament was read. Tikhon loved the prophecy of Isaiah and often wept when it was read. In the evening the New Testament was read and Tikhon commented upon it. Taking his place at the table, Tikhon used to say: "Glory be to God. I have good while some of my brothers in Christ languish in prisons, others have poor food and still others have not even salt for their meal. Woe to me, miserable man!" Tikhon did not sleep at night but went to bed at sunrise. The night he spent in prayer with many prostration and much compunction. He even used to say aloud: "Lord, have mercy on me! Lord, pardon! Giver of life have mercy on me!" At midnight he used to go out and walking around the church, knelt before every door, praying and singing softly. If the bishop was sad he sang: "It is good for me that I am humbled." When he was glad he sang: "Praise the Lord in heaven."

The bishop began his night vigils after his first mystical experience, when he was still a lay tutor. He said once to Chebotarev: "When I was yet tutor I developed a liking for staying up all night to read spiritual books and meditate. Here is something I tell you in strict confidence: you must not repeat it. One night in May was pleasant, quiet and clear. I went out of my room to the balcony which faced the North. I stood and meditated on eternal beatitude. Suddenly heaven opened and I saw such a sea of light that no corruptible tongue nor mind could ever comprehend it. This wondrous vision started in me a burning desire for the solitary life. Long after that vision I was full of joy and even now when I remember it I feel in my heart a peculiar gaiety and joy."[7]

The bishop attended Mass daily. He received Communion

7. Ibid., p. 7.

on Sundays and feasts, first in the sanctuary, vested, and later in his rooms, even in bed, when he became weak. He never pontificated after his retirement and, it seems, never celebrated the Mass himself either. Why he did not do so is difficult to say. Apparently he thought that once he retired he must not pontificate, while to celebrate as priest was considered in those times unseemly for a bishop. Some suspected that the Synod suspended him from celebrating once he retired, but there is no shred of evidence for that. Tikhon always approached the Holy Table in tears and after went out in joy. In this he was a true mystic. St Simeon The New Theologian, the greatest Byzantine mystic, would heartily approve of St Tikhon. Simeon said once that those who celebrate without tears and receive Communion without tears are not worthy either to celebrate or to receive Communion. Tikhon assisted at the Divine Office and often sang in choir, nearly always in tears. His keleinik states: "There was in him a peculiar gift of tears. Always two streams were flowing from his eyes." He rarely smiled at anything and if he did, he said at once: "Lord, forgive me, I have offended you! " St Isaac the Syrian, perhaps the greatest mystic who ever lived, taught that no one can reach pure, perfectly recollected prayer and attain transfiguration unless he passes first by the valley of tears. The gift of tears is a sign of a very high spiritual state.

Tikhon lived in Zadonsk in great simplicity. He slept on the carpet with two pillows, without a blanket, covering himself with a fur overcoat. His cassock was the poorest, as well as his socks and shoes. He often used to walk in peasant footgear. The bishop had neither a box nor sack but only a leather bag for his books when he travelled. The walls of his cell were bare but for pictures of Christ's passion and of a dead man in the coffin. Tikhon often looked at the latter picture and sang: "Tell me, Lord, my end and what is the number of my days, to give an account of them." Even this humble life seemed too lofty for him. He often said: "If it were possible I would lay down my episcopacy and not only that dignity but also my cowl and would say to others I am a simple peasant. I would go then to the remotest monastery as a laborer, saw wood, carry water, bake bread. It is misery that here in Russia, this is impossible to do! " He also often spoke of Mount Athos. "There many of our brethren, bishops, who have left their dioceses, live in monasteries as solitaries." When he was visited by passing Greek archimandrites from Mount Athos, he had long talks with them about their monasteries and monastic life. He listened to them with great attention. When they were leaving him, he used to bless them and say: "Farewell, beloved, behold I bow low to the Holy Fathers on Mount Athos. And I ask you to request them with insistance to mention me, a sinner, in their holy prayers."[8]

St Tikhon was exceedingly charitable. He used to help the poor from his pension and from large sums which were given to him by Cossack officers, noblemen and merchants. With these funds he used to buy clothing for the poor and shoes and cattle for the peasants. He also distributed cash.

In the days when the bishops in Russia were great magnates St Tikhon was very simple and humble. He dined with simple peasants, consoled their widows and orphans, maintained the poor for long periods. He liked to give the last sacraments to sick peasants and to bury them. When the town of Livny was burned down in 1768, the bishop collected a large sum of money to rebuild it. St Tikhon helped his relations from time to time but moderately. "My brothers," he used to say, "must work themselves and not look to me. To give them money is to make them frivolous." The bishop lived more or less like a solitary. He went out very rarely and travelled still less.

In Zadonsk St Tikhon experienced several raptures and visions. In 1775 he prayed, "Lord, show me the place prepared for those who love you and what is pity." And coming before the altar he prayed. Then he saw heaven open and the entire monastery illuminated and there was a voice saying: "Look what is prepared for those who love God." He beheld a scene of indescribable beauty and fell in fear to the earth. He could only crawl back to his cell with difficulty. [9]

8. Ibid., pp. 10-11.   9. Ibid., p. 34.

In 1778 and in 1779, St Tikhon saw Our Lady. On Christmas day of 1779, St Tikhon went to the monastic church for the last time. There was a great crowd and he was very tired. After that date the bishop never left the monastery and even his cell and also ceased to receive people. He became silent and ceased to comment on the Bible to his keleiniks. The date of his death was revealed to Tikhon three days before it occurred. The saint died at 6:45 AM on August 13, 1783. St Tikhon prepared his coffin five years previously and requested to be buried as a monk but his admirer, Tikhon III, bishop of Voronezh, ordered him to be buried in the pontifical vestments according to the rubrics. This bishop buried him. Soon after the death of St Tikhon, a people's pilgrimage to his grave began and soon assumed vast proportions. A few decades later, in the reign of Nicholas I, the Russian Church canonized Tikhon. He became a very popular saint, particularly among the monks.

St Tikhon left numerous writings. The best edition of them is the *Collected Works,* published by the Russian Synod in Moscow in 1898-99 (sixth ed.). There are five volumes. The first volume includes St Tikhon's writings as rector of Tver Seminary and diocesan bishop. These writings are chiefly instructions to the clergy; sermons preached in churches; meditations on various subjects and the like. The second and third volumes contain the chief work of St Tikhon, *On True Christianity.* The fourth volume is devoted to *Spiritual Treasure Gathered in the World.* The last volume contains his letters and the memories of him written by B. Chebotarev and T. Efimov.

St Tikhon was quite alien to post-Tridentine Catholicism which so influenced St Demetrius of Rostov. The Hesychast spirituality of St Nilus of Sora is equally absent from his works. St Tikhon's spirituality may be best termed evangelical. It is exclusively based on the Scriptures. References to the Fathers and mystics are rare. The evangelism of St Tikhon is not Protestant but there was in him, nevertheless, some warm sympathy for German pietists and English evangelicals.

On True Christianity was written by the saint in 1770 and 1771. The book was published in 1785 in St Petersburg by the Moscow merchant Timothy Polezhaev, who gave it exactly the same title as the famous work of the German pietist, Johann Arndt. The work appeared, therefore, under the title: *On True Christianity, that is, the true faith, holy living, salutary penance, devotion, sorrow for sins, and of the state of true and sincere Christians as well as instructions how the true Christian may escape sin, death, the devil, the world and every disaster.* Although St Tikhon knew of the work of Arndt, his book has very little in common with it beyond the title. In the *Collected Works* the title is given simply as it was in the manuscript: *On True Christianity.*

The book was much appreciated in Russia and highly praised by the best theologians and prelates of the next generation, particularly by the Metropolitan of Moscow, Plato Levshin; the Metropolitan of Kiev, Eugenius Bolkhovitinov; and the Metropolitan of Novgorod, Michael Desnitsky.

It is quite impossible to sum up in a chapter these two thick volumes. The book stresses the need to study the Scriptures and to live according to them. The first chapters discuss the heart and the good and evil coming out of it, various sins and passions and the results of them. Penance and its fruits, death and the last judgment are then studied. An exposition of Christian virtues follows this. The second part of the work deals with the Scriptures, faith, sacramental life, prayer, Christian duties and so on. The language of the work is simple and pleasant and the teaching sound. The best way to illustrate the mind of St Tikhon is to quote him in his own words.

"Prayer," he says in his chapter on that subject, "comes from hope. We do not ask a man for something we desire if we do not hope to obtain it from him, as, for instance, we do not ask money of a beggar or a mean person, advice from a fool or assistance from the weak. So also those who do not hope to obtain from God what they want do not implore him but turn to helpless creatures. On the contrary, as many turn to a good and generous man because they hope to obtain from him what they need, so those who have a firm, untroubled trust in God, rich in charity and generosity, beg from him pardon and assistance. Prayer is a request for something good, addressed to God by pious men. St Basil the Great so describes prayer in the sermon on Yulitta the Martyr. Any time is suitable for prayer, day and night, morning and evening. To ask a man something is not always possible because he might be busy, or ill, or sleeping; with God it is not so. He is available at every moment and is always free. His door is always open when we want to approach him while still living in this world. He is ever ready to listen to our request and is always ready to grant grace to those who ask for it." [10]

"Because God knows hearts he hears our innermost desires and our aspirations although our lips may be silent. The desires of the poor the Lord hears and his ear is ready to accept the aspirations of their heart (Ps. 9:18). God does not demand words from us. While it is impossible to present our request to a man without speaking with our lips and using words, God knows our thoughts even without words. This word and the thought are equal before him. He knows even our future thoughts. 'You have understood my thoughts from afar' (Ps. 131:2) the Psalmist says. Prayer can be said by the mind without words. It is said in the Scriptures of Anna, the mother of Samuel: 'She prayed in her heart, her lips moved but her voice was not heard' (1 Sam 1:13)." [11]

"As prayer of the heart may be without voice and without words so movements of the lips without the heart, and words without the mind, external voice without any interior voice, prayer without the attention of the heart are all useless. The outward voice and word must correspond to the interior intention because the word is nothing more than the manifestation of the interior state. God sees through our heart. He looks at our heart and not at our words. Therefore words without the consent of the heart are nothing. It happens that

10. *Tvorenija*, 2:323-325.
11. Ibid., p. 325-326.

the tongue says one thing while the mind thinks of something else. Therefore, we must try our best to make our heart pray when our tongue prays and make our mind meditate on the words pronounced by the tongue. The heart must listen to the word and vice versa, while the mind must meditate on what is said."[12] In another chapter, speaking of prayer St Tikhon says: "It is possible to pray sitting, walking, sleeping, working, alone and in company. Everywhere, at all times, in all our activities, eating and drinking, in devout conversation, we are able to raise our minds and hearts to God, to present our needs with faith and humility and ask him pardon saying: Lord, have mercy upon me." He says further: "He who reads many prayers, or psalms, or prostrates frequently but without reason, without attention, humiliy of heart and fervor, such a one never pray."[13]

Although St Tikhon does not mention the Prayer of Jesus, his doctrine on prayer is akin to Hesychasm. A prayer without the attention of heart and mind is nothing, whether it is said vocally or mentally. The reading of the office in the same way is useless. Prostrations and mortifications do not help if they are divorced from true prayer.

Higher prayer and indeed the only prayer is that of aspirations, when the mind and heart, without words, even interior words, elevate themselves to God. This is, of course, true contemplative prayer. It is not an ejaculatory prayer where there is a need of attention and perseverance. It is infused prayer in which the Spirit of God utters in the heart. The grace of this Spirit cannot be exacted by any effort of man, but it will come by itself when man purifies himself of his sins and replaces his vices by virtues, particularly by charity and humility. Then the heart will be prepared for the descent of the Holy Spirit and for infused contemplation.

Although never discussing the Prayer of Jesus, St Tikhon propounds the same view on the all-sacredness and power of this Divine Name as the Hesychasts. "The Divine Name," he

12. Ibid., p. 326.
13. *Tvorenija,* 3:105.

writes, "is so holy, glorious and worshipped that it does not need our worship. Just as the sun, whether it is praised or blamed, shines just the same in the sky and illuminates with its rays everything under heaven, so the Divine Name whether it is praised or blamed by men remains always the same, ever glorious, ever holy and awful, shining with the rays of its glory. . . . The glory of this Divine Name is eternal, boundless and permanent as God himself. Therefore it can neither be increased in itself nor decreased. The great Divine Name contains in itself Divine attributes, incommunicable to any creature, proper only to God as, for instance, unity and eternity of substance, almightiness, goodness, wisdom, omnipresence, omniscience, truth, holiness, veracity, spirituality, and so forth. These attributes of his the Holy Spirit reveals to us in his Word and manifests them in various ways for our instruction and the glorification of the Divine Name."[14]

The fourth volume of the *Collected Works* contains various treatises written from 1777 to 1779, that is, much later than *On True Christianity,* and just before the final retirement of the saint into complete seclusion. The most important treatise in the volume is *Spiritual Treasure Gathered in the World.* Tikhon worked on it for nearly three years. It was printed for the first time in St Petersburg in 1784. It was republished many times. The Metropolitan Eugenius Bolkhovitinov of Kiev in his enumeration of the writings of the saint, which is added to the life of the latter,[15] observes that this treatise is very similar to a small book in Latin, published by Joseph Hall, an Anglican bishop of Oxford. This booklet was also printed in Russian in Moscow in 1786 (three years after the death of Tikhon) under the title *Improvised meditations produced instantly after looking at something.* Although the saint knew this booklet, there is nothing in common between his work and that of Hall, except the method and the way of speaking. *The Treasure* contains a great many meditations produced by considering the world,

14. Ibid., p. 73.
15. E. Bolkhovitinov, *Svjatitel' Tichon Zadonsky* (St Petersburg, 1820), pp. 99 and 109.

the sun, spring, a traveller, a shepherd, father and sons, a wedding, and so on.

A long meditation, "Water flowing by," is worthy of quotation because it gives us some insight into the mind of Tikhon and enables us to understand him better. "What water flowing by is," the saint says, "so is our life and everything happening in it. We see that water in the river flows unceasingly and passes by and everything floating upon the water, like wood or refuse, likewise passes by. Some years ago I did not exist and behold I am in the world like other creatures. 'Thy hands created me and formed me' (Ps. 118:73). I was a baby and this passed by. I was an adolescent and this passed by. I was a youth and this left me. I was a mature and strong man, and I am no more. Now my hair is white and I am weary with old age but this is also passing by. I approach my end and I will go the way of all flesh. I was born in order to die. I die in order to live. 'Remember me, O Lord, in your Kingdom!'

"What happened to me happens to everybody. I was in good health and ill, again in health and again ill. All that passed by. I was happy and unhappy. Time passed by and with it everything disappeared. I was honored; the time came when honor left me. People honored and revered me. Time passed and I see this no more. I was sometimes gay and sometimes sad. I was joyful and I wept. The same happens to me also now. Days go by and with them sadness and gaiety, joy and weeping. People praised and glorified me, then they blamed and abused me. Those who praised me the same damned me and those who abused me also praised me. Time passed by and all that disappeared. Praise and abuse, glory and dishonor, all that passed by . . . .

"Such is the world and such is its consistency, such is our life in this world. Where is the time when I was happy, healthy, joyful, honored, praised, revered; the time when I enjoyed delicate meals and music and a carriage drawn by many horses. Time passed by and with it all my happiness and consolation. Where is the time when I was unhappy, ill, sad, sorrowful, abused, blamed, reproached, reproved? Those days passed by and with them all my unhappiness. Everything that happens now will pass by too. Everything disappears with time. We see our past like a dream and with it all our former happiness. In the end of our life we will see likewise, as a dream, what still remains to us. Then we will remember and dream of all that happened to us. . . .

"Quite different will be the life of the world to come as the Word of God and our faith assure us. There our life once begun will never end. Our life will be unceasing and changeless. Our body will be free of illness, old age, death and putrefaction. Our body will be spiritual, unchangeable, immortal, strong, ethereal, flourishing. Likewise, glory, honor, rest, peace, consolation, joy, gaiety and every beatitude will be there forever. The elect of God will constantly see God face to face and from this they will always be consoled, joyful, gay. They will reign with Christ forever as members with the head."[16]

Another meditation of great depth is on the vessel: "The vessel full and empty." "The heart of man is like a vessel. The first similar to the second. A vessel full of water or something else cannot contain anything more. On the contrary, the empty vessel is ready to be filled by anything. For this reason people empty the vessel if they want to fill it with something else. The heart of man is like that. When it is empty of wordly and fleshly desires, it is ready to receive the God of love. But when it is filled with love of this world, fleshly desires and sinful inclinations, then divine love cannot fill it. . . . If we want, Christian, to have our hearts filled with divine love we must first empty them of the love of this world, its frivolous and sinful customs and then turn our hearts to the One God, our only good and happiness and eternal beatitude. Then only divine love shall penetrate our hearts and we shall taste and see how good is the Lord (Ps. 33:9)"[17]

16. *Tvorenija,* 4:196-198.
17. Ibid., p. 354.

The fifth volume of the *Collected Works* contains *Letters from the Cell: Keleinyia Pisma,* meditations and discussions on various subjects. They were published in 1784 in St Petersburg. They deal with such things as the number of the saved, joy in the cross and Christian duties. The volume also includes some prayers and instructions. There are altogether 125 such letters. By the end of the last century they were reprinted forty-two times which proves their popularity. The volume also includes sixty-two selected letters to various persons. They are of very varied contents: catechetical, apologetical, moralistic, and so forth. Some letters give us a good insight into the mind of Tikhon. To a monk in a Moscow monastery who was persecuted for no reason, the saint wrote: "Know well, that anywhere you will be, he (the devil) will always disturb you either through men or through yourself. You will live in tranquillity and have interior peace if you can endure patiently, silently and without rebellion anything which may happen to you from men and from yourself. A pious soul living in this world is always in a strange land, where troubles are ever present. They will stop when the soul will return to its heavenly fatherland."[18]

In letter thirty-one the saint stresses the importance of peace of mind. "Serenity," he writes, "is the principal happiness in this world. Without peace of mind nothing is pleasant to us. This we learn during spiritual struggle when we are dominated by evil, fear, or confusion, as we learn what a blessing health is when it is taken away from us. But in this world it is impossible to find rest. The sea is ever restless. It has its high and low tides and is hardly ever still. Such is our life. Man seeks rest and wanders from place to place to find it but fails because he looks for that which is absent in this world. From the vanity of the world he retires to solitude and he is met there with more numerous and cruel temptations from the invasion of various thoughts and attacks of the devil. In cities and in villages we are surrounded with scandals which always disturb and inflame our hearts. Woe to the

18. *Tvorenija,* 5:354.

world for scandals! The Christians, although they do not find rest outside, because they are always disturbed by external or interior temptations, yet they can and must possess rest always and everywhere. The good conscience which is undisturbed by evil deeds, words and thoughts and the soul that resists every temptation, enduring everything and is thus fortified, are always in rest, like a ship in a safe port. This is our happiness in this world."[19] In the same letter Tikhon recommends reading the works of Johann Arndt, showing that he studied them: "Read Arndt."[20]

Advising a certain Ivan Mikhailovich, a lover of solitude, Tikhon describes the ways of the spiritual life: 1. Knowledge of self and of our own heart comes from reading the Sacred Scriptures and other Christian books. But the best and truest knowledge of ourselves we gain from temptations which come either from the outside from the devil and evil men or from the inside, from our own evil thoughts. Temptations are like medicines which make us vomit to expel from the stomach juices and food. Temptations show what is hidden in our heart. Temptations are permitted so that we may learn what is in our heart. Often we think that we are something but temptation shows us that we are nothing. 2. We see from this that there is no true rest in this world. If we live in a town, among people, we are troubled by scandals and evil men. If we flee into solitude we face still greater and more unprecedented attacks from Satan and evil thoughts. 3. If there is any rest in this world, it is only in a pure conscience and patience. This is the haven for us navigating the sea of life. A pure conscience is unafraid, therefore man is quiet. Patience masters and humbles the troubled and stormy heart and makes man serene. 4. To learn patience without sorrows and temptations is impossible. Patience comes from enduring evil and disasters and not from happiness and well being. In the same way it is impossible to have a pure conscience unless man truly repents and corrects his life according to the Word

19. Ibid., p. 357.
20. Ibid., p. 358.

of God. 5. A pure conscience and patience are inseparable: a pure conscience keeps the Word of God while patience stands against all that which resists the Word of God and keeps the conscience from being defiled by crime and, consequently, disturbed. 6. True, eternal and undisturbed rest is reserved for us in the world to come and, therefore, it is called rest in the Scriptures.[21]

The fifth volume also includes the memoires of Basil Chebotarev and Ivan Efimov, which we quoted above. The personality of St Tikhon was much admired in Russia not only by the masses and monks but by several eminent Russians as well. It particularly struck the great Russian genius, Theodore Dostovesky, who modelled on him the Staretz Zosima in his greatest novel, *The Brothers Karamazov*. In Zosima Dostoevsky tried to express Tikhonian spirituality but only partially succeeded. Zosima includes several features of the great Optino Staretz, Father Ambrose, whom Dostoevsky personally visited. Into this combination of two very dissimilar men Dostoevsky injected some elements of his own personality. Still the Staretz Zosima is undoubtedly inspired by St Tikhon as Dostoevsky himself admits.[22]

All the novels of Dostoevsky are now reprinted in Soviet Russia and are very widely read. In a time when publication of religious or theological books is not allowed and none can be sold in bookshops, the great novels of Dostoevsky keep before the Russian masses, and especially the youth, the image of Christ and the figures of the Russian Staretz. The great Optino Staretzy whose influence on the life of many prominent Russians, like Gogol, Dostoevsky, Tolstoy, Leontiev, Soloviev and Rosanov was very considerable, were themselves disciples of another Staretz, Paisius Velichkovsky, a contemporary of St Tikhon, who initiated in his Neamtu Monastery in Moldavia the astonishing revival of Russian monasticism in the nineteenth century which also became the Golden Age of Russian mysticism.

21. Ibid., p. 360-361.
22. N. Gotodetzky studied the influence of the personality of St Tikhon on Dostoevsky as reflected in the Staretz Zosima: *Saint Tikhon Zadonsky, Inspirer of Dostoevsky* (London, 1951).

CHAPTER V

ARCHIMANDRATE PAISIUS VELICHKOVSKY
AND HIS DISCIPLES

ARCHIMANDRITE PAISIUS VELICHKOVSKY,
Peter by birth, was born in 1722 in Poltava in the
Ukraine, where his father, John, was dean of the
Cathedral. Peter was only four years old when his father
died. He remained under the care of his mother, Irene, and
his brother, John, who succeeded his father as dean. Peter
was a very bright boy and studied well. He read avidly the
bible and ascetical works, particularly those of St Ephrem the
Syrian, Abbot Dorotheus and St John Chrysostom. Peter was
only thirteen years old when his brother died. Rafael, Metropolitan of Kiev, reserved the deanery for Peter and sent him
to the College of Kiev to study. The eighteenth century in
the Ukraine was still an age when some church livings "ran in
the family" and small boys were appointed deans just as they
were appointed abbots and canons in France of the same
century. These boys, of course, did not exercise any office or
authority until they reached the proper age and were duly
ordained. In the meantime some other priest assumed the
responsibilities, being paid a salary by the holder of the bene-
fice. This kind of ecclesiastical abuse has long since disappeared.

Peter had no desire whatever for a deanery in Poltavia. He
wanted to be a monk and to enter the strictest possible monastery. Knowing full well that his mother would not approve
his project and would try to stop him, Peter decided to leave
Kiev secretly. This he did. His disappearance greatly upset his

mother who learned that he had fled to some monastery.
Indeed she became gravely ill. During her illness she had a
vision. A voice told her that she was being punished because
she preferred a creature, her son, to God. "Your son will be a
monk, and you will be a nun or you are lost." Irene repented
and recovering became a nun with the name of Juliana. She
died ten years later. Peter meanwhile arrived to Lubech Monastery where the abbot received him well and straightway
made him cellarer. Abbot Nicephoros, a kind and simple
man, died immediately after Peter entered the community as
a novice. His successor, a learned and capricious monk,
Germanus Zagorovsky, at once disliked Peter and sent him
away.

   In no way upset, Peter crossed the Dnieper into the Polish
Ukraine and entered Nikolaevsky Medvedovsky Monastery.
The superior, Father Nicephoros, received him kindly, made
him rassophoros,[1] a kind of regular oblate, and renamed him
Plato. The new rassophoros, who was only nineteen, was appointed cantor and refectorian. Plato had left Russia in 1741.
He died in Moldavia in 1794, fifty-three years later. Although
nearly all his life was spent abroad, he did more for Russian
monasticism than anyone among his contemporaries. Indeed he
can be likened to St Sergius of Radonesh for his importance
in the history of Russian monasticism. Plato was unable to
remain for long in Medvedovsky Monastery. The Ruthenian
Catholics assisted by the Polish government were taking over
one Orthodox monastery after another. The turn of Medvedovsky Monastery came. Its church was closed down. Plato
returned for the last time to Kiev and worked for a while in
the printing press of Kievo-Pechersky Laure under Father
Macarius. He learned then of his mother's death.

   Although the reign of the Empress Anne over the position
of the clergy and monasteries improved, Plato foresaw the
new tide of anti-monasticism, which indeed came twenty-two
years later and ended in the secularization of monastic estates, the suppression of many monasteries and the limitation
of the number of monks. The time was very uncertain for

---

1. A person who has received the monastic habit but has not made vows. He
may go on to take vows, becoming a *stavrophoros,* or he may remain *rassophoros.*

monks in Russia. Plato decided, therefore, to migrate into the Rumanian Orthodox Principalities of Valakhia and Moldavia which, although under the overlordship of the Turkish Sultans, were de facto more or less independent. The Orthodox Church there was strong and religious life flourishing. He left Kiev in 1743 for good and settled in the Rumanian Monastery of Treihsteni, the superior of which, Father Demetrius, received him well. The Staretz or spiritual director of Treihsteni, Michael, was away, in the Ukraine, when Plato arrived at the monastery. Soon after, however, the Staretz Basil, whose disciple Michael was, came to Treihsteni from his Skete of Merlopolyani. Basil used to live formerly in Russia in the Moshen hills. Basil greatly impressed Plato. Yet when Basil invited Plato to go with him to the skete, the latter refused, afraid of being pressed to be ordained. Plato, as many Russian monks, considered priesthood as far too great an honor for a monk, as something contrary to the exercise of proper humility.

In the Orthodox monasteries in Russia, Greece, Bulgaria, Rumania, and elsewhere, the number of ordained monks was always strictly limited. They were there in order to celebrate the holy Liturgy, to preside at the Divine Office, and to administer the Sacraments but that was all. The Orthodox monks still look upon priests in the monastery as St Benedict did.[2]

When Father Michael returned to Treihsteni, Plato started to study under him what he had to know in order to be professed. In Western parlance, Father Michael was Plato's novice-master. In the East there is no single novice-master for all the novices. The abbot entrusts the novices to experienced men, each of whom might have charge of one or two, or more. Plato was a fervent novice, and the smallest failure in his duties used to upset him greviously. He writes of this himself. When Plato was in Treihsteni, the monastery was visited by the celebrated ascetic and mystic from Kuirkul,

2. St Benedict wrote his Rule for a predominantly lay community. Monks in general became priests at a much later date, and this necessitated the introduction of lay brothers (*conversi*) unknown in the East.

Onuphrius. Plato understood at once, after a talk with
Staretz Onuphrius, that the latter could teach him far more
about the spiritual life than he was ever likely to learn in
Treihsteni. So he left Treihsteni for Kuirkul.

The Skete of Kuirkul enjoyed perfect solitude. Mountains
and forests surrounded it on every side. No one lived in the
vicinity. The monks lived as hermits. They congregated only
on Sundays and festivals. On these occasions they sang
Matins, Liturgy, and Vespers in choir together, had a meal in
common and a spiritual conference.

In the evening each of them returned to his solitary cell.
Plato liked this kind of life which gave him plenty of opportunity for meditation. For work he carved wooden spoons
which were in general use in those days and were much in
demand. The carving of spoons was a simple business which
permitted meditations and the practice of the Prayer of
Jesus.

Onuphrius taught Plato what the passions of flesh and mind
are and how to overcome them. He also described to him in
detail the terrible, unceasing, invisible war with the devil who
attacks solitaries. There is no salvation in this war and no
victory except in Christ to whom we must pray unceasingly.
Plato was an able and willing pupil. He remained three years
in the skete. Basil and Onuphrius called him the "Young
Staretz" because he was only twenty-four.

While in Kuikul, Plato realized that all the ascetical and
mystical teaching which Onuphrius imparted to him came
from Mount Athos where holy monks wrote treatises on all
aspects of the spiritual life, exercising themselves in self-
denial and interior asceticism, in spiritual combat with the
passions and the devil and practicing prayer in its ultimate
perfection. He decided thereupon to go to Mount Athos himself in search of greater perfection, as St Nilus had done three
centuries before.

Plato went to Mount Athos accompanied by Father
Triphon in search of a renowned Staretz and ascetical and
mystical writings. The Monastic Republic was in a period of

decay when Plato landed on its coast.[3] Twenty sovereign monasteries continued to exist with a number of dependent houses but their membership was small and common life had been abandoned altogether. All the monasteries by this time had become idiorrhythmic. Under this rule the monastery is managed by a Council which is elected periodically. The monks are permitted to possess property and money. For their work for the monastery, as priests, cantors, managers, and the like, they are paid a salary. Idiorrhythmic monks may also possess estates which, however, pass to the monastery on their death. They take their meals each in his own cell, or rather in his apartment of several rooms. They practise austerity according to their taste. The system of administration is oligarchical. The monks are divided into two classes, the proistamenoi and the paramicroi. Only the first take part in administration. These would correspond to the "Fathers" of the Latin Church, while the second are similar to the Western "Lay Brothers."

Meat is allowed in idiorrhythmic monasteries, life is easier, freer and, perhaps corresponds better to Greek individualism. In the beginning all the Athonite monasteries were cenobitic. The idiorrhythmic system made its first appearance in the fourteenth century and reached its peak in the eighteenth century. The Ecumenical Patriarchate never approved of this abuse and tried to extirpate it. In the nineteenth century many monasteries went back to cenobitic living. At present out of twenty sovereign monasteries only nine are idiorrhythmic. While the idiorrhythmic monastery is encouraged to become cenobitic, the opposite process is forbidden.

When the idiorrhythmic system began to spread on Mount Athos, the monks who wanted an austere life left the monasteries and started to form sketes. The skete is a small village, where each monk or two or three monks live in their own small house. A common church stands in the middle of the village.

3. One of the latest and in many ways the best study of Mount Athos is Emmanuel Amand de Mendieta, *La Presqu'île des Caloyers: le Mont Athos* (Bruges: Desclée de Brouwer, 1955).

Another form of Athonite living is the *Kellion*, monks living
in huts gathered in a group under a superior. The severest
form of life is that of the hermits. The first half of the
eighteenth century was even on Mount Athos a period of
intellectual standstill and ritualistic formalism. Nothing, it
seems, augured for good. Yet the astonishing revival of
Mount Athos was not far off.

Plato and Father Triphon, another monk of Kuikul, went
first to the Great Laura of St Athanasius where the Greeks
welcomed them. They preferred, however, to move to Pantocrator Monastery, where Slavs were numerous. Father
Triphon suddenly fell ill and within a few days died. Plato
was left alone. He settled alone in Cypress Calyva. He tried at
first to find a staretz for spiritual direction as he was used to
having one in Moldavia, but found none. Plato started then to
live alone and very strictly indeed. His only food was water
and dry bread every other day, except Saturdays, Sundays,
and feasts. He wore nothing except his cassock and shirt. The
door of his hut was always open. He obtained ikons and
books from the Bulgarian monks of the neighborhood. In this
manner Plato lived three and half years, struggling alone with
his thoughts and temptations and the devil. Father Basil of
Merlopolyani visited him on Mount Athos and professed him
with the name of Paisius. Basil had a few talks with Paisius on
various aspects of monastic life before he returned to Moldavia. Paisius was then twenty-eight years old.

About three months after the visit of Basil of Merlopolyani,
a young monk, Bessarion, visited Paisius. Like the latter he
had tried to find a staretz on Mount Athos and failed. He
asked Paisius to be his staretz. After some hesitation Paisius
agreed, seeing in this the divine will. In this way Paisius lived
a few more years. Other men came and he accepted them as
pupils. Soon they were eight and their two small houses
became far too crowded. Paisius acquired the Kellia of St
Constantine with a church. He had by this time eight Rumanians and four Russians. The celebrations were in Rumanian
and Slavonic. The disciples persuaded Paisius to be ordained
and to act as their confessor.

More and more disciples came. The small kellia was soon inadequate. Paisius bought the empty and much larger Kellia of St Elias, which was transformed subsequently into a skete, it continued to grow, reaching six hundred in the twentieth century. When Paisius bought it, St Elias' Kellia possessed a church, sixteen houses, each for three men, a refectory, a bakery, and other buildings. There were already fifty monks, and more and more were coming. Paisius did not refuse to take in those who begged him for a place. However busy he was with the administration of his community, he did not give up his study of the Fathers and mystics. Learning Greek from a certain Macarius, he began to translate Byzantine manuscripts from Greek to Slavonic. He never slept more than three hours nightly. Becoming more and more known as a spiritual director, Paisius gradually formed a large number of disciples in the various Athonite monasteries. He became spiritual adviser to the retired Ecumenical Patriarch Seraphim who resided at Pantokrator Monastery. The general respect paid to Paisius excited the envy of one Moldavian monk by the name of Athanasius. The latter disparaged the Prayer of Jesus practiced by Paisius and even called him a heretic. Paisius replied to Athanasius by an answer in fourteen chapters where he defended the Prayer of Jesus and stated his doctrine on prayer. This had the desired effect and the attacks ceased.

The community of Paisius increased so much that he could not lodge them any longer at St Elias. He settled a number of his monks in Simono-Petra Monastery but because of debts he could not acquire this monastery. Moreover, the Russian-Turkish Wars complicated matters for Russians in residence in the Turkish Empire. He could not take his monks to Russia where recently monastic estates had been confiscated, many monasteries suppressed and the number of monks drastically reduced. Paisius decided, therefore, to return to Moldavia. Leaving some of his monks on Athos, he took the majority to Moldavia. Paisius hired two ships to transport them from Athos, via Constantinople, to Galaz in Valakhia. Wisely he divided his community putting the Russians in one ship and the Rumanians under Father

Bessarion into another. They were sixty-four in all. After a
stay in Varzareshti Skete, the monks arrived at Yassi where
they were well received by Metropolitan Gabriel and Gregory
Kallimakh, Prince (Voivoda) of Moldavia.

Metropolitan Gabriel gave Paisius Dragomirna Monastery
while the Prince granted to them various privileges. Soon
Father Alexis, a former schoolfellow of Paisius and disciple
of the Staretz Basil, came to Dragomirna from Merlopolyani
and professed Paisius as a megaloschemos. Paisius introduced
a severe rule in the community. The monks possessed everything in common. Strict obedience and silence were enjoined.
Besides attending numerous services in church, the rule prescribed long prayers in the cells as well as an obligatory reading of suitable books. Paisius also introduced the daily confession of thoughts, the starchestvo. Paisius was severe with
the obstinate and violent but kind to the rest. Those who
quarreled were forbidden to enter the church unless they
were first reconciled. Paisius forbade his monks to go out of
the monastery except in obedience. As on Mount Athos,
Paisius continued to make translations from Greek, assisted
by Fathers Macarius and Hilarion.

After the Austro-Turkish Wars Northern Moldavia or
Bukovina passed in 1774 to Austria. Paisius decided to leave
Dragomirna, unwilling to live under the Hapsburgs and ex-
pecting persecution from them because of his faith. The
abbot of Sekul in Moldo-Valakhia invited Paisius to settle in
his monastery with the permission of the Metropolitan and
Prince Gregory Ghika. Paisius arrived with his 350 monks
only to find out that the monastery was far too small and
unsuitable for his community. He went to visit Prince Constantin Murusi and begged for another monastery. The Prince
granted to Paisius the vast Laura of Neamtu, the largest
Rumanian monastery.[4] The Neamtu monks, however, did
not take kindly to the newcomers. Paisius again returned to
the Prince explaining the situation. The Prince told Paisius to

---

4. Neamtu still flourishes. It has 150 monks now and a monastic seminary.
Neamtu was founded in the fourteenth century. "Na gosti v Rumnija," *Chekven
Vestnik* (Sofia, Jan. 1, 1956).

go on. There was nothing left to Paisius but to submit. Finally, in 1774 the Neamtu Community submitted to him. Paisius also retained Sekul, for by this time the community of Paisius had reached five hundred monks; four hundred lived in Neamtu, and one hundred in Sekul.

Paisius ruled both monasteries as well as several sketes. He was obliged to reside alternately in various places. The basic observances of Paisius' community were the practice of the Prayer of Jesus, study of the Bible and the Fathers, strict cenobitism and starchestvo. Paisius continued his translations from Greek, particularly the *Philokalia*, St John Climacus and St Isaac the Syrian. He experienced great difficulties in this work because of the lack of good manuscripts and dictionaries. Fathers Hilarion and Macarius translated into Rumanian. Paisius was in correspondence with Gabriel Petrov, Metropolitan of Novgorod and St Petersburg, who published in Russia the Slavonic translation of the *Philokalia* by Paisius. In 1790, when the Russians occupied once more the Rumanian principalities, the Russian archbishop, Ambrose of Ekaterinoslav, holding the Metropolitanate of Valakhia, visited Neamtu and created Paisius archimandrite. Paisius died on November 15, 1794.

The chief importance of Paisius in the history of Russian monasticism lies in his Slavonic translations from Greek. Although the Russian monks possessed numerous translations from the Fathers, for centuries the latter were scattered, unclassified, difficult to get and by no means easy to read. Ascetical and mystical treatises were particularly rare. Indeed many classics of Byzantine spiritual literature were completely unknown. These classics were very little read even among the Greeks because they were not in print. The patristic and mystical revival started again on Mount Athos. The eighteenth century was, as we have seen, a time of decay in the Monastic Republic. It was the age of the idiorrhythmic communities, characterized by ignorance and by the absence of spiritual directors, nevertheless, better times were at hand. Already in 1743 the Patriarch of Constantinople, Cyril V, tried with the assistance of a learned monk of Vatopedi,

Meletius, to found on Mount Athos a theological college.
This attempt failed. A new effort was made in 1753, when a
Sigillion was published opening the Academy. Ample means
were provided. A fine building was constructed. The program
was most ambitious. The students were to study Greek and
Latin literature, mathematics, philosophy and theology. A
brilliant scholar, Eugene Voulgaris (1753-58), was appointed
rector. Voulgaris' Western outlook and sympathies for
German idealist philosophy made him quickly suspect in the
eyes of the Athonite monks. The disappointed Voulgaris
retired and went to Russia where he became an archbishop.
Nicholas of Metzovo, who succeeded Voulgaris as rector of
the Academy, tried in vain to check the process of decadence. In the end excited monks rioted and burned the
Academy as a place of heresy and iniquity.[5]

The monastic revival of Mount Athos came from quite a
different source. An Athonite monk, Nicodemus, surnamed
the Hagiorite, undertook in company with a saintly and
learned prelate, the retired Metropolitan Macarius of Corinth,
to gather and to publish in a collection the best classics of
ascetical and mystical literature known in Greek. After some
years of work this collection was published in Greek, at
Venice. This is the celebrated *Philokalia.* In includes treatises
of Abbot Dorotheus, Hesychius, Nicephorus, Nilus and
Philotheus of Sinai, Gregory the Sinaite, Gregory Palamas,
Callixtus and Ignatius, Kanthopoulos, Simeon the New Theologian and many others. Nicodemus the Hagiorite also translated and published in a modified form *The Spiritual Combat*
of an Italian mystic of the sixteenth century, Lorenzo
Scupoli. He even translated the *Exercises* of Ignatius Loyola.
Nicodemus has recently been canonized in the Orthodox
Church. Paisius translated only the *Philokalia,* naming it in
Slavonic, *Dobrotolyubie — Love of Good.*

Paisius' translations became known to the leading prelate of
the Russian Church, Gabriel Petrov, Metropolitan of Novgo-

---

5. The Ecumenical Patriarch, Athenagoras I, restored the Academy. It now has
dozens of students, all from the Athonite monasteries.

rod and St Petersburg, a great lover of monastic life who did much to revive it in Russia. The son of a Moscow priest, Gabriel was born in 1730. Graduating from Moscow Theological Academy, he worked for a while in the Synodal Printing Press and taught in the seminary. Becoming a monk and priest in 1758 Gabriel was made at once rector of the seminary. Three years later he was promoted to the rectorship of the Theological Academy and on December 6, 1763 he was consecrated Bishop of Tver. A very gifted man, he was respected by Catherine II who consulted him on many state affairs. Transferred in 1770 to St Petersburg, Gabriel took over, in addition, the vast archdiocese of Novgorod. In 1783, as the First Member of the Holy Synod, he became in fact the Primate of Russia. He opened several clerical schools and seminaries, built churches and monasteries. He greatly loved monks of spiritual attainment. Paul I much respected Gabriel and showered on him honors and estates. After some years Gabriel wanted to retire. He was urged to change his mind, but finally the Emperor released him from his onerous duties. He died on January 26, 1801, about a month before Paul I. Gabriel left various writings. His chief contributions to Russian monasticism are his restoration, or rather revival, of Valaam Monastery, the foundation of Russian missions in America, and the publication of *Dobrotolyubie*.

When Paisius received the request of the Metropolitan of Novgorod for his Slavonic translation of *Philokalia*, he became uneasy. Remembering the Palamite controversies in the fourteenth century, Paisius was afraid of their repetition in Russia, particularly in connection with Hesychast prayer. The Metropolitan prevailed however and in 1791 Paisius sent Father Athanasius to Moscow with the Greek copy of *Philokalia* and his own translation. Paisius' translation was compared with the Greek text by a board of monks, including the abbot of Valaam, Nazarius, Father Theophan, afterwards abbot of Novoezersk, Father Filaret, later abbot of Novospasky Monastery and James Nikolsky, afterwards dean of the Assumption Cathedral in Moscow. The first edition of *Dobrotolyubie* appeared in Moscow in 1793, the second in

1822 and the third in 1832. Their influence on Russian monks was astonishing. All the Russian contemplatives and mystics of the nineteenth and twentieth centuries were brought up either on the Paisius Slavonic *Dobrotolyubie* or on its Russian version prepared by the greatest Russian mystic of the nineteenth century, Bishop Theophane the Recluse.

Paisius also left writings and letters of his own. The most important among his treatises is his defence of Hesychast prayer.[6] This treatise is divided into six chapters. It was written in Dragomirna Monastery against a monk who lived in the Moshen hills and depreciated the Prayer of Jesus. In the first chapter Paisius asserts that the Prayer of Jesus dates from the earliest times and was well known to the Fathers. Many manuscripts concerning this prayer were destroyed by the Moslems and, therefore, it was largely forgotten. Barlaam attacked this prayer but Palamas vindicated it. Chrysostom says that it is useful and salutary to appeal to the name of the Savior. In the second chapter Paisius shows how Hesychast prayer began, and quotes Scripture and the Fathers to support his view. Prayer has two degrees. The first is proper to beginners and the second to the perfect. The first corresponds to the active life and the second to the contemplative life. According to St Gregory of Sinai there are eight primary visions: the Formless, eternal, uncreated, Cause of everything, the Unity in Trinity, the supra-substantial Godhead; the degrees and organization of the Angelic Host; the structure of beings; the providential descent of Logos; universal resurrection; the dreadful second advent of Christ; eternal torments; and the Kingdom of Heaven.

All vocal prayers, fasting, tears, vigils, meditation and mental prayer are characteristic of the active life. After purifying the ascetic, divine grace raises him by degrees to contemplation not by his own will, but by the divine will. Those who want to attain to contemplation by their own efforts

---

6. This treatise is printed in *Žitie i pisanija moldavskago starca Paisija Veličkovskago* (Moscow, 1892).

will fall into delusion. Prayer in the Spirit is the highest degree of prayer.

In the third chapter Paisius shows that Hesychast prayer is a spiritual art.[7] Everyone can read Church prayers but to pray with the mind within the heart, offering them in sacrifice to God is an art for those called to it. The fourth chapter discusses the preparations for those who want to learn the Hesychast way of prayer. In order to learn this prayer one must find an experienced guide and entrust oneself to him, surrendering one's own will. If no teacher is available, a thorough and humble study of the Scriptures and the Fathers may replace him. The fifth chapter studies the quality and the effects of Hesychast prayer. This prayer is, according to Paisius, the co-existence and the union of God and man. The effects of this prayer are peace of mind, reconciliation with God, compunction and satisfaction for sins. The Jesus Prayer is a refuge from temptations, a bulwark against sorrows, victory in struggle, the work of angels, food of bodiless beings, heavenly joy, endless work. Paisius ends the chapter with suitable quotations. In the sixth chapter Paisius describes the Hesychast method.

"Sit down," Paisius quotes from St Simeon the New Theologian, "in a quiet room, in a selected corner, and do what I advise you. Lock the door and detach your mind from all vanity. Press your beard to your breast and synchronize your sensible eye with your mind. Breath slowly and try to find mentally within your body the place of the heart. You shall see things which you never saw. You shall see the air in the heart and yourself all in light and full of wisdom. After that, whatever distracting thoughts may come, before they can produce any impression, the appeal to Jesus Christ will expel and destroy them. Thus the mind, alert to resist the devil, rises naturally against him and in a hot pursuit destroys invisible foes. You will learn many other things watching after

7. I Hausherr, *La méthode d'oraison hésychaste* (Rome: Pontifical Institute for Oriental Studies, 1927) is a good summary of Hesychast prayer. The fruits of rhythmical breathing for contemplation are discussed in J. M. Déchanet, *Christian Yoga* (New York: Harper and Row, 1960).

your mind and keeping Christ in your heart." Paisius quotes afterwards similar passages from Nicephorus and Gregory the Sinaite.

In his letter to Father Theodosius, Paisius states that he studied the Scriptures and its commentaries by the Fathers while he was still in Mount Athos. He also studied the canons and rites and began to read Hesychius, Philotheus, and Isaac the Syrian. He learned Greek on Mount Athos and looked everywhere for rare books. In the Skete of St Basil he found twenty-four books of the *Philokalia,* and obtained copies of them. He could not correct them, however, because his Greek was poor. He had studied in Kiev for four years and then only Latin. He also lacked lexicons. Yet he began to prepare Slavonic translations as far as he was able. In his letter to Theodosius, Paisius described the history of his translations. In his other surviving letters Paisius gives various spiritual counsels to monks and nuns.

The secularization of the monastic estates reduced the number of the Russian monasteries for men to 225 "Shtatnuie" monasteries, supported by the state, and 160 "Zashtatnuie" monasteries, without any assistance from the state.[8] The same reform limited the membership of the "Shtatnuie" monasteries. They were divided into three classes. Fifteen monasteries of the first class were allowed to have thirty-three monks each. Forty-one monasteries of the second class were permitted to have seventeen each, while one-hundred monasteries of the third class were reduced to twelve monks each. The "Zashtatnuie" monasteries were treated far worse. Only four received permission to have thirty monks, while 154 were reduced to seven monks, the superior included. In these conditions many aspirants to monastic life, unable to enter Russian monasteries, migrated abroad, a few to Mount Athos but the majority to the Rumanian principalities. According to the Archimandrite Theophane Novoezersky, by 1778, Paisius' community numbered over 1,000 monks,

---

8. A. Zavyalov, *Vopros o tserkovnuikh imeniyakh pri imperatritse Ekaterine II* (St Petersburg, 1900) describes the situation of the monasteries quite adequately.

mostly Russians. A number of these Russian monks returned home in 1779, 1787 and 1801. These monks revived Russian monasticism.

Among the disciples of Paisius the most remarkable are Staretz Cleopas, Staretz Theodore, Staretz Basil Kishkin and Staretz John of Moldavia. The Staretz Cleopas lived on Mount Athos and in Dragomirna with Paisius whose disciple he was. Returning to Russia before 1778, Cleopas was appointed abbot of Ostrov-Vedensky Monastery, where he introduced the Athonite Cenobitic Rule. Ignatius and Macarius, two disciples of Cleopas, introduced his rule into the celebrated Pesnoshsky Monastery near Moscow. Macarius became abbot of Pesnoshsky Monastery in 1788. He died in 1811. Several monasteries were reformed according to the Pesnoshsky pattern by the superiors coming from that monastery. Among these monasteries were Davidov, Berlyukov, Ekaterinin, Medvedov, Krivoezersky, Golutvin, Moscow-Stretensky and the renowned Optina Pustuin. Ignatius became in 1788 successor of Cleopas and afterwards abbot of Tikhvin and in 1795 archimandrite of Moscow Simonov Monastery where he died in 1796. All these communities were inspired by the spirituality of Paisius.

Staretz Theodore, born in 1756 in Karachev, province of Orel, was son of a merchant. He wanted to become a monk and twice ran away to monasteries but both times his mother forced him to return. At home Theodore was very pious and kind. He did much for the poor. Meanwhile Theodore became manager of a big firm, owned by a widow and her four beautiful daughters. Circumstances led him to lose his chastity which upset him very much. Theodore left Russia and went to Moldavia where Paisius received him into Neamtu Monastery and entrusted him to Staretz Sophronius. The latter suspended him for five years from communion on account of his sins and made him work hard. After some years in Neamtu Theodore became a disciple of Father Onuphrius. Onuphrius was a Chernigov nobleman, who, after being for ten years a fool for Christ's sake, became a monk. He lived with another monk, Father Nicholas. One day, in the absence of Theodore, robbers attacked both monks and beat them without pity. Onuphrius soon died and Theodore returned to Neamtu where he helped Paisius in his translations. After Paisius died Theodore returned to Russia and entered Cholnsky Monastery near Orel. In that monastery Theodore made many changes and introduced starchestvo.

From Cholnsky Monastery Theodore went to Belo-Berezhsky Monastery, where he met two priests, Cleopas and the celebrated Leonide Nagolkin, who was to become the first Optino staretz. With these two companions he started to live in a hermitage. This excited the suspicions and envy of other monks who forced Theodore to retire with his disciples to Novoezersky Monastery. The Metropolitan of Novgorod sent Theodore to reform Paleostrovsky Monastery on the Lake of Onega. The monks there did not like the austerities of Theodore and persecuted him. So he was obliged to leave them and went to Valaam Monastery and finally to St Alexander Svirsky Monastery, where he died in 1882, saying: "Thanks be to God, thanks be to God. I see at last the shore of the sea of life in which my soul, as a small boat, has endured many storms."[9] In every monastery in which he lived, Theodore introduced the Athonite rule, Hesychast prayer and starchestvo. He did much to form Staretz Leonid Nagolkin. In this way Theodore greatly influenced the spread of Paisius ideas in Russia.

Staretz Basil Kishkin did even more for Russian monasticism than Cleopas and Theodore. Born in the Province of Kursk in 1745, Basil (in the world Vladimir) was attracted at a very early age to monastic life. Indeed he was just seven when he entered the celebrated Sarov Monastery together with Nazarius, later abbot of Valaam, who was seventeen. After four years in Sarov Basil went to Kiev as a pilgrim. Basil became a professed monk at fifteen. In 1764 Miropolsky Monastery, where he was professed, was suppressed. Basil migrated to Korenny Monastery where he learned Hesychast

9. "Skhimonakh Fedor Aleksandro Svirsky," *Zizneopisanija* (Moscow, April, 1907), pp. 77-80.

prayer. He often visited Zadonsky Monastery and talked with St Tikhon. Basil was told that if one will pray earnestly and with attention laziness will pass off and the heart will be filled with divine love. All prayers must be said clearly and slowly and words like "forgive and have mercy" in the plaintive tone of a beggar.

Unsatisfied in his search for perfection in Russia Basil went to Mount Athos, accompanied by his disciples, Arsenius and Israel. They settled in the Skete of St Elias, founded by Paisius. Basil visited many Athonite mystics and spent several years on Mount Athos in profound peace of mind. Circumstances obliged him to leave Mount Athos and to come to Neamtu Abbey after the death of Paisius. From Neamtu Basil returned to Russia to Korenny Monastery. In 1800 Basil was appointed superior of the decaying Belo-Berezhsky Monastery, which had seven monks and no priest. The monastery was in ruins. With the utmost difficulties Basil was persuaded to be ordained. Within a very short time he raised the number of monks to sixty. Among the newcomers were several remarkable monks, including Serafim of Ploshansky, Melchisedek of Moscow-Simonov, Filaret of Glinsky, and Leonid of Belo-Berezhsky, who introduced the ideas of Paisius into their monasteries. Basil wrote rules for four other monasteries. In 1802 Basil obtained from St Petersburg the permission to introduce strict cenobitic life.

Basil opposed the wandering of monks outside their monasteries, demanded general confession from all entering his monastery and insisted on manual labor. "Work hard, brethren. God so much appreciates labor for obedience's sake that for him every drop of perspiration is like martyr's blood."[10] Basil prescribed the reading of the Fathers and Hesychast prayer together with meditation on death every evening. After putting into order Belo-Berezhsky Monastery Basil resigned. In 1811 he left the abbey saying to the monks: "Be saved, brethren. When God shall inspire you, remember me and my love for you. Presently I leave you to go where God

10. "Stroitel o. Vassilij, nastojatel Belo-Berežskey pustyni," Ibid., p. 260.

guides me." Basil visited one after another, Sevsk Convent,
Ruizhovsky Monastery, Livnui, Zadonsk, Voronezh and
Kremetsky Monastery. The latter numbered but eight monks.
Basil within a short time increased this number to sixty-five.
Finally, he visited Ust-Medvedtsky Monastery and Tolshevsky
Monastery. After settling in Korenny Monastery for a while,
Basil decided to migrate to Glinsky Monastery. He went there
in the springtime when the rivers were in floods. With some
danger, Basil reached Glinksy Monastery where he remained
for ten years. When he arrived at Glinsky Monastery it had
but ten monks of a poor sort. Basil obtained the nomination
of his disciple, Filaret, to be superior and together with him
reformed the monastery which numbered several hundred
monks before the Revolution and is still flourishing. From
Glinsky Basil went in 1827 to Ploshansky Monastery. He died
there on April 27, 1831, eighty-six years of age. Basil called
himself a tramp. In a sense he was such. Wandering from one
monastery to another, he spread the ideas of Paisius all over
Russia.

The Staretz John of Moldavia was, perhaps, the greatest
mystic among the disciples of Paisius. A Great Russian, John,
like Basil, wandered all over Russia looking for outstanding
spiritual directors. Finding none according to his heart, John
went to Paisius in Moldavia. After the death of the latter, the
new abbot, Sophronius, began to change the Rule. This displeased many of the monks. Seventy Russians returned
home, while John went to Mount Athos to Lack Skete. War
prevented John from remaining there for long.

He returned to Neamtu where he met Father Plato, one of the
most renowed disciples of Paisius. John wanted to enter his
skete but was not admitted. After a new stay of three years on
Mount Athos, John returned to Moldavia and was, at last,
accepted into the skete of Plato. He remained twenty years in
the skete. When Plato died, the monks started to visit John
for spiritual direction. This did not please John and he went to
live alone in the solitude of Vorona. Parthenius, afterwards
abbot of Guslitsi, visited him in Vorona and left a remarkable

record of his talk with John concerning Hesychast prayer.[11]

"Listen to me, a sinner," Father John said, "I reveal to you a secret but keep it while I am alive. I reveal to you a part of my treasure, do not hide it, but when the time comes share it with others. Listen! After my arrival at Neamtu Monastery, hearing from Staretz Paisius about Hesychast prayer, I asked the Staretz how to begin it and how to do it. And I began to experiment with it. This prayer appeared to me so sweet that I liked it above everything else in the world! For this reason I isolated myself from the brethren, I loved silence and went often to solitude avoiding all scandals and particularly, vain talk. For the sake of this prayer I traveled twice to the Holy Mountain. I mortified myself with obedience, labor, fasting, prostrations and all-night vigils in order to master unceasing mental prayer. For the sake of this prayer, I often became a recluse. I spent all my strength in order to attain it, even to the point of prostration. Many years passed by in this kind of living and little by little prayer began to deepen.

"Afterwards, when I lived in Pokrovsky Skete, the grace of the Lord visited me thanks to the prayers of Father Plato. Undescribable joy overshadowed my heart and prayer began to function. This so much pleases me that I cannot sleep. I sleep hardly one hour in twenty-four, and then sitting. When I rise again, it seems as if I never slept. And even when I sleep my heart is watching. The fruits of prayer began to appear. Truly, child, the Kingdom of Heaven is within us. An indescribable love for everyone, along with tears, was born in me. If I wish, I can weep without stopping. The divine Scriptures, particularly the Gospel and Psalter, have become so sweet to me that I can never cease to enjoy them. Every word leaves me lost in admiration and makes me weep copiously. O, God, you have manifested to me your unknown and mysterious wisdom! Often I rise in the evening to read Psalms or say the

---

11. Parthenius left a work worthy of note: *Skazanija o Stranstvii i putešestvii po Rossii, Moldavii, Turcii i Sv. Zemle ostriženika sv. Gory, inoka Parfenija,* 4 vols. (Moscow, 1855).

Prayer of Jesus and I become enraptured, drawn out of myself I know not where, in the body or out of the body, I do not know, God knows. Only when I come to myself it is already light. But a sting of the flesh is given to me—to disturb me—to keep me humble. In no wise can I be with people, still less with laymen. With women I cannot even talk. For more than forty years, in Moldavia, no woman has visited me although many wanted to have a talk with me. But I refuse, saying that I am ill."[12]

Among the disciples and friends of Paisius we should note Theodosius, archimandrite of Sophroniev Monastery; Father Cleopas, who died in Valaam Monastery in 1816; Father Athanasius Zakharov, who died in Ploshansky Monastery in 1823; another Athanasius, who brought *Dobrotolyubie* from Athos to St Petersburg in 1791 and died in Svenksy Monastery in 1811; Father Paul, who died in Simonov Monastery, Moscow; Father Gerasim, who died in Sophroniev Monastery; Father Arsenius, who died in 1844, and many others. Over 160 monasteries experienced the influence of Paisius through his immediate disciples or through their pupils. Paisius revived in Russian monasteries Hesychast prayer, starchestvo and the study of the Bible and of the Fathers. The result of his efforts was strikingly manifested in a truly astonishing revival of Russian monasticism in the nineteenth century which also proved to be the Golden Age of Russian mysticism.

12. Pathenius, *Skazanija,* 1:400-401.

CHAPTER VI

RUSSIAN MONASTICISM IN THE NINETEENTH CENTURY

THE REIGN OF CATHERINE II was a critical period for Russian monasticism. After the secularization of Church estates, the number of monasteries was drastically reduced as well as the number of monks and nuns. While there were 12,444 religious in 1762, no more than 5,105 were allowed after that. In fact, the true numbers were much smaller because it was impossible for many communities to maintain the allocated number of religious on the vastly decreased income. Before the secularization, the Church received in a poll tax alone, from the 910,866 taxable peasants on its estates, 1,366,299 roubles a year. Several communities became greatly impoverished. Buildings were soon delapidated and everything decayed. The superiors were afraid to report this state of things to the government which would only use this as a pretext to close many more monasteries.

Only learned monks who became professors, rectors of theological colleges, and bishops lived well. They were paid good salaries and formed a privileged class. Plato Levshin, Metropolitan of Moscow, developed and fostered this group of monks, which did much to raise the standing of monks in society.

Paul I (1796-1801), the son of Catherine II, was a religious man. He doubled state subsidies to the monasteries and was even more generous to the learned monks. In his reign a few new monasteries were founded. The total number of all the monasteries in the Empire, old and new, reached 452 by 1810, 358 for men and 94 for women.[1] In 1701 there were 965 monasteries for men and 236 for women, 1201 altogether, excluding Southern and Western Russia. On the eve of the secularization there were 954 monasteries in existence, excluding Southern and Western Russia. After the secularization only 387 monasteries were left, 319 for men and 68 for women, excluding Southern Russia. Secularization was effected there in 1786 and 1788.

Still later the same process was repeated in Western Russia and in the Caucasus. Alexander I (1801-1825) greatly respected the monks and rarely refused them. During his reign by the decrees of 1805 and 1810 the monasteries were allowed again to acquire estates but without peasants. The spread in Russia, from the West, of free thought and revolutionary ideology alarmed the Tsars. They began to look on the Church as a bulwark against the Revolution. The more revolutionary ideas spread, the more attention was paid to the Church. The government was, however, unwilling to free the Church from its control by reestablishing the Patriarchate.

Nicholas I (1825-1855), a strong, authoritarian ruler, realized the value of the Church for the regime. Twice during his reign, in 1835 and in 1838, the monasteries received from him new properties, partly arable, partly wooded, from fifty hectares to 150 hectares each. Alexander II (1855-1881) granted the monks an annual subsidy of 168,200 roubles to hire workers. Alexander III (1881-1894) increased the state subsidy still farther. At the same time the monasteries began to benefit from private benefactors. The Countess Anne Orlov alone bequeathed to 340 monasteries 5,000 roubles each, besides vast donations to Yuriev, Solovetsky and Pochaev Monasteries. In 1858 the Society of Assistance to the Poor Churches and Monasteries was founded. Gradually, several suppressed monasteries were restored. In 1799 the

1. The figures given are chiefly from P. Znamensky, *Učebnoe rukovodstvo po istorii russkoj cerkvi* (St Petersburg, 1904).

celebrated Bratsky Monastery was reopened in Kiev. Sorsky Monastery, reduced to the status of an annex, was reestablished in 1850 as an independent monastery. Maksakovsky Monastery, closed in 1786, was reopened in 1803. In 1801 the renowned Spaso-Kamenny Monastery, suppressed in 1775, was reestablished. In 1827 Divnogorsky Monastery, suppressed in 1786, was revived. In 1844 Svyatogorsky Monastery was reopened. Twenty-nine closed monasteries were reopened in the eighteenth century and sixty-five in the nineteenth century. Only twenty new monasteries were founded in the eighteenth century but in the nineteenth over 300 new monasteries were founded. Over 160 new monasteries were founded between 1880-1890, a record in Russian history.

The women's communities developed best, both monasteries and the so-called communities. The latter appeared in 1764 when the numbers of nuns were drastically reduced and many novices and oblates were expelled from the cloister. The expelled religious continued to live together as well as they could, without vows. They usually tried to live near churches and to make their living by teaching children, looking after the sick and the aged, and the like. Later communities were formed. Gradually they became organized into convents.

Several of these convents rendered distinguished services to the Russian Church, particularly in the mission field among the Old Believers and in Western provinces of the Empire. In the latter area Lesninsky and Radochnitsky Convents particularly distinguished themselves.

Lesninsky migrated abroad after the Soviet Revolution and is now in France, near Paris. Since 1881 the foundation of new monasteries was left to the Synod. The consent of the government became unnecessary unless a subsidy was requested. Sixteen years earlier, in 1865, the diocesan bishops had received permission to authorize monastic professions, a function previously reserved to the Holy Synod. By 1900 there were 800 monasteries in Russia, of which 300 were nunneries. There were 17,000 professed monks and nuns and nearly 30,000 novices of both sexes. Convents, although

fewer than the monasteries for men, were much more populous. While there were fourteen monks and eleven novices in
the average male monastery, there were thirty nuns and
ninety novices in the average convent. Among the male monasteries four enjoyed the title and the privileges of the
Lauras. They were Pechersky Monastery in Kiev, Troitse-
Sergiev Monastery near Moscow, Alexandro-Nevsky in St
Petersburg and Pochaev in Volynhia.

Of these Lauras three still exist as regular monasteries while
that of St Petersburg houses a theological Academy, seminary
and the residence of the Metropolitan of Leningrad, with a
number of monks. There were also seven stavropigiac monasteries, subject not to their diocesan bishops as all the others,
including the Lauras, but to the Holy Synod directly. Four of
them were in Moscow: Novospassky, Simonov, Donskoy and
Zaikonospassky. Three others were in the provinces: New
Jerusalem, Spaso-Yakovlev in Rostov and Solovetzky. None
of these monasteries survived but Donskoy is still open for
worship.

The growth of monasteries in the nineteenth century is well
illustrated by the figures. In 1810 there were 452 monasteries
(358 for men and 94 for women). By 1825 the number increased to 476 (377 male and 99 female). In the same year
these monasteries numbered 3,272 monks and 2,015 novices
and 1,882 nuns with 3,456 novices. By 1850 the number of
monasteries reached 597 (408 of men and 119 of women).
Five years later there were already 544 monasteries (415 of
men and 129 of women) with 5,174 monks and 5,274
novices and 2,508 nuns and 6,606 novices. In 1879, at the
end of the reign of Alexander II there were 619 monasteries
(449 of men and 170 of women) with 6,688 monks and
3,490 novices and 4,371 nuns with 12,496 novices. In 1893,
at the end of the reign of Alexander III the number of monasteries reached 742 (507 of men and 235 of women). In
1890 the number of religious was estimated at 12,712 men
and 27,574 women.[2] In the nineteenth century the number

2. Igor Smolitsch, *Russisches Mönchtum, Entstehnung, Entwicklung und Wesen*
(Würzburg: Augustinus, 1953), p. 538.

of nuns grew much faster than that of monks. There were several convents with 500 nuns or more, even up to 1,000. Among the monks monasteries of this size were rare. Both monks and nuns maintained schools, hospitals, homes for the aged, printing presses, and so forth.. Several communities were engaged in missionary activities. In the single reign of the Empress Elizabeth, in the former Kingdom of Kazan on the Volga, over 430,000 people, Moslems and pagans, were baptized. In the nineteenth century there were on the Volga several monasteries both of men and women, entirely made up of the Volga Finns and Turks, Czuvazh and Cheremissi. Their influence on the natives was very strong indeed. The Orthodox Czuvashs survived the Soviet Revolution as well as the Russians, if not better, and form now a special diocese corresponding to their own Soviet Guvash Republic. The great Sarov Monastery rendered considerable service to another Volga Finn tribe, the Mordvinians.

Igor Smolitsch in his study of Russian monasticism stresses the importance of monasteries in the Russian colonization of the Volga lands. In the sixteenth century thirty-one monasteries were founded there, four in Nizhni Novgorod, five in Kazan, three in Arzamas, two in Astrakhan, three in Sviazhsk, and so on. In the next century in twenty-four towns there were already in existence twenty-eight monasteries and forty-four new ones were founded. Two more monasteries were founded in Astrakhan, making the total number there seven. There were two in Cheboksaris, three in Arzamas, two in Ufa, two in Samara. Altogether 101 monasteries were founded in the Volga lands within two centuries.[3] The foundations became even more numerous in the nineteenth century. Indeed the Volga dioceses, in the era of the Revolution, became prominent for the number of monasteries and religious.

The nineteenth century produced a great number of Russian mystics, some Orthodox and some not. A few words may be said of the latter. Already in the eighteenth century, as a reaction against the rationalism and free thought that

3. Ibid., pp. 536-537.

was strong at the Court, non-Orthodox mystical literature made its appearance in Russia. The Russian, non-Orthodox mysticism of the century was promoted by two Free Masons, Professor Schwarz and A. Novikov. The latter did his best to spread mystical books in the society.

In 1782 the Free Masons founded the Friendly Learned Society with educational and charitable activities. They published religious books, helped gifted young men and assisted schools and hospitals. The Russian Free Masonry of the age professed mystical theism, free of all denominational teaching.[4] It aimed at union with God through wisdom and morality outside the Church. Free Masonry considered itself above all the Churches. It admitted to its membership people of all denominations. Anxious to placate the Orthodox Church, Russian Free Masons selected Plato, Metropolitan of Moscow, as their protector. The Free Masons assisted the clergy in their struggle against militant atheism yet they remained alien to the Church. In 1785 the Empress requested Metropolitan Plato to find out whether the Free Masons were sectarians or not. The Metropolitan after a long study of the relevant literature reported to the Empress that some of the Masonic books were ordinary literature. Mystical books, he stated, he could not understand, while those of the encyclopedists were harmful. The Empress thereupon prohibited Masonic mystical books. In 1791, when the French Revolution was in the ascendancy, the Empress closed the Masonic lodges and their printing press and ordered the burning of the Masonic mystical books. In 1792 Novikov was imprisoned in Schlüsseburg. Paul I, who was himself a Free-Mason, freed Novikov and called another Free-Mason, Lopukhin, to Court.

Alexander I, the son of Paul, was inclined to mysticism by his nature and circumstances. He knew of the plot to depose his father in 1801 and reproached himself for the latter's assasination by the plotters. This tragedy led him to seek consolation in mysticism. He assiduously visited Russian monks, hermits and recluses, as well as Russian sectarians,

4. Cf. S. Bolshakoff, *Russian Nonconformity.*

Protestant pietists and Catholic divines. The victory over Napoleon in 1812-15 made the Emperor still more mystical. Alexander I found many followers in Russian high society. The writings of Jacob Boehme, Meister Eckhart, Jung-Stilling, Saint Martin de Toit, Madame Guyon and Swedenborg became popular and were widely read. All these writings are slightly or, even pronouncedly, pantheistic; none of them has anything to do with Byzantine or Russian mystics. Although many treatises of the Orthodox mystics existed already in Russian or Slavonic translations, including those of St Macarius of Egypt, St Isaac the Syrian, St John Climacus, St Gregory of Sinai, St Simeon the New Theologian, St Nilus of Sora, as well as *Dobrotolyubie,* they were not in fashion in high society, which wanted something esoteric, wonderful, almost magic.

In the nineteenth century the Free Masons remained, as previously, inspirers and leaders of the society's mystical movement. Lopkhin published a book *Some Featurers of the Interior Church,* while Labzin published in 1806 and in 1817-18 *Sionsky Vestnik.* When the Russian Bible Society was founded the aristocratic mystics used it for spreading their ideas. They sent their tracts and leaflets to schools, shops, parishes and monasteries. This aristocratic mysticism preached immediate communion of man with God, a universal, exclusively affective, subjective religion without dogma and Church, based on immediate illumination by the Holy Ghost and on the pronouncements of the interior word in the spirit of man. This mysticism rejected all the externals of religion, hierarchy, sacraments, rites and even the obligatory teaching of the external, only true, revelation. It acknowledged the unique "interior" Church, having no dogma but that of conversion and the union of man with God, admitting no differentiation among its members or among denominations except that between the old and the new man. According to these aristocratic mystics this interior church existed since the creation of the world, in all times, in all religious, mysteries and philosophical systems.[5]

5. Znamensky, *Učebnoe rukovodstvo,* p. 440.

The members of the Bible Society supported various Russian sects, prayed together with the visiting British Quakers, listened to Linde and to Gosner, visited the meetings of Baroness von Krüdener, Madame Tatarinov, Khluisty and Dukhoborui. This non-Orthodox mysticism infiltrated even into Church publications, like *Khristianskoe Chtenie.* The salons of Princess Meshchersky and of Princess Galitsuin became centers of this aristocratic mysticism. During this period Prince Galitsuin, the Minister of Education and of Cults, deprived the translator, Smirnov, of his job because he wanted to criticize unorthodox mystical books. In 1818, Archimandrite Innocent, rector of St Petersburg Seminary, obtained the suppression of *Sionsky Vestnik.* He allowed, as censor, the publication by Stanevich of a book *Discussions on the Grave of a Child,* which attacked the aristocratic mystics. Prince Galitsuin, greatly irritated by the publication this book, which dared "to defend the external Church against the interior one which is against the principles which guide our Government," suggested to the Synod that they send Innocent to Penza. The Metropolitan of St Petersburg, Ambrose Podobedo, was reprimanded. His successor, Metropolitan Michael Desnitsky, although himself influenced by the theories of the aristocratic mystics, had many difficulties with them. He died early. A coalition of the influential Archimandrite Photius of the Novgorod Yuriev Monastery and Count Arakcheev, the Minister of War, a confidant of Alexander I, led to the dismissal of Prince Galitsuin and to the dissolution of the Bible Society. Nicholas I was extremely hostile to non-Orthodox mystical literature published in the reign of his brother. All such books were confiscated and destroyed.

The eighteenth and nineteenth centuries produced a number of non-Orthodox mystics in Russia, like the Ukrainian Gregory Skovoroda, Professor Schwarz, Novikov, Lopukhin, Labzin and much later Vladimir Soloviev and Nicholas Fedorov. Although some of these people, particularly Skovoroda, Soloviev and Fedorov were powerful thinkers and nominally members of the Orthodox Church, they were hardly Christians in fact but lonely thinkers professing a curious blend of theosophic and pantheist theories. Skovoroda greatly influenced the Russian sect of the Dukhoborui, while Vladimir Soloviev, who was at once a member of the Orthodox and of the Catholic Churches, much impressed the Russian Catholics with his works *Russia and the Universal Church*[6] and *God, Man and the Church, the Spiritual Foundations of Life.*[7] None of these non-Orthodox mystics except Soloviev made much impression on the Russian Orthodox clergy or the faithful. To the monks their treatises were simply unknown and when known, abhorrent. In addition to the aristocratic and learned mystics the Russian masses produced quite a number of their own non-Orthodox mystics, who spread their ideas among Russian sects, like the Khluistui, Skoptsui and Dukhoborui Begunui.

The Orthodox mystics appeared in great numbers when non-Orthodox mysticism had already spent its force. Although the majority of the Russian Orthodox mystics of the period belonged to the school of Paisius Velichkovsky, there were also several exceptions. One of the most interesting among them was George Mashurin, Recluse of Zadonsk Monastery, where St Tikhon lived and died. The spirituality of George Mashurin is akin to that of St Tikhon. Mashurin, a nobleman, was born in Vologda in 1789. His father was murdered by robbers before he was born. Brought up by his mother, George entered the cavalry in 1807. He served as an officer for eleven years, being very popular with his superiors, fellow officers and soldiers for his honesty, modesty and fine sense of duty. While still an officer George Mashurin lived as a recluse, reading continually the Sacred Scriptures, meditating and praying. On September 7, 1818 Mashurin arrived at Zadonsk Monastery and was received as a novice. He was twenty-nine years old. After a short stay in the monastery he again became a recluse, living first in an underground cell but later in a house specially built for him. His manner of life was

6. London:Bles, 1948.
7. London:Clarke, 1937.

very austere, full of long prayers, night vigils, incredible fasts and mortifications. George died, after seventeen years of seclusion, on May 25, 1827, before the ikons in prayer. He was only thirty-eight years old.

George the Recluse occasionally received people for spiritual direction. He also wrote letters of direction. Several short treatises, poems and letters found after his death were collected and published in a single volume.[8] The spirituality of George, like that of St Tikhon, is evangelical but rather on the dark side. George was dominated much more by the contemplation of Calvary, suffering, mortifications and the expiation of sins than by the joy of the Resurrection, the light of Thabor and delight in God and his creatures. He has something in common with the French mystics of the seventeenth century, Port Royal, Marie de l'Incarnation and the Abbé de Rancé. Man is sinful and perverse, always inclined to be selfish. Only by suffering can man be purged from his sinful inclinations. Penance and mortifications are salutary. Life in this world is like a smoke. It passes speedily and leaves no traces. The true life is in the world to come.

In one letter George writes: "Be reasonable and wise. Be prepared well in advance to meet the hour of death with penance and compunction of heart. Be prepared for the hour when the gates of eternity will open to everyone. This hour is terrible not only to sinners but also to the saints, who always, looking upon him, sorrowed and wept. In that hour everyone must go either to eternal life or to eternal perdition. Remember death and you will not want to enjoy this world. Truly all the vanity and pomp of this world will disgust you. You will seek rather weeping and tears than gaiety and dissipation."[9] In another letter George writes: "Only prayer to the most sweet Jesus may sweeten your sorrowful heart and raise your soul to the rapture of heavenly joy.... All the worries of the sea of life are merely vanity.... He who is

8. The writings of George the Recluse are contained in *Pisma v Boze počivajuš-čago zatvornika Zadonaskago Bogoridcskago Monastyrja Georgija* (Moscow, 1844).
9. Ibid., pp. 257-258.

today on the throne, is tomorrow in the grave. He who today wears a crown, is buried tomorrow. He who is today sitting with friends, is eaten up tomorrow by worms. Such is our life."[10]

While all earthly life is vanity and suffering, the Kingdom of Heaven is not so. Our salvation consists in finding our way thereto. The recluse gives advice to those who seek the Kingdom of Heaven. "Those who want to penetrate the Kingdom of God must know the commandments of the Lord Jesus Christ, live accordingly and remember that it is impossible to enter the Kingdom of God except by many sorrows. This Kingdom is not found in something external and visible but in our heart after many labors and frequent prayers to Jesus Christ. You will find the way, if you read with attention the lives of the saints glorified by God, Jesus Christ, and by the Orthodox Church. These saints truly found the Kingdom of God within themselves, by faith, hope and love. This is possible for you too in the Lord."[11]

In his letters to Mary Koluichev, the recluse asserts that no learned theologian can understand heavenly things unless he is humble and indifferent to earthly pleasures. Those who live comfortably have not the Spirit of God living in them. Only those who live in true solitude, detached from all sensible things, only they really understand themselves and realize their own frailty and nothingness and at the same time the power and providence of God who calls us to salvation. As soon as anyone surrenders himself to the Providence of the Heavenly Father, he changes for the better and seeks nothing more but his holy and good will for us. His will be done in heaven and on the earth!

After surrender to Divine Providence, man finds peace of mind and true serenity. For the sake of the latter he runs away from the crowd and from every vanity. Sorrow and sadness always precede great consolations and indescribable joys. In order to live in abandonment to God we must pray

10. Ibid., p. 269.
11. Ibid., p. 398.

unceasingly and never lose time in vain doings. The lost time can never be recovered.

The recluse recommended frequent communion and meditation on death. The poems of George the Recluse remind us of the wonderful poems of St John of the Cross. George often experienced the dark night of the soul. In one place he writes: "Heavenly sadness overwhelmed me. I ask myself from where this dark cloud came to my soul. Everything is depressing and sad. I do not know what to do, what to undertake to disperse this heavy obscurity. I suffer in this gloomy darkness. Thought hardly moves in my heart. Life, however, encourages and strengthens me to the continuous endurance of things to come, whispering: 'Be patient a little while and the Omniscient will have compassion on you and will console you with eternal salvation. Pray with the heart. The repentant heart is a true sacrifice.' "[12]

Like the great Syrian mystic, St Isaac of Ninite, George the Recluse thought highly of tears: "As after rain air is purified and the earth exudes perfumes, so tears purify the soul and fill the heart with consolations. Therefore, tears are needful. Like water from stone, so tears from a strong heart are pure. When they come you can hardly dry them! As a fresh wind pleasantly dries up the face heated by sun, thus the soul heated by love accepts suffering. In the same way as the warmth of the sun is pleasant to the body in need of it, so the words of pure love are pleasant and sweet to the soul."[13] In a poem George writes: "All the treasures of the world are nothing to me if love is absent, all the honors of the world are lowly and dead without love. Love is for me life, light and joy. This sad world does not know this love and calls darkness light."[14] The life and poems of the recluse ended in a hymn to Divine Love.

Among the Russian mystics not directly connected with the disciples of Paisius Velichkovsky, those of Kiev are the most renowned. Staretz Parthenius of the Laura of Kiev must

12. Ibid., p. 253.
13. Ibid., p. 265.
14. Ibid.

be mentioned first. Born in 1790 in the Province of Tula, Peter Krasnopevtzev entered the local clerical school. One night he saw in a vision a white dove floating above him. "Since that time," Parthenius wrote afterwards, "my heart was filled with indescribable sweetness and with a desire of something unearthly. Nothing on this earth attracted me any longer. Everything was tasteless. I became indifferent to everything. To live with people became a burden to me."[15] After another vision Peter entered the Seminary in Tula. His brother, Basil, was already a monk. Although young, Peter was so wise that his parents always asked his advice and did nothing without his guidance. In 1814 Peter went to Kiev for a pilgrimage and remained in the Laura for several months. He could not, however, enter it until 1819, because his parents did not want to lose him. Professed as a monk in 1824 by Archimandrite Anthony with the name of Paphnutius. Peter was made in due course deacon and priest. Several astonishing visions belong to this period. On December 26, 1830, Paphnutius was appointed confessor of the Laura. As confessor Paphnutius sorrowed and wondered at the corruption of human nature. Personally he never knew the temptations of the flesh, although he believed the Devil tempts man continually and prayer is the only salvation. On June 1, 1838, Metropolitan Philaret of Kiev, professed Paphnutius Skhimnik, changing again his name into Parthenius. Parthenius, becoming a Skhimnik, started to celebrate Liturgy daily and say dutifully all the prescribed offices and prayers.[16]

In a vision Our Lady told him that to be a Skhimnik is to dedicate oneself to prayer for the entire world. Anthony, Archbishop of Voronezh, himself a profound mystic, wrote once to Parthenius: "The great *skhema* is the unmeasurable depth and height of Christian humility, founded on the very words of Jesus Christ, our Savior: Learn from me that I am

15. *Skazanie o žizni i podvigach starca Kievo-Pečerskija Lavry ieroschimonacha Parfenija*, (Kiev, 1856), p. 6.

16. Russian priests, even monks, do not celebrate the Eucharist daily as a rule. Only a few very spiritual men do. It is considered unworthy to celebrate without a due preparation and to celebrate daily before receiving the gift of tears.

meek and humble in heart. Thus you shall find rest for your souls. In these few words all the mystery of our salvation is stated."[17] Parthenius was tired before long of his duties as spiritual director and at one time ceased to receive people, but a vision obliged him to resume his duties. He died on Good Friday of 1855 and was buried on Easter Monday. Parthenius left numerous short spiritual counsels, which were collected and published after his death.

The spirituality of Parthenius is very different from that of the recluse of Zadonsk. There is nothing morbid and gloomy about it. It is radiant and serene. "Solitude and prayer are above every good thing," Parthenius writes. "He who has acquired prayer has no time to think of anything earthly. Meeting people and talks with them are a burden to him as well as everything which separates him from God. It is unspeakably difficult to gain true prayer. The soul who tries to do this will approach the gate of death several times. But when prayer is mastered, it will be like a wound in the heart. None can take it away. The love of God can be earned only by unceasing prayer. Although we must make every effort to acquire unceasing prayer, these efforts come to nothing without grace."[18] Man cannot dispose either of his external life or of the state of his soul without the cooperation of God. Without the will of the latter, we cannot even reach the threshold of our room. Our human will is only to desire good and to find the appropriate means to attain it, but God alone can complete and realize any good. Any evil, on the contrary, comes from us. In order to avoid confusion and preserve the spirit of prayer, we must avoid conversations and visits, prefer solitude to everything and often meditate on death. In order to attain to perfect purity we must have no attachments, not even spiritual ones, neither to persons nor to things. We must love everybody with a perfect love, as we love ourselves but without any attachment. We must not desire the sight or the company of the beloved and we must not

17. *Skazanie o Žizni . . . . Kievo-Pečerskija,* p. 44.
18. Ibid., p. 88.

deliberately seek pleasure in thinking of him. We must use every means to acquire peace of mind. It can be earned only by prayer and solitude. If peace of mind cannot be gained without grace, the loss of it is the greatest disaster."[19] The loss of grace is the most terrible of all losses. There is nothing more miserable than the state of a man who has lost grace. Only a few are able to regain it with heroic deeds. We must always take care to preserve grace. Grace is given freely by divine mercy but to keep it we must use every effort.[20]

Total abandonment to the divine will is the summit of the spiritual life. "Total poverty for Christ's sake is a great treasure for the soul but it can be attained by man only if he has a firm, unhesitating, trust in Divine Providence. Keep this confidence without failing and God will never allow you to die of hunger or to lack anything; but if you begin to doubt, however little, or seek human help, or trust in yourself, Divine Providence will leave you. Peter, while yet in darkness, could walk upon the waves as long as he did not doubt in his heart. Divine Providence for us knows no limits. God invisibly leads us. Nothing happens except by the will of God: a day and an hour are fixed for everything. Trust in God and he will care for you, but start to worry about yourself, he will help you still but his almighty Providence will desert you."[21] Total abandonment to Divine Providence is impossible without the Holy Spirit dwelling in the heart. "The Holy Spirit dwells in simple hearts. Interior simplicity must manifest itself in our exterior: in speech, manners, and so forth. Meekness and simplicity attract divine mercy and grace more than all other virtues. .. To the monk the safest way of salvation is solitude with unceasing prayer. Without prayer solitude is unendurable. Without solitude it is impossible to acquire prayer. Without prayer we can never unite ourselves with God and without such a union our salvation is doubtful."[22]

The Laura of Kiev had two other monks of high spirituali-

19. Ibid., pp. 89-91.
20. Ibid., p. 85.
21. Ibid., pp. 93-94.
22. Ibid., pp. 95-99.

ty, both fools for Christ's sake, Paisius Yarotzky (1821-1893) and Hieroschimnik Theophilus Gorenovsky (1788-1853).[23] The life of the latter is so full of miracles that it might be taken for a medieval legend if it were not so recent and so well attested by irreproachable documents and witnesses. Some profound sayings of his have come down to us: "Our life is a time for trading. We must hurry to acquire as much as possible. When somebody brings to the market merely wooden shoes, he does not sit crossing his hands but tries to find buyers in order to sell everything and afterwards to buy for himself what he needs. ... Study yourself well and you will find quickly what you have and what you can gain in exchange for what you have. ... At the terrible judgment you will be asked about everything: Did you possess hands? What did you acquire with them? Did you have brains and a tongue? What did you gain with them? And the reward will be not for the passing objects of time that you gained but for what you gained for eternity."[24] On simplicity Theophilus said once: "God sees my simplicity. I say the Liturgy according to the rubrics, read all the prescribed prayers revering the first concelebrant as my chief, but when I begin to meditate on the sacrament which is performed I forget myself and everything around me. I see during the Divine Liturgy a ray, like a cross, descending from above and overshadowing the first celebrant and those around him, but sometimes not all of them. I see something like dew descending on the Holy Gifts and luminous angels flying above the altar and saying: Holy, Holy, Holy, Lord Sabaoth, heaven and earth are full of his glory. And then all my being is indescribably enraptured and I have no power to detach myself from such a sweet vision."[25] The description of the death of Theophilus and the phenomena witnessed by those present would, by themselves be worthy of study.

23. The lives of these two monks are written by Vladimir Znosko: *Christa radi jurodivji starec Paissij* (Kiev, 1911); *Christa radi jurodivyj ieroschimonach Feofil* (Kiev, 1906)

24. Znosko, *Feofil*, pp. 51-52.

25. Ibid., pp. 122-123.

Archbishop Anthony of Voronezh and Archimandrite Lawrence, Superior of Iversky Monastery in Novgorod were also monks of the Laura of Kiev. The latter was spiritual director of Taisiya Solopov, abbess of Leushin, perhaps the most profound woman mystic in Russia.[26] Born in 1841, daughter of a nobleman, a Naval officer, Maria Solopov, received a good education in Pavlovsky Institute in St Petersburg, a school for daughters of nobles. Already in school Maria had remarkable visions and lived like a nun.

When Maria left school and received a good inheritance after her grandfather died, her mother wanted to marry her off but the daughter wanted to be a nun. After a long struggle the mother gave in and Maria entered Vedensky Convent in Tikhvin. She was nineteen years old. Archimandrite Lawrence was already her spiritual director. The Archimandrite blessing her on her admittance to the monastic life, said: "The life of the Religious is an unceasing interior prayer." For the wealthy society girl, life in the austere convent was very hard in the beginning. Her mother many times called her home but the daughter, although still a novice, resisted. Maria received several astonishing visions at this period. Then she experienced a severe conflict of loyalties: her mother, desperately ill, called her home. Maria preferred Christ and remained. She returned home only after her mother was dead in order to arrange for her brother and sister, who were still small children.

Maria was already a Rassophoros, having received the name Arcadia, when she experienced a great temptation. The abbess transferred her to a dark, wet, unhealthy cell, giving her former one to a newcomer. Arcadia was in that cell for several months and risked losing her health forever when she was called to Novgorod on business. Archimandrite Lawrence, her spiritual director, whom she visited, said to her: "The Holy Ghost teaches us that even a hair from our head does not fall without the will of the Heavenly Father. Do not think, there-

26. The abbess left an autobiography written by order of her confessor: *Zapiski Igumenii Taisii, Nastoyatelnitsui Pervoklassnago Leushinskago Zhenskago Monastuirya* (St Petersburg, 1916).

fore, that your transfer from your beloved and favorite cell into a bad one that is damp is done without the divine will. Your wise and good abbess could not do that if the Lord did not inspire her. You needed to experience this monastic cross in order to gain greater wisdom in your later life. Seven years did you spend in your favorite cell. As you yourself say, you became accustomed to its solitude, so profitable for monastic exercises and secret interior prayer. All this means that the time of your training is over. You needed to learn more sacrificial patience. You have now learned a little. At the same time this is an appeal to you to advance to another manner of life, to undertake new labor for the common good. As gold in fire, you are now tested. In due course the Lord will fulfill in you his will. I tell you: He leads you as by the hand. Surrender yourself to him altogether. He knows better than I and you by what way to lead us to the Heavenly Kingdom. You will not return to Tikhvin."[27]

Arcadia was translated to Zverinsky Convent. She was there for four years, when she visited Lawrence again. The Archimandrite was very old and lived in retirement. He told her: "We must endure and struggle even to the shedding of our blood and not lose our courage during the relatively insignificant storms on the sea of life. The Lord teaches you by these unavoidable commotions a higher degree of patience, in order to face greater sorrows which come in due course to yourself and to the souls who will demand from you consolation and support. Sorrows are the fate of monastic life, its inalienable property from the begining till the end. With the spiritual growth of the monk his sorrows grow as well, that is in degrees. For the child—childish sorrows, for the mature man—mature sorrows. There are no sorrows so heavy as those of superiors, but the subjects somehow do not believe them. They think, on the contrary, that the life of the superior is pleasant and light-some. In fact the life of the Superior is the heaviest cross of all the monastic crosses which ground us to the earth before our time. Time will come and you will learn this by experience."[28]

27. Ibid., pp. 67-68.
28. Ibid., pp. 74-75.

When Arcadia the Archimandrite whether such a cross awaited her, Lawrence answered: "Yes, indeed! This cross, to my regret, awaits you. You are predestined to it. Those whom the Lord elected he will also justify and make wise. Meditate on your life, understand where to the Lord leads you. Then you will understand his providential ways. You, for instance, since the first minute of your entry into the cloister, have remained all the time near the abbesses. You have had the opportunity to observe closely their administration, their relations with the sisters and reciprocally the sisters' dealings with them. This gives you an experience which will be very useful to you in due course. Observing good and evil in those relations, guide yourself by what you see. Example is better than any book of instructions. I do not recommend you to spy on your superiors or criticize their orders, God save you from that. Still it is impossible not to notice what takes place before your eyes. From all that we must learn lessons for ourselves."[29] The Archimandrite gave Arcadia his own abbatial staff during their last meeting.

Professed as nun with the name of Taisiya she was appointed in 1881 to stabilize the recently founded Leushim Community. In 1885 Taisiya was made abbess. Within a few years she built a magnificant church, gathered a great number of nuns and was gratified by seeing her community raised to the degree of a first class monastery.

The spiritual teaching of the abbess is well expressed in her memoires: "Time has passed by and taken with it the past, all I have experienced, the good, the evil and the painful. Storms have ceased, stillness reigns and then the sea of life is again agitated and again calmed as before. The same thing has happened in my little life. But everything which I considered hard and terrible before was merely an introduction to the pains and sorrows which I was called by Divine Providence to endure later on. We must, however, thank the Lord for everything. He showed us, by his own example, there is no other way but that of the cross."[30]

29. Ibid., p. 75.
30. Ibid., p. 72.

Among the many mystical visions and raptures of Taisiya, one, that of November 8, 1885, during the Liturgy, may be quoted: "The Cherubim Hymn was sung. My heart was filled with joy but I restrained myself and continued to direct the choir in order not to betray my feelings and to disturb others. When the choir began to sing 'Let us abandon now all worldly care,' I lifted up my eyes unintentionally, and saw something which I am unable to describe or even to picture in any orderly way. I saw that over the solea, just opposite to the Royal Gate of the ikonostasis, some sacred rites were being performed. It seemed to me that the Savior, surrounded with angels, was there and something was going on, but what and how I am quite unable to describe although I saw and heard something unusual. I felt myself enraptured in the beginning of the vision. When the singing of the hymn was finished and the Great Entrance was over, I saw and understood nothing . . . I remember nothing. I came to myself only when the last requests of the Ektenia before the Creed was sung. Tears streamed down my face. Only then I noticed that everyone was looking at me."[31] The visons of Abbess Taisiya and their interpretation would require a special chapter. We pass on to two other Russian abbesses who may be mentioned here: Theophana Gotovtsev, foundress of Novodevichi Convent in St Petersburg, and Mary Tuchkov, foundress of Spaso-Borodin Convent, the only Russian abbess of the nineteenth century who was ordained deaconess according to the old Pontifical.[32] Both these abbesses belonged to the highest society, both were widows. Mary Tuchkov was close to the Court. Her life is most interesting.

Describing the Russian mystics of the nineteenth century, who are not associated directly with the disciples of Paisius Valichkovsky, it is impossible to omit Staretz Daniel of Achinks.[33] He was born in 1784 in the Ukraine. Becoming

31. Ibid., p. 115.
32. The life of Theophana is described by V. Askochensky, *Feofaniya, Igumeniya Voskresenskago Devičjago Monastyrija* (St Petersburg, 1866). The life of Mary Tuchkov was written several times. The best biography is by Elizabeth Shakhov, *Pamjatnyja Zapiski o Zisni Igumenii Marii* (St Petersburg, 1865).
33. The best study of Daniel was published in Moscow in 1901: *Skazanie o Žisniipodvigakh v Boze pučivshago Stratza Daniila.*

an artillery soldier in 1807, he fought at Borodino in 1812 and was for three years with the Russian army of occupation in Paris and France. While reading the Bible, and perhaps influenced by Protestants or Russian sectarians, Daniel Demenko came to the conclusion that a true Christian must not kill people, even in war. Already a senior non-commisioned officer, on the eve of a new promotion, Daniel left his battery without receiving permission. He retired to a monastery. Arrested as a deserter, Daniel Demenko was sentenced in 1823 by the military court to penal servitude in Siberia. After completing his term, Daniel settled in the small Siberian town of Achinsk, where he rapidly became known as a holy man. In 1843 he moved to Eniseisk, where he died on April 15, 1843, Easter Thursday.

Daniel was never a priest or monk. He remained always a layman, a solitary, a recluse and a spiritual director.

A contemporary has left us a striking description of Daniel: "Prayer streamed out of his heart like one of the rivers of paradise! His mind was always occupied in prayer. Often prayer stopped his conversation and he became enraptured. All his talks were useful to the soul and salutary. He spoke of God and of the Savior of the world, his teaching and his passion, or of the beatitude of the just and the punishment of the sinners. All his talks and instructions were mingled with tears and love in such a way that he hardly could discuss anything without tears. His body seemed transparent, his face pleasant and gay, a little flushed. Often he fasted for a week and more. He went very often to confession and to the reception of the Holy Mysteries of the Body and Blood of Christ. A multitude of people visited Daniel and asked his direction. They included bishops, abbots, abbesses, monks and nuns, priests and layfolk of all ages, professions and classes. He was particularly sought by people who wanted to test their vocations.

"Susanna, abbess of Irkutsk Znamensky Monastery, when she was yet in the world, could not make up her mind where to become a nun. She visited several convents and all looked equally good to her. She then came to Daniel: 'I asked him to indicate a convent for me to settle in.' But he said: 'I am a man and not God. I shall send you to a convent but the life there may appear to you unendurable and you will say: 'I would never remain here but for his order,' and you will suffer. But when God himself shows anyone where to live, in that place all sorrows are light.' I asked again his blessing and he said: 'You will know yourself, your heart will tell you. You will feel that in the same moment. There you shall remain thanking the Lord.' During my long journey from Achinsk to Irkutsk I wondered how the things the Staretz told me might happen. I visited many monasteries in Russia but my heart remained unmoved. It never told me where I am to stay. All those monasteries seemed to me equally good.

"I went to Irkutsk to venerate the holy relics of the great miracle-worker, St Innocent of Irkutsk. I had made a vow to do so when cured of a disease. After a short stay in Voznesensky Monastery, in fulfillment of my vow I went to the town. En route I saw a convent. It had a low wall and I could see buildings behind it. The garden appeared to me as a paradise. I did not return from the town to Voznesensky Monastery straight away but decided to visit the convent. When I came to the Holy Gate a strong perfume of flowers met me. I even stopped as someone ordered me to remain and not to return. I experienced a peculiar joy in my heart. The voice, it seemed, told me: 'Remain here.' I immediately remembered the words of Fr Daniel as though he himself were present on the spot. When I entered the church the sight of the great crucifix so much impressed me that I could not move for quite a while."[34]

To his disciple, Dorotheus, Daniel said once: "Go, brother, follow Christ as an apostle, by the narrow way. Do not take with you on your journey either bag, or staff, or money. The Lord will not abandon you and will feed you. On your way you will meet a bishop who will take you with him and make you a monk."[35] All this happened in Kungur, midway from Achinsk to Kiev. Bishop Eulampius of Ekaterinburg, translated to Orel, met Dorotheus and took him to European

34. Ibid., pp. 24-25.
35. Ibid., p. 30.

Russia and made him a monk in Beloberezhsky Monastery. Daniel was greatly respected by St Serafim of Sarov, the greatest Russian canonized mystic of the nineteenth century.

In Siberia, at the same time, lived and died the mysterious hermit, Feodor Kusmich. There are many serious grounds to suppose that he was the Emperor Alexander I.[36] The latter was a mystic by nature. All his life he reproached himself for the assassination of his father, Paul I, in 1801 although he was never directly implicated in this crime. In 1825, according to tradition, the Emperor left Russia for the Holy Land by sea while a dead soldier was buried in his place. Returning to Russia during the reign of his younger brother, Nicholas I, he settled as a hermit in Siberia. Feodor Kusmich certainly was very like Alexander I in his countenance, stature and character. He preserved, even in Siberia, many features of the mentality of the aristocratic mystics of that reign.

36. The literature on the Staretz Feodor Kusmich is very vast. The latest studies, like that of Professor M. Zazuikin, incline to the identification of the Staretz with Alexander I.

CHAPTER VII

ST SERAPHIM OF SAROV

S T SERAPHIM OF SAROV is the most popular Russian mystic of the nineteenth century.[1] He is the representative of the mysticism of light, joy and resurrection as opposed to the mysticism centered on Calvary, the dark night of the soul and spiritual torment. St Seraphim is the flower, or rather, the final fruit of Sarov spirituality, having been preceeded by many others. Sarov Monastery was founded during the worst period of Russian monastic history, in the reign of Peter the Great. In 1664 the monk Theodosius settled as a solitary in the great forests of the Arzanas district, which was inhabited mostly by the Mordvinians, a Volga Finnish tribe. Later another monk, Gerasimus, dwelt in the same place although as yet there was no monastery.

Sarov Monastery was founded around 1700 by John, abbot of Vedensky Monastery, Arzamas. Born in 1670, John became a monk of Arzamas in 1689; he visited Sarov in 1691 and, having been drawn by its solitude, settled there together with several monks. Elected abbot of Arzamas in 1700, John turned Sarov into a skete of the latter. In 1709 he became abbot of Sarov. The period was a difficult one for the monks. They lived in isolation and were often attacked by robbers who looted the monastery and killed the monks. However, worse times were to follow. In 1734, during the reign of the

---

1. The best book on St Seraphim so far is that by N. Levitsky, *Žitie, podvigi, čudesa i proslavlenie prep. i bogonosnago otca našego Serafima, Sarovskago čudotvorca* (Moscow, 1905).

Empress Anne, John was arrested under the suspicion of having cooperated with the well known ecclesiastical antagonist of the regime, Fr Marcel Rodiushevsky. Abbot John died in 1737 at St Petersburg in the prison of the Secret Chancery. After the death of John a number of abbots succeeded each other in Sarov, each remaining in office for a few years. The situation improved under the leadership of Ephrem. A member of a Tula merchant family, Ephrem became a monk in 1712 at the age of nineteen. Four years later he was ordained. In 1727 he came to Sarov and remained there until 1734 when he was arrested with Abbot John. Sentenced to be laicized, Ephrem was imprisoned in the fortress of Orsk where he remained as sexton till 1755, when his innocence was proved. He was reinstated in the priesthood and in 1758 elected abbot of Sarov. Ephrem corresponded with St Tikhon of Zadonsk, who respected him greatly in his suffering for the truth. Ephrem ruled till 1777 and was succeeded by Pachomius (Boris Leonov), a Kursk merchant, who became a monk at Sarov in 1762. Among the remarkable Sarov contemplatives of this period was Theodore Ushakov, afterwards abbot of Sanaksar.

The reign of Pachomius is made memorable for Sarov by reason of various mystics whom he attracted to the monastery. The most renowned among them were Nazarius, afterwards abbot of Valaam, Mark the Solitary, Madarius, Pitirim, and especially St Seraphim, the first canonized Russian mystic of the nineteenth century. Seraphim, or Prokhor Moshnin as he was called, was born on July 19, 1759, the son of a Kursk merchant. He was a very pious boy, and decided to become a monk when he was only eighteen years old. He went to Kiev to the well known Staretz Dositheus to ask him to indicate what monastery he should enter. Dositheus recommended Sarov. It was there on November 20, 1778 that Prokhor was admitted as a novice, his training being entrusted to Fr Joseph, treasurer of Sarov. During the reign of Catherine II it was impossible for anyone to become a monk without the express permission of the Holy Synod;

this permission was ordinarily granted only after long delay. Consequently Prokhor was twenty seven years old when he was professed on August 13, 1786; he was given the name of Seraphim. Made deacon in the same year, Seraphim was ordained to the priesthood in 1793. Already at this time he was known for his holiness and mystical visions.

Abbot Pachomius died in 1794. Soon thereafter Seraphim asked the new abbot for permission to retire into solitude and devote himself to the eremitical life. This was granted and the focal period of the life of the saint began.

During his years of solitude St Seraphim observed the long and difficult Rule of St Pachomius. His reading and meditation was centered on the Bible and the Fathers. His abode was a small house in the virgin forest about seven kilometers from Sarov. Very little is known of this period of the saint's life. Besides the observance of the Rule and exercises in unceasing prayer, Seraphim occupied himself in a small garden adjacent to his hut and also tended bees. Every Saturday he went to Sarov in order to receive Holy Communion on Sunday.

As is the experience of all hermits, Seraphim was subjected to various diabolical attacks. In time he overcame them and reached such purity of spirit that animals came to him in large numbers to be fed by him and share his company. The saint fasted a great deal. At first he ate bread brought from the monastery together with vegetables from his own garden. Later he limited himself to vegetables. For three years he once abandoned even vegetables and lived on grass alone.

At the start of his solitary life Seraphim received a few visitors, including his friend Timon, founder of Nadeev Monastery. He did not turn away monks who wished to share his solitude. None of them however was able to remain with him for long because of the severity of his way of life.

The holiness of Seraphim became manifest to all who visited him. As a result, in 1796, he was offered the abbacy of Alatuir Monastery. He declined the offer. Later the abbacy of Krasnoslobodsk Monastery was offered to him. He again refused. During this period the saint undertook yet another spiritual exercise: he prayed on a stone for 1,000 days and

nights, usually kneeling and reciting the prayer of the publican, "God, have pity on me, a sinner." Although the devil
could inflict no harm on the saint, evil men did. On
September 12, 1804 three robbers attacked him and demanded money. When he said that he had none, the robbers
started to beat him. Seraphim, a strong man and armed with
an axe, could easily have killed the robbers; but remembering
the word of the Scripture that those who take the sword shall
perish by it, he did not resist them. After leaving Seraphim
half dead, the robbers searched his hut thoroughly but found
nothing. After the robbers left, Seraphim came to himself
and found strength enough to reach Sarov. There the doctors'
examination revealed so many serious wounds that his condition was considered hopeless. It was then that he was healed
during an astonishing vision of Our Lady. Although he was
restored to life, the effects of his wounds remained with him
till the end of his life. He had become an old and feeble man.

After a stay of five months in the monastery, Seraphim
returned to the solitude of the hut. The robbers were apprehended but at the request of the saint they were pardoned.
When Isaiah retired from his position as abbot of Sarov in
1806 the community elected Seraphim but he declined the
honor. When Isaiah died, Seraphim undertook the practice of
perfect silence, both external and internal. He spoke to no
one and increased the intensity of his prayer. Seraphim wrote
a true hymn to silence: "When we remain silent then the foe,
the devil, cannot penetrate the heart of man; herein lies the
wisdom of silence. Solitude and silence engender fervor and a
meekness which flows through the heart of man as the waters
of Siloe, without sound or disturbance. Life in the cell in
silence, in prayer and in the study of Divine Law, day and
night, these make a man devout."[2] For two years, Seraphim
observed complete silence, then he returned to Sarov and
became a recluse. The new abbot, Nifont, had been displeased that Seraphim, on account of his sickness, ceased to
visit the abbey on weekends to communicate. He told him

2. Ibid., p. 90.

that he must either visit the monastery regularly or come to live there. The saint elected to return to the monastery on May 8, 1810. He lived in such strict seclusion that in 1815 he even refused admittance to his cell to the saintly Bishop Jonas (Vasilevsky) of Tambov.

During this period of seclusion Seraphim experienced a rapture which lasted five days and five nights; he contemplated the heavenly mansions. Later he described this vision to Ivan Tikhonovich: "If you knew what sweetness awaits the souls of the just in heaven, you would be resolved to endure all the sorrows, persecutions and insults in this passing life with gratitude. Even if your very cell were full of worms and they gnawed on your flesh throughout your entire life, you would accept it all in order not to lose that heavenly joy which God has prepared for those who love him. If the Apostle Paul himself was unable to describe heavenly glory and joy, what other human tongue could describe the beauty of the heavenly abode which the souls of the just inhabit? . . . . I cannot tell you of the heavenly joy and sweetness which I experienced there." It was during this conversation that the first recorded transfiguration of St Seraphim took place. Ivan Tikhonovich describes it: "Fr Seraphim became silent and bowed forward slightly. His eyes were closed and his head was bowed. He gently massaged his breast around the heart with the palm of his right hand. His face began gradually to change and to give forth a wonderful light. Finally it became so bright that it was impossible to look on him. Such joy and heavenly rapture were expressed on his face that he could be called an earthly angel or a heavenly man."[3]

For five years Seraphim lived in his cell, never leaving it and never receiving visitors. Then he had a vision of Our Lady who ordered him to begin to receive people and give them spiritual advice. He began to receive people daily but still remained in his cell. The first person whom he received was A. M. Bezobrazov, Governor of Tambov. This was in 1815. On November 25, 1825 Our Lady again appeared to

3. Ibid., pp. 99-100.

Seraphim and told him to give up his reclusion and to return to his solitary hut. He did this but as his old age and feebleness did not permit him to walk any distance, a new solitary hut, nearer to Sarov, was erected for him. He went there every morning and remained nearly the entire day. He practised Hesychast prayer and worked in the kitchen garden and in the forest. He also received visitors. From time to time Seraphim visited his former, more remote hermitage. At this time the saint ate only one meal a day and hardly slept at all. He received Holy Communion every Sunday and feast day. The celebrating priest, accompanied by all the clergy and people, solemnly brought the Holy Gifts to Seraphim in his cell. He himself did not celebrate. However, after a time, human envy and jealousy obliged the abbot to change this procedure, and St Seraphim was ordered to go to church to receive Communion.[4]

Once Seraphim had abandoned his silence and seclusion, he became a Staretz or spiritual director and immediately he began to attract enormous crowds of people. On certain festivals as many as 5,000 people visited him, but great crowds were a daily occurrence. The saint was always meek, friendly and full of compassion. He addressed those who came to him as "my father" or "my mother" or "my joy." The latter expression Seraphim preferred to all others. Occasionally when receiving visitors the saint prostrated himself before them, as he did on the occasion of receiving General L., who was so overwhelmed by the gesture that he wept like a child.[5] Seraphim was a remarkable spiritual director. He readily discerned the spiritual disease from which his visitors were suffering and what remedies to provide. He advised some to become religious, and others to marry. He gave counsel in the presence of the most baffling circumstances. Seraphim was particularly kind and compassionate with the poor, the sick and the unhappy, the serfs, the oppressed, abandoned wives and children. He was most taken by the

4. Ibid., pp. 116-117.
5. Ibid., pp. 129-130.

latter. In the last year of his life Seraphim was exhausted from having received so many people and, to avoid them, he retired deep into the forest. But even there if children came with the adults he would go out and speak with them.

Recorded and authenticated cases of clairvoyance, prophecy and healing of the sick by St Seraphim are so numerous that it is impossible to give even a summary account of them in one chapter. A few cases, however, may be cited to illustrate the methods of the saint. Once an officer came to him and asked his blessing to enter a monastery. Seraphim, after listening to his story, said to him: "Do not become monk. You must marry and your fiancée is here. Go at once to the guest house for women. You will find there a mother and daughter. The latter is your fiancée. Tell them to come to me at once." The officer went to the guest house but he found neither mother nor daughter. He decided to take a walk and while doing so met a carriage on the road to the monastery. In the carriage were the two women whom Seraphim had described. The officer told them to go to the Staretz at once and he accompanied them himself. When they came before him, Seraphim immediately gave his blessing for the marriage of the two young people.[6]

In 1825 Seraphim advised another visitor, who was later to be a monk of Ufa Monastery, to remain at Sarov. The visitor did not want to and went away. Within a few hours he became so ill that he could go no farther. He returned to Sarov and there became a monk.[7] To monks with spiritual experience Seraphim always suggested Starchestvo, that is, spiritual direction. To Timon, founder of Nadeev Monastery, the saint said: "Son, Fr Timon, sow everywhere the good seed given to you. Sow in good ground, sow in sand, sow among the stones, sow on the road, sow among the weeds. Perchance some of these seeds will open and grow and bring forth fruit, albeit not at once. Do not bury the talent given to you, otherwise you will be punished by your Lord. Give it to merchants. Let them trade with it."[8]

6. Ibid., pp. 157-158.
7. Ibid., p. 159.
8. Ibid., p. 160.

The saint sometimes read men's thoughts, and thus knew the names and life history of his visitors. Cases of this are so numerous that only a few will be cited. In 1830 a monk of Sarov was appointed abbot of a monastery in the archdiocese of Kazan. Before leaving he went to Seraphim to ask for his blessing and advice. The saint asked him: "Where are you going? " "I am called to Kazan." "You are misled," Seraphim replied, and added: "Do not go to Makariev Monastery." "But I am appointed to Raif Monastery," was the monk's reply. "I tell you." Seraphim insisted, "do not go to Makariev. Remain here for a while. When you leave, you will return again in due course to die."[9] All this came about. The monk arriving in Kazan found that he was in fact appointed to Makariev. He declined this abbacy and was made abbot of Tsivilsk Monastery. Many years later he resigned this post and returned to Sarov to die.

To another monk, Anthony, abbot of Vuisokogorsk, Seraphim made a remarkable prophecy. In 1831 the abbot became suddenly obsessed with the expectation of imminent death. He went to consult the saint. "Father," the abbot said to Seraphim, "tell me when I shall die. It seems to me my hour has come and I want to retire and prepare for death." Seraphim looked at him and said: "Not so, my joy. God is going to entrust you with the administration of a great Laura." The abbot, believing that Seraphim was trying to make him feel better, insisted. But the saint repeated the same words and added that in his new position he should receive pilgrims from Sarov with kindness. Within two months Anthony was appointed abbot of the Laura of the Holy Trinity near Moscow.[10]

Seraphim healed many people who were suffering from the most dangerous and incurable diseases. Among the most striking are the cases of M. Manturov and N. Motovilov. Manturov, a nobleman and landowner, had contracted a rare disease which doctors were unable to treat. In fact he became a living corpse. In 1823 Seraphim healed him, but in return

9. Ibid., pp. 233-234.
10. Ibid., pp. 245-248.

asked that he distribute his estate to the poor and freely
adopt poverty, even though Manturov was a married man.
—"Leave everything and do not worry about the future. The
Lord will forget you neither in this life nor in the next. You
will never be rich but you will always have your daily bread."
Manturov obeyed.[11]

The case of Motovilov is even more extraordinary. The latter was, if one can so speak, a decaying corpse. No doctor
could help him. He was brought to Seraphim in 1831. The
saint, upon meeting him, said that he was not a doctor and
advised the sufferer to look for one. Motovilov answered that
he had tried everything but without success. Whereupon the
saint asked the nobleman if he believed that Christ was the
incarnate God and that his Mother was ever a Virgin. The
nobleman answered: "Yes." Seraphim then asked him
whether he believed that Christ, who had healed people by a
simple touch, could do so now at the request of his Mother.
Motovilov said that he believed it to be so. Seraphim then
told him that if he believed he was already whole. And thus
he was healed.[12]

After his cure, Motovilov became a close friend of the saint
and Seraphim revealed to him many mysteries as well as his
own high spiritual estate. In the "Notes" of Motovilov the
doctrine of Seraphim is well summed up.[13] One winter's day,
Motovilov visited Seraphim near his solitary hut, and they
discussed the aim of the Christian life. "Prayer, fasting, vigils
and all other Christian exercises," Seraphim said, "however
good in themselves are not the goal of our Christian life,
although they are necessary means to its attainment. The true
goal of Christian life consists in the acquisition of the Holy
Spirit. Note, my Father, that only the good deed which is
performed for Christ's sake brings us the fruits of the Holy

11. Ibid., p. 273.
12. Ibid., pp. 288-290.
13. The "Notes" of Motovilov remained unpublished for sixty years. S. A. Nilus
published then in July, 1903, in *Moskovskiya Vedomosti*: "Duch božij javno
počiušij na otce Serafime sarovskom v besede ego. o celi christianskoj žizni." The
quotations here are translated from V. N. Iliin, *Prep. Serafim Sarovsky* (Paris,
1925).

Spirit. Everything which is not done for Christ's sake, however good, fails to win compensation in the future life. Even in this life it does not give us the grace of God. For this reason the Lord Jesus Christ said: 'He who does not gather with me, scatters.' Still a good deed is the same as gathering and is good even if not done for Christ. The Scripture says: 'In every nation he who fears God and does right is pleasing to him.' We see from sacred history how the performer of good deeds is so pleasing to God that he sent his Angel to the praying centurion Cornelius, who feared God and was just, and told him: 'Send someone to Joppa, to Simon the tanner; there you will find Peter and he will tell you the words of eternal life by which you and your house will be saved.'

"So it is, lover of God. The true aim of our Christian life consists in the acquisition of the Divine Spirit; prayer, vigils, fasting, alms, and other virtues practiced for Christ are merely means to the acquisition of that Divine Spirit." When Motovilov asked for further explanations, Seraphim continued: "Acquisition is the same as gathering. You understand what is meant by the acquisition of money. The same is true concerning the acquisition of the Divine Spirit. Do you understand what worldly gain means? The goal of the worldly life of the ordinary man is the acquisition of money. In addition noblemen want honors, decorations and other rewards for their service to the state. The acquisition of the Spirit of God is also capital but eternal capital, full of grace. This capital is gained in much the same way as money and temporal honors.

"God the Word, our Lord, the God-man Jesus Christ, likens our life to a market place. Our life on the earth he calls trading. He says to all: Trade until I come, redeeming the time because the days are evil. That is, use time to obtain heavenly goods by means of the earthly. The earthly goods in this trading are the virtues practiced for Christ's sake. They bring to us the grace of the Holy Spirit without whom salvation is impossible because: Every soul lives by the Holy Spirit, is elevated by purity, and is brightened by the mystery of Tri-unity. The Holy Ghost himself takes up his abode in

our soul. This entry of the Pantocrator himself into our
souls and his co-habitation with our spirit is granted to us
only when we strive to the best of our ability to acquire the
Holy Spirit. This effort prepares in our soul and body the
throne where God our Creator co-habits with our spirit according to the unchangeable Divine word: 'I shall enter into
them and live in them and I shall be their God. They will be
my people.' Certainly, every virtue, practiced for Christ's
sake, acquires for us the grace of the Holy Spirit but prayer is
the most effective of all because it is always at our disposal as
a means to acquire the grace of the Spirit.

"For instance, you cannot go to church whenever you like—
there may be no church available or the liturgy may be over.
You might wish to give alms to the poor but there might be no
poor or you may have nothing to give. You might desire to remain a virgin but because of your constitution, or because of unavoidable occasions, you may not have the strength to do this.
You would like to practice some other virtues for Christ's sake
but either you have not the strength or no opportunity. No such
obstacles stand in the way of prayer. Everyone, rich and
poor, nobleman and commoner, strong and weak, healthy
and sick, just and sinner, has the opportunity to practice
prayer. The power of prayer is great. It brings to us the Spirit
of God. It is the easiest virtue for everyone to practice.

"Through prayer we are honored with the conversation of
our all-good and lifegiving God and Savior. But we must pray
only until the time when God the Holy Ghost overshadows
us by his heavenly grace. When he is pleased to visit us we
must cease to pray. There is no sense in praying then. Why
pray: "Come and live in us and purify our souls of every evil
and save, O God, our souls," when he has already come to us
to save us, who trust in him and appeal to his Holy Name in
truth. To call upon his name in truth is to go humbly and
with love to meet him, the Consoler, within the temple of
our souls which hunger and thirst for his coming."

When Motovilov asked what to do about the practice of
other virtues for Christ's sake, Seraphim answered: "Acquire
the grace of the Holy Spirit with all the other virtues. For
Christ's sake, trade with those which give you the highest

return. Gather the capital of divine grace, put it into the divine eternal bank. You will receive not four or six percent but one-hundred percent and infinitely more for a single spiritual rouble. If prayer and vigils acquire you more divine grace, then pray and watch; if fasting—fast; if alms—then give alms. In this way judge every virtue practiced for Christ's sake. Please trade in this way in spiritual virtues. Distribute the gifts of the grace of the Holy Spirit to those who ask for them. Be like a lighted candle which itself gives light, burning with earthly fire, and light other candles, without losing its own flame, so that they can give light elsewhere. If this is so of earthly fire, what can we say of the fire of grace of the All-Holy Spirit of God? "

Motovilov then asked Seraphim how it might be possible to receive the grace of the Holy Spirit, how might he know whether the Holy Spirit were with him or not. In the following talk the greatest heights in Russian mysticism are reached. "At the present time," the staretz answered, "because of our universal coldness to faith in our Lord Jesus Christ and because of our lack of attention to his Divine Providence for us and to the union of man with God, we have fallen so low that it can be said that we have altogether abandoned true Christian life. The words of Sacred Scripture seem strange to us when they say that the Spirit of God spoke through the mouth of Moses, or when Adam saw the Lord walking in paradise, or when we read the Apostle Paul saying: 'We went to Achaia and the Spirit of God did not come with us, we returned to Macedonia and the Divine Spirit went with us.' Elsewhere in the Sacred Scripture we hear of the manifestation of God to men. Some people say that these texts are incomprehensible. How could men see God so clearly? There is nothing incomprehensible! We cannot understand these texts because we have departed so far from the breadth of the original Christian vision! Under the pretext of enlightenment we have entered into such a darkness of ignorance that we are unable to understand what the ancients understood so clearly. To them the manifestation of God, even in familiar converse, did not appear strange.

"People saw God and the grace of his Holy Spirit not in

dreams, or in hallucinations, but in actual fact. We have become so indifferent to the work of our salvation that we understand many passages of Scripture only in a weak and watered-down sense. The reason is that we do not seek divine grace, do not allow it to enter our souls because of our pride. Therefore, we are not truly enlightened by the Lord. The Spirit is sent into the hearts of those people who hunger and thirst for truth.

"When our Lord Jesus Christ accomplished the work of our salvation, after his resurrection, he breathed on the Apostles, renewing the breath of life lost by Adam. He gave to the Apostles Adam's sonship, the grace of the All-Holy Divine Spirit. On the day of Pentecost he solemnly sent to the Apostles the Holy Spirit in storm and tongues of fire. The Spirit descended on every one of them and filled them with the strength of flaming divine grace, which breathes like dew and makes joyful those who participate in its strength and actions. This same firelike grace of the Holy Spirit is given to all of us, the faithful of Christ, in the sacrament of Holy Baptism. It is impressed on all the principal parts of our body by the Holy Spirit. But where do we put our humble seals, Father, Lover of God, but on vessels which keep the jewels which we highly appreciate?

"If anyone, inspired by Divine Wisdom which seeks our salvation, decides to watch and to serve God, he must follow the voice of wisdom and truly repent of all his sins and try to practice the opposite virtues for Christ's sake. In this way he will acquire the Holy Spirit, who works within us and establishes in us the Kingdom of God. The grace of the Holy Spirit, given to us in baptism in the name of the Father, and of the Son, and of the Holy Spirit, in spite of human sins and the darkness around us, still shines in the heart by the ever present divine light of the priceless merits of Christ.

"When a sinner is converted to the way of repentance, this light of Christ destroys altogether the very traces of committed crimes and clothes the former criminal once more with the garment of incorruption woven by the grace of the Holy

Spirit. The acquisition of the Holy Ghost is, as I have often said before, the goal of the Christian life. Lover of God, I shall tell you how to understand easier what is the meaning of Divine Grace, how to distinguish it and in what way it manifests itself particularly in men illuminated by it.

"The grace of the Holy Spirit is a light which enlightens man. The Lord manifested many times, before many witnesses, the action of the Holy Spirit in those men, whom he consecrated and illuminated by his great coming. Remember Moses after his talk with God on Sinai. People could not look upon him because he shone with a wonderful light which surrounded him. He was even obliged to appear before the people covered with a veil. Remember the transfiguration of the Lord on Mount Tabor. 'And his robe shone like snow and his disciples prostrated themselves out of fear.' When Moses and Elijah came to him then, in order to hide the shining light of divine grace which blinded the disciples, a cloud, it is said, overshadowed them. In this manner the grace of the All-Holy Spirit of God manifests itself in an indescribable light to all those to whom God manifests its action."

When Motovilov asked Seraphim how he could know whether he was in the grace of the Holy Spirit or not, Seraphim answered him: "This, Lover of God, is very simple. The Lord says: 'Everything is simple to those who understand.' Being in this state the apostles always saw whether the Holy Spirit was present in them or not. Penetrated by him and seeing this, they asserted firmly that their work was good and pleasing to God. This is the explanation why they wrote in their Epistles: 'This was pleasing to the Holy Spirit and to us.' Only on this basis they offered their Epistles as incontrovertible truth for the benefit of all the faithful. You see how clearly the holy apostles sensed in themselves the presence of the Divine Spirit. Do you understand now, Lover of God, how all this is simple?" When Motovilov asked for further explanation Seraphim took him firmly by the shoulders and said: "We are both now in the Divine Spirit. Why do you not look at me?"

The description of Motovilov of the transfiguration of St Seraphim is something unique in Russian mystical literature: "I said: 'I cannot look at you, Father, because lightenings stream from your eyes. Your face has become more brilliant than the sun and my eyes cannot bear it.' Fr Seraphim said: —'Do not be afraid, Lover of God, because you are now shining just as brightly as I am. You are now in the fullness of the Divine Spirit because, otherwise, you could not see me in that state.' And inclining his head toward me he whispered quietly into my ear: 'Thank the Lord God for his undescribable mercy to you. You saw I did not even cross myself but only prayed mentally in my heart to the Lord God saying: 'Lord, grant him clearly and with bodily eyes to see that descent of the Holy Spirit by which you honor those servants of yours to whom you appear in all your magnificent glory.' You see, Father, the Lord granted at once the humble request of the poor Seraphim. How much we must thank him for his indescribable gift to both of us. Rarely the Lord God manifests himself in this way, even to the greatest hermits. Divine Grace has condescended to console your sorrowful heart, like a fond mother, at the prayer of the Mother of God herself. Why do you not look me in the eyes? Look simply and be not afraid; the Lord is with us.'

"After these words I looked at his face and even greater respectful fear overcame me. Picture in the midst of the sun at its noon-day brightest the face of the man who talks to you. You see the movement of his lips, the changing expression of his eyes. You hear his voice and feel that someone's hands are grasping your shoulders. But you do not see those hands, nor yourself, nor the body of the speaker but only the blinding light which spreads a good many meters, illuminating with a brilliant light the snow covering the meadow and the snow falling down on the great staretz. Picture my state then! 'How do you feel now?' Fr Seraphim asked. 'Extremely well,' I said. 'But how well? In what way?' I feel such a stillness and peace in my soul that I cannot express them in words,' I answered.

" 'This, Lover of God,' Fr Seraphim said, 'is that peace of which the Lord spoke to his disciples saying: "I give you my peace but not as the world gives do I give to you. If you were of the world the world would love you; but as I have chosen you from the world, the world hates. But be of good cheer because I have overcome the world" To these people whom the world hates but whom the Lord has chosen, he gives that peace which you feel in yourself now. "Peace," according to the Apostles, "is beyond all understanding."

" 'What else do you feel?' Fr Seraphim asked me. 'Extraordinary sweetness,' I answered. And he continued, 'This is the sweetness about which the Sacred Scripture says: "They will be inebriated with the fullness of your house and with the stream of your sweetness you will fill them." This very sweetness fills us and streams through our bodies with inexplicable pleasure. Our hearts melt from this sweetness and we are filled with such beatitude that no language can describe it. But what else do you feel? '

" 'Overwhelming joy in all my heart.' Fr Seraphim continued: 'When the Spirit of God descends on man and overshadows him with the plenitude of his coming, then the human soul is filled with an indescribable joy because the Divine Spirit makes joyful everything he touches. This is the same joy about which the Lord said in his Gospel: "A woman when in travail has sorrow because her hour has come; but when she has brought forth the child, she does not remember the sorrow because of the joy that a man is born into the world. In the world you will be sorrowful but when I shall see you, your heart will be in joy and no one can take away from you this joy." Nevertheless, this present joy, which you feel in you heart as consoling, is altogether insignificant in comparison with that joy about which the Lord himself said through his Apostle, "That joy no eye has seen, nor ear hear, nor a heart pictured, the joy which God has prepared for those who love him." The foretaste of this joy is given to us now. If the foretaste is so sweet and good and such a joy in our souls, what can we say of that joy which is prepared in heaven for those who weep here on the earth? You, Father, have wept much in your life. See with what joy the Lord consoles you even in this life? '

" 'What else do you feel, Lover of God? ' 'An extraordinary

warmth.' I answered. 'How can it be, Father? We are in the forest. It is winter now. The snow is under our feet; we are covered with snow and it still falls on us. What warmth could be here?' 'Such as it happens in the bath when water is thrown on the hot stones and steam rises up.' 'And the scent' he asked me, 'is it also like a bath?' 'O, no,' I answered. 'There is nothing on the earth like this wonderful perfume. When my mother was still alive, I liked to dance and went to balls and parties. Mother used to spray me with perfumes which she bought in the best and most fashionable shops in Kazan. But those perfumes never smelled like this!'

"Fr Seraphim smiling radiantly, said: —'I know myself, Father, that this is so, but I asked you about it for a purpose. This is perfect truth, Lover of God! No scent of the earth can be compared with the perfume which we smell now because we are surrounded with the perfume of the Holy Spirit. What on the earth could be like him? Note, Lover of God, you told me that it is as warm around us as in the bath, but look around; the snow does not melt either upon us nor under us. Therefore, this warmth is not in the air but in ourselves. This warmth is that for which the Holy Spirit makes us ask the Lord in prayer: "Warm me with the heat of your Holy Spirit." Hermits, men and women, warmed by this heat, do not fear the winter's cold. They are clothed as if in warm furs by the clothing of grace made by the Holy Spirit. This must be so because the Lord said: "The Kingdom of God is within you." By the Kingdom of God, the Lord meant the grace of the Holy Spirit. This very Kingdom of God is now in you while the grace of the Holy Spirit illumines and warms you also from the outside and fills the air around us with many different perfumes. Our senses are mightily pleased and our hearts are full of inexplicable joy. Our present state is that of which the Apostle said: "The Kingdom of God is neither food nor drink but truth and peace in the Holy Spirit." Our faith is not in the persuasive words of human wisdom but in the manifestation of spirit and strength.

" 'The Lord meant exactly this state when he said: "There

are some here present who will not taste death until they see the Kingdom of God coming in power." What undescribable joy, Father, Lover of God, the Lord God has granted to us. This is what it means to be in the fullness of the Holy Spirit about which St Macarius of Egypt writes: "I was myself in the fullness of the Holy Spirit." The Lord has now filled us, his poor, with the fullness of the Holy Spirit. I think there is no need to ask more, Lover of God, concerning how men come into the grace of the Holy Spirit. Will you remember the present manifestation of the indescribable mercy of God which has visited us? '

" 'I do not know, Father! ' I answered, 'whether the Lord will allow me to remember this mercy always so vividly and clearly as I see and feel it now.' 'But I think,' Fr Seraphim answered 'that the Lord will help you to retain this forever in your memory because otherwise his goodness would not so quickly have answered my humble prayer nor would he have let the poor Seraphim know that this would happen. Moreover, this is given not only for you to understand but through you, for the entire world, in order that you may be strengthened in the work of God and may be useful to others. The fact that I am a monk and you are a layman is secondary. God seeks those who have faith in him and in his only begotten Son. For this the grace of the Holy Spirit is given in abundance from above. The Lord seeks out the heart that is full of love for God and neighbor. This is the throne upon which he likes to sit and where he appears in the plenitude of his heavenly glory. "Son, give me your heart," he says, "and everything else I shall add unto you," because the Kingdom of God is in the human heart. "The Lord is near to everyone who calls upon him in truth. He does not look at the face but at the heart. The Father loves the Son and gave everything into his hands." We must only love him, our heavenly Father, truly, like sons.

" 'The Lord listens equally to the monk and to the layman, the simple Christian, if they are both Orthodox and both love God with all their hearts and have faith in him even as a grain of mustard seed. Both monk and layman, can move mountains. The Lord himself says: "Everything is possible to him who believes;" while the Apostle Paul cries out: "I can do everything in Christ who strengthens me." Even more wonderful is that which our Lord Jesus Christ says of those who believe in him: "He who believes in me, the works which I do, he shall do as well and he shall do much more because I go to my Father and will pray to him for you that your joy may be full. You have asked nothing in my Name until now; ask now and you shall receive." Therefore, Lover of God, everything you ask the Lord God, you shall receive, but this should be for the glory of God or for the benefit of your neighbor, because everything done on behalf of the latter he relates to himself, saying: "Everything you did to anyone of these little ones, you did for me." Therefore, never doubt that the Lord God will grant your requests if they are directed to the glory of God or to the benefit and the edification of your neighbor. But whenever something might be necessary for your own use or benefit or profit, this the Lord God will grant you quickly and readily, provided there is a real need for it because the Lord loves those who love him. The Lord is good to all who fear him. He acts according to their desire and accepts their prayer.' "[14]

The conversations of Seraphim with Motovilov are the summit of Russian mysticism. In 1832 the Staretz began to prepare himself for eternal life. He selected the place for his burial and often meditated before the coffin which stood at the entrance to his cell. Seraphim began to take leave from various people, beginning with Arsenius, Bishop of Tambov, who visited him. Certain remarkable facts are reported about these days. One monk of Sarov used to visit the cell of Seraphim to get a light from the sanctuary lamp which burned before the ikon of Our Lady of "Umilenie." This monk came to Seraphim a short time before his death. The staretz, finding that the flame of the lamp had gone out, said: "Oh, my lamp is out when it should be lighted." He began to pray before the ikon of Our Lady. A blue light appeared before the ikon and turning toward it started to circle around the big candle before the ikon. The candle was lit by this flame.

14. Iliin, *Prep. Serafim Sarovsky*, pp. 104-124.

The saint taking a small candle lighted it and gave it to the monk. He started to talk with him. The face of Seraphim was illuminated. He told the monk that his time had come. When the monk began to cry, Seraphim said: "My joy, now it is time for joy and for sorrow."[15]

On January 1, 1833 the saint came to the chapel of the infirmary, lighted candles before the ikons, received Holy Communion and took leave from the community saying: "Be saved, be courageous and watchful. Today crowns are ready for us."[16] After receiving a few visitors, Seraphim spent his last hours in his cell singing solemn and joyful hymns of Easter. The next day he was found dead kneeling before the ikon in prayer.

The popular veneration of Seraphim as a saint immediately spread far and wide. In July, 1903 a solemn canonization of him was performed in Sarov. The last Russian Emperor, Nicholas II, with the Grand Dukes carried the coffin of the new saint. There were several bishops, headed by the Primate, Metropolitan Anthony of St Petersburg, crowds of clergy and many hundreds of thousands of the faithful. St Seraphim is still the most popular saint in Russia. Although Sarov has now been closed by the Soviet Government and the whereabouts of the relics are unknown, the fiftieth anniversary of his canonization was solemnly observed in the Russian Church. Seraphim is beginning to be known also in the West. There are books and articles about him in various languages and his portraits can be found in Western monasteries. However, there is not yet a really satisfactory study of St Seraphim, of his life and of his teaching.

A number of instructions, meditations, and counsels were left by the saint. These instructions were published in 1839 in an appendix to the life of the Sarov hermit, Mark. The spiritual counsels of St Seraphim are profound and true. Some quotations from these "Instructions" can give us a good idea of the mind of St Seraphim.

About hope the saint writes: "All those who have a firm

15. E. Poselyanin, *Prepodobnui Serfaim, Sarovsky čudotvorec* (St Petersburg, 1908), pp. 124-125.
16. Ibid., p. 130.

hope in God, are raised to him and are illuminated by eternal light. If a man does not worry about himself for the love of God and for the practice of virtues, knowing that God will take care of him, such a hope is true and wise. But if man worries about his business and appeals to God in prayer only when he is assaulted by unavoidable misfortunes, or if he does not look to the means within his power and begins to rely solely on divine assistance, such a hope is vain and false. True hope seeks solely the Kingdom of God and is certain that everything needful for this temporal life will be undoubtedly given. The heart cannot have peace before one acquires this hope."[17]

Speaking of the love of God, Seraphim says: "He who has attained to perfect love for God, exists in this life as if he did not. He considers himself a stranger to everything visible, awaiting in patience the invisible. He has changed all into love for God and he forgets every other love. He who loves himself cannot love God."[18]

Concerning peace of mind, the saint says: "It is a sign of a wise soul when a man turns his mind to within himself and acts in his heart. Then divine grace overshadows him and he is at peace, that is to say he enjoys a good conscience. At the same time he attains supernatural peace, contemplating within himself the grace of the Holy Spirit according to the word of God: 'His place is in peace.' When one is in peace he is fed with spiritual gifts as though with a spoon. The Holy Fathers, being in peace and overshadowed by divine grace, lived to a great age. Only when a man comes to peace of mind, can he illumine himself and others with the light of wisdom. . . . Peace of mind is acquired by sorrows. . . . Nothing so much helps the acquisition of interior peace as silence and, as far as possible, unceasing meditation and infrequent converse with others."[19] On other pages Seraphim describes how to resist evil thoughts, how to use the Prayer of Jesus, how to repent, and so on.

17. Letopis Serafimo, *Diveevskago Monastuirya* (Moscow, 1836), pp. 113-114.
18. Ibid., p. 114.
19. Ibid., p. 120.

St Seraphim left no disciples among the monks but he greatly influenced the nuns of the neighboring convent of Diveevo which he helped found. To these nuns he left many remarkable counsels. It may be said that the nuns of Diveevo were closer to the spirit of St Seraphim than the monks of Sarov. The Abbey of Diveevo grew and flourished. In 1893, during the rule of the Abbess Mary Ushakov, the number of sisters reached 900. Like Sarov, Diveevo was destroyed by the Soviet Revolution.

CHAPTER VIII

BISHOP IGNATIUS BRYANCHANINOV

IN RUSSIAN MYSTICISM Bishop Ignatius Bryanchaninov represents a striking contrast to St Seraphim. While
the latter was always serene and cheerful, often gay, the
Bishop was sad, melancholic and occasionally morbid. The
mysticism of St Seraphim centered on the Resurrection, on
light, and the descent of the Holy Spirit, while that of Ignatius is centered on Calvary, the vanity of life, suffering and
sins.

Ignatius never reached the heights climbed by St Seraphim
but he was a theoretician of Russian mysticism and its popularizer. Dimitry (the secular name of the bishop) was born on
February 6, 1807 in a manor house in the Vologda province.[1] His father, Alexis Bryanchaninov, was a nobleman.
Delicate by constitution, Dimitry received a good education
at home. Already as a child he was very devout and once,
when asked by his father what he would like to do when he
grew up, the boy answered: "I would like to become a monk."

When he had been duly prepared, Dimitry entered the
Imperial School of Engineers in St Petersburg. He passed with
honors the exams of admission, attracting the attention of

1. My principal source for this chapter has been the account in *Žizeopisanija
otečestvennuikh podvižnikov blagočestija 18 i 19 vekach* (Moscow, April, 1908):
"Episkop Ignaty Bryanchaninov." L. Sokolov published a two volume study on
him: *Episkop Ignatij Brjančaninov. Ego žizn, ličnost i moralno-asketičeskija
vozzrenija* (Kiev, 1905).

144

the Grand Duke Nicholas, afterwards Emperor Nicholas I, who introduced Dimitry to his wife, the Grand Duchess Alexandra. Dimitry was a brilliant pupil. He was very popular with professors and students alike. Introduced into the house of Olenin, President of the Imperial Academy of Arts, Dimitry came into contact with the elite of the Russian society of the age. Yet he was not satisfied. The students went to communion only once a year. This was not enough for Dimitry. He started to visit the chaplain of the school and tell him that he was assaulted by various sinful thoughts. The latter thinking that Dimitry had, perhaps, joined a secret political society and was looking for a way out, reported him to the authorities. Nothing was found but Dimitry was reprimanded. He then started to visit the monks of the Valaam Priory in St Petersburg for a weekly confession and communion, an unheard of thing for noblemen in those days. Another student, Chikhachev, also a favorite of Nicholas I, started to accompany Dimitry. The Valaam monks, being simple and humble men, did not know what to do with the two young noblemen. They directed them to a learned confessor of the Laura of St Alexander Nevsky in St Petersburg, Fr Athanasius.

Under the direction of Athanasius, Dimitry started to read the Fathers, and other theological and mystical books. His desire to become a monk increased. Alexis Bryanchaninov, hearing of the intention of his son, wrote to the director of the school, Count von Sivers, and to the Primate, Metropolitan Seraphim (Glagolev) of St Petersburg, complaining that Fr Athanasius was trying to persuade his son to become a monk. The Primate reprimanded Fr Athanasius and forbade him to receive his young nobleman. Dimitry thereupon visited the Primate personally explaining his position. The Metropolitan then allowed the young people to visit the Laura. Here Dimitry met the afterwards celebrated Fr Nagolkin, the first great Staretz of Optino, a disciple of Staretz Basil Kishkin, the popularizer of Paisius' ideas in Russia. This meeting decided the issue. Dimitry said to Chikhachev: "Fr Leonid has won my heart. I have made my decision. I shall resign and become a disciple of the Staretz."

The decision of Dimitry was strongly opposed by his parents and his superiors alike. When Dimitry passed his final examinations with the highest honors, the Emperor entrusted his brother, Grand Duke Michael, with the mission to persuade Dimitry to remain an officer. When Dimitry still sent an application to resign, it was refused and he was appointed, as an officer in the engineers, to the fortress of Dünaburg. Shortly after his arrival at Dünaburg, Dimitry fell ill. In 1827 the Grand Duke Michael visited Dünaburg and finding Dimitry unsuitable for the military service on medical grounds granted him the discharge. Chickhachev also applied for a discharge intending to follow Dimitry to Svirsky Monastery, where the Staretz Leonid lived. His application was turned down.

Dimitry, meanwhile, dressed as peasant, deprived of all assistance by his wealthy parents, went to Svirsky Monastery. He was kindly received there by the monks and sent to work in the kitchen under a monk who was a former serf of his father. A year later, Staretz Leonid moved to Ploshchansky Monastery in the province of Orel. Dimitry went with him. Chihachev rejoined them. Then Staretz Leonid left Ploshchansky Monastery for Optino where he became in due course its first great Staretz. Both noblemen followed him. The abbot of Optino, however, received them unwillingly and the community was suspicious. The extreme austerity of Optino soon made the two friends ill.

Unable to continue in Optino, Dimitry returned home. His parents, thinking that he was disgusted with the monastic life, received him kindly. Chikhachev also came to stay with his friend. Alexis Bryanchaninov insisted on his son resuming his career in the world.

Finally, the two friends, wearied with life in the world, reentered the cloister in 1830, becoming postulants in Kirilov Novoezersky Monastery. Again they fell ill. Dimitry returned to Vologda, while Chikhachev retired to his Pskov estates. Stephen, bishop of Vologda, noticing the rare perseverance of

Dimitry, admitted him into Semigorodsky Monastery and himself received his profession as monk on June 28, 1831 giving him the name of Ignatius. Ordained in the following year, Ignatius was sent at once to revive the decaying Pelshem-Lopotov Monastery. Within a short time he did a great deal. The faithful Chikhachev rejoined Ignatius. Finally the parents became reconciled with their son. Soon afterwards Ignatius' mother died, and Ignatius fell ill again. The cold climate and marshy lands around his monastery were too much for him. The Metropolitan Filaret (Drozdov) of Moscow offered Ignatius the abbacy of Ugreshsky Monastery, but the Emperor intervened and called him to St Petersburg.

"I have not lost my affection for you," the Emperor said to Ignatius. "You are my debtor for the education which I arranged for you and for my love for you. You did not want to serve me, where I intended to send you. You selected another road by your own free will. You will repay your debt to me in that very field. I appoint you to Sergiev Monastery. I want you to live there and to make that monastery a model for the capital."[2] The Emperor then introduced Ignatius to the Empress and asked him to bless the Imperial children. The Holy Synod, on the request of the Emperor, appointed Ignatius Superior of Sergiev Monastery raising him to the dignity of an archimandrite. The new abbot arrived at his monastery on January 5, 1834. He found the monastery much neglected. There were only thirteen monks. For years the monastery had been ruled by the coadjutor bishops to the Primate who had neither much time nor desire to look after the monastery. Gradually Ignatius put the monastery into good order.

The Emperor and his family often visited the monastery. Once Nicholas I came to the monastery from the neighboring Imperial Palace, the Peterhof. "Is the archimandrite at home? " he said. "Tell him that an old friend wants to see him." The Emperor inspected the new buildings, the farm, and so forth. He promised a new subsidy. Ignatius introduced

2. *Žizeopisanija*, p. 321.

magnificent services, organized a first-class choir, gave lectures and conferences. He wrote much for monks and for laymen. He also taught by the example of his life. Yet life in the wealthy monastery, frequently visited by the Court and high society, wearied him. He wanted to retire to a distant and austere monastery. He applied once for such a transfer but the Emperor strongly opposed it. The Synod turned down the request, granting him instead a leave of eleven months to repair his shattered health in Nicolo-Babaev Monastery in the diocese of Kostroma. In 1856, after Nicholas I died, Ignatius applied once more for permission to retire to Optino Monastery. Instead Alexander II, Ignatius' admirer, requested the Synod to make him bishop. On October 23, 1857 Ignatius was consecrated in St Petersburg as bishop of the Caucasus and the Black Sea.

The episcopal period of the life of Ignatius lasted only ten years, but he did much in this relatively short time. The ascetical and mystical doctrine of Ignatius received its final elaboration during this period. Ignatius arrived at his episcopal city in 1858. He nearly died en route. The bishop had much to do in this vast newly-founded diocese. There was no episcopal residence. The seminarists were undisciplined as were the clergy. Even the churches were kept in a poor order. The parallel with the life of St Tikhon of Zadonsk is striking. The latter also was appointed to bring a vast new diocese into better order. Quickly Ignatius was struck down by smallpox which shattered his already poor health. Like St Tikhon he decided to retire. The Synod accepted his resignation and gave him Nikolo-Babaev Monastery for residence. The bishop arrived there October 13, 1861 as superior. He did much to rebuild and beautify this monastery. He erected a new church. Fr Michael Chikhachev, Ignatius' old friend who remained in Sergiev Monastery, paid a last visit to the bishop. In 1862, P. Bryanchaninov, the brother of the bishop and former Governor of Stavropol, settled at the monastery where eventually he died as a monk. On August 14, 1866, the bishop was visited by the Tsarevich Alexander, afterwards Emperor Alexander III, and his brother, Grand Duke Vladimir. In his retirement the bishop continued his literary work and prepared the publication of his *Opera Omnia*. In 1867 his health began to deteriorate rapidly. On April 16, 1867, Easter Sunday, soon after Vespers, the bishop took leave of the community, telling the monks that he would not receive any more visitors and would begin his preparation for death. Within a fortnight, on April 30, 1867, Bishop Ignatius Bryanchaninor died.

Ignatius left four volumes of writings which were published between 1865 and 1867 in St Petersburg.[3] These books were written chiefly for monks but they are useful for devout laymen as well. The first volume describes how one should follow Christ. It discusses how we should read the Gospels and the Fathers and how we must avoid the reading of false and dangerous books. The Bishop also gives instructions concerning prayer, including the Prayer of Jesus, tears of grace and various virtues. The volume also contains many meditations. While it is quite impossible to describe the contents of a thick volume with any adequacy, some insight into the spirituality of Ignatius can be given through the selected quotations.

"When reading the Gospel, do not look for pleasure, for ecstasy, for brilliant ideas; look for the unerring sacred truth. Be not satisfied with a mere sterile reading. Try to practice its commandments. The Gospel is the book of life and it must be read by life. . . . When you open the Holy Gospel to read it, remember that it will decide your fate in eternity. We will be judged according to that book. According to our relation to this book on earth, we shall receive as our lot either eternal beatitude or eternal perdition."[4]

"The Holy Fathers teach us how to become familiar with the Gospel, how to read it and how to understand it, what helps and what opposes its understanding. Therefore, at first you must devote more time to reading the Holy Fathers. When you have learned from them how to read the Gospels,

3. Episkop Ignatij, *Sočinenija,* 4 vols. (St Petersburg, 1865-1867).
4. Ibid., 1:23-24.

then give your preference to them.

"Do not think that the reading of the Gospel without that of the Fathers is enough! This is a proud and dangerous idea. It is far better that the Holy Fathers guide you to the Gospel as their beloved child who seeks his preliminary education and training in their writings. Everyone should select for reading that Father who corresponds to his manner of living. The hermits should read the Fathers who wrote about solitude, while those living in monasteries should read the Fathers who wrote instructions for cenobites. Christians living in the world should read those Fathers who preached to all Christians.[5] . . . We must read unfailingly only that which is suitable to our own manner of life. Otherwise, our mind will be filled with ideas that are doubtless holy but unpracticable, inspiring sterile activity in imagination and desire. Meanwhile good works, suitable to our manner of life, will go by. Moreover, there is danger you will become a sterile daydreamer. Your thoughts, being in permanent opposition to your life, will leave your heart troubled and your behavior uncertain in ways harmful to you and to your neighbors."[6]

"Learn first to pray to God correctly. After learning to pray correctly, pray always. You will thus be saved without difficulty. Salvation comes from God, and an unshakable conviction of this is granted to those who pray well, and pray always. The beginning of prayer must consist in the confession of our sins before God; the middle, in glorifying God and in thanksgiving for his numberless mercies to us; the end, in requests, with great humility, for our needs, bodily and spiritual, leaving to God with all submission the realization of these requests.[7] . . . The soul of prayer is attention. As a body without soul is dead, so is prayer without attention. Prayer said without attention is vain speech. He who prays in this way calls on God in vain. The mind during prayer must be carefully kept formless, rejecting all imagination, because God is formless and cannot be pictured in any form. Images,

5. Ibid., pp. 30-33.
6. Ibid., p. 35.
7. Ibid., p. 49.

if the mind admits them, become a curtain and a wall which separate the soul from God. Those who see nothing during their prayer see God, according to St Meletius the Confessor."[8]

"The feeling of the divine presence is a high state. Retain your mind there free from contacts with alien ideas which try to pervert prayer."[9]

"Offer to God prayers that are silent and humble and that are not heated and inflamed. . . . Devils inspire men to attack the man who prays much. People condemn him for strange behavior. They will call him useless. They accuse him of laziness, hypocrisy, pseudo-holiness. They attribute to him evil and cunning intentions, vicious deeds. They will trouble and disturb his solitude and force him to activities contrary to his manner of life, activities full of dissipation that interrupt peace of hear."[10] Make a vow in your soul never to give up prayer until the end of your life and with it to pass to eternity."[11]

"St Pimen the Great said, on the death of St Arsenius the Great: 'Blessed are you Abbot Arsenius because you wept so much in your lifetime. Those who do not cry here will weep for all eternity.' It is impossible not to weep either here, voluntarily, or thereafter involuntarily and in torments."[12] "Tears are natural to fallen man. Consolation lives mysteriously in tears and joy in weeping."[13] . . . The gift of tears is one of the greatest divine gifts. It is an essential gift, necessary for our salvation. The gifts of prophecy, clairvoyance and miracle-working are signs of a special vocation to serve God, to which service a reward is promised. But the gift of a warm heart and tears is the sign that one's penance is pleasing to God. Weeping is a teacher. It teaches everyone what is useful to him. . . . Without tears everything is useless."[14]

8. Ibid., pp. 57-58.
9. Ibid., p. 59.
10. Ibid., p. 76.
11. Ibid., p. 79.
12. Ibid., p. 217.
13. Ibid., p. 219.
14. Ibid., p. 227.

"Our own cross is in the sorrows and sufferings of our earthly life. They are particular to each. Our own cross is fasting, vigils and other religious exercises which humble the flesh and subject it to the spirit. Such exercises must correspond to the strength of each one. They are personal to each. Our particular sinful inclinations and passions are also crosses. With some of them we are born and with others we are infected in the course of our earthly life. The cross of Christ is the teaching of Christ. Our own cross is vain and sterile, however heavy it is, unless through our following of Christ it is transformed into his cross. Our cross is heavy, but when it becomes the cross of Christ, it is light."[15]

"A brother once sorrowfully asked Sisoes the Great: 'Father, what can I do? I have fallen into sin.' The Staretz answered him: 'Rise again.' The brother said: 'I rose up and fell' The Staretz answered: 'Rise again.' The brother answered: 'How often must I fall and rise up? ' The Staretz said: 'Until your death.' "[16]

In his long meditation, Ignatius, reflecting on his own life, gives us the key to his spirituality. Meditating on his childhood, Ignatius writes: "My birth in sin (original) was a misfortune worse than non-being. What a misfortune to be born for the sorrows of a short earthly life and then for eternal existence in the darkness and torments of hell? I was strengthened in Baptism, but I was not grateful. I did not think of death and eternity. I knew dogma and doctrine but with a dead knowledge, not by faith. My childhood was full of sorrows revealed to none. I read the Gospels and the lives of the Saints. The first I did not understand but the second comforted me. The military school's two years of training were filled with hunger and heaviness of spirit; then came promotion to officer's rank. I regretted that I could not stand in the church among the soldiers and simple folk and cry. Indifference to the world overcame me. I meditated on natural science but it could not reveal the mystery of the Cos-

15. Ibid., p. 228.
16. Ibid., p. 344.

mos. .... Mathematics only hints at the existence of infinite quantities as an idea beyond matter. The exact definition and understanding of this idea is logically beyond any finite being. Mathematics shows numbers and measures, some of which because of their bigness and others on account of their smallness cannot be adequately explored by man. Mathematics indicates the existence of a body of knowledge toward which man has an inborn attraction. Science has, however, no means to bring man there."[17]

"Those who are satisfied with the knowledge obtainable by philosophy, not only fail to obtain a true notion of God, self and the spiritual world, but on the contrary, are infected with false notions which corrupt the mind and make it unable, because of its infection and corruption with falsehood, to enter into communion with truth. . . .[18] True philosophy (the love of wisdom) is expressed only in the doctrine of Christ. Christ is Divine Wisdom. Anyone who looks for wisdom outside of Christ, renounces Christ and rejects wisdom. He acquires and assimilates false wisdom and enters a state of spiritual damnation. Geography, surveying, philology, letters and other sciences and all arts are not worthy of mention in the same breath with spiritual wisdom. They are all earthly. The need of man for them ends with his earthly life, more often much earlier. If I spend all the time of my earthly life in the acquisition of knowledge which ends with the earthly life, what can I take with me? Give me, if you can, something eternal, positive, something important and not to be taken away, something worthy to be called the property of man. Science has no answers."[19]

"I looked then for faith. I rejected fanaticism which separates one from the Church and lacks meekness. . . . I turned to the Holy Fathers. What surprised me most in the writings of the Fathers of the Orthodox Church? Their agreement among themselves is wonderful, splendid! Eighteen centuries witness unanimously through their mouths to the one same

17. Ibid., pp. 635-636.
18. Ibid., p. 639.
19. Ibid., pp. 640-641.

divine teaching! I find this doctrine repeated by all the
Fathers, the doctrine that the only way to salvation consists
in following the Holy Fathers without compromise. They
say: 'Suppose you have met someone seduced by false teaching, who perished because he chose the wrong spiritual exercises? You will see that he followed his own ideas, his own
reasoning, his own opinions and not the teaching of the
Fathers.'[20] The reading of the Fathers has convinced me of
the truth of the Orthodox Church. I left the world and went
to the cloister. There were many obstacles, including my
health, but an interior voice said: 'This is your duty.' The
Holy Fathers were my guides. . . .[21] The Fathers compared
the sorrows of a monk before his entrance into solitude with
the suffering of Christ before Calvary. They compared the
monk's solitude with crucifixion and burial, after which follows resurrection. . . . Soon after my entrance into the cloister, sorrows poured over me like purifying water. There were
interior sorrows and sickness, poverty, crises due to my own
ignorance, inexperience, unreasonableness. Sorrows from
men were bad enough. . . . In 1833 I was called to Sergiev
Monastery and made abbot. The monastery did not welcome
me. I fell gravely ill in the very first year of my abbacy. I was
ill again the second year and the third. These illnesses took
away the remnant of my already delicate health and strength,
exhausted me with continual suffering. Then jealousy,
slander and false accusation rose up against me. I was subjected to painful, protracted, humiliating punishments,
without judgment, without the slightest inquiry. I was treated
as a speechless animal, as a senseless statue. I saw foes,
breathing with irreconcilable hostility, thirsty to destroy
me.[22] . . . Here the merciful Lord honored me and I experienced indescribable joy and peace of mind. The Lord allowed
me to taste spiritual sweetness and love in my very encoun-
ters with my enemy who sought my head. And the face of
this enemy became in my eyes as the face of the angel of

20. Abbot Doretheus, Sermon Five.
21. Episkop Ignatij, *Sočinenija,* 1:646.
22. Ibid., p. 649.

light. By experience I understood the mysterious silence of Christ before Pilate and the High Priest of the Jews. What a happiness to be a victim like Jesus! Or, rather, what a happiness to be crucified next to the Savior, as the blessed robber was, and like the robber, with full conviction of soul to confess: 'I receive according to my deeds. Remember me, O Lord, in your Kingdom.'[23] Although I was ill I did not envy others, I thirsted to die in expiation. The doors of repentance, open to me, O Lord."[24]

The second volume of the *Collected Works* is devoted to the bishop's "Ascetical Essays." It is made up of meditations and instructions. Some of them are striking. In the meditation "On the image and likeness of God in men" the bishop writes: "Man is the image and likeness of God himself. In him, like the sun in a drop of pure water, the Deity in Three Persons is clearly reflected. . . . Our minds have given birth and continually bring forth thought. Thought, being born, never ceases to be reborn and at the same time remains born and hidden in the mind. Our minds cannot exist without thought and neither can thought exist without the mind. The beginning of one is also inevitably the beginning of the other. The existence of a mind is inevitably the existence of thought as well. Likewise our spirit proceeds from the mind and assists thought. Therefore every thought has its own spirit. Thought cannot be without spirit, the existence of one unavoidably follows upon the existence of the other. Through the existence of both the existence of the mind is made manifest. . . . What is the spirit of man? The totality of the feelings of the heart, which belong to the rational, eternal soul. The moral strength of man is his spirit. Our mind, word and spirit, by their origins and mutual relations represent the Father, Son and Holy Spirit without beginning, equal in honor and of one nature."[25]

" True prayer is the voice of true repentance. When prayer is not inspired by repentance, it does not fulfill its purpose

23. Lk 23:42.
24. Episkop Ignatij, *Sočinenija*, 1:690.
25. Ibid., 2:119, 122-123.

and God does not accept it. He accepts only the broken
spirit, the broken and contrite heart. . . .[26] If someone were to
reach the summit of perfection, yet if he did not pray as a
sinner, his prayer would be rejected by God.[27] 'In that day
when I did not weep for myself,' said one blessed man of true
prayer, 'I would consider myself deluded. . . .'[28] The baby ex-
presses with cries all his desires. Let your prayer be always
accompanied with tears. Not only when saying prayers but
also when you are silent, express with tears your desire of
repentance and reconciliation with God, your extreme need
of divine mercy."[29]

"Meditate when you pronounce the words of a prayer; you
will then be attentive. Direct your eyes toward your mouth
or close them. This will assist you in the realization of the
union of mind and heart. Pronounce the words very slowly.
This will help you to be attentive to them. No word of your
prayer will then be pronounced without attention. . . . When
the mind meditates on the words of the prayer it attracts the
sympathy of the heart. This sympathy of the heart for the
mind manifests itself by warmth in the heart, a pious feeling,
which unites in itself sadness and quiet and meek consolation. . . . Dissipation robs prayer of its value. He who prays
with a distracted mind feels in himself an inexplicable
emptiness and dryness. He whose prayer is always full of
distractions deprives himself of all the spiritual fruits which
are born of an attentive prayer. He enters into a state of
dryness and emptiness. This state produces coldness toward
God, depression, a darkening of the mind and a weakening of
faith which results in the death of the spiritual life. All this
shows most clearly that such a prayer is not acceptable to
God."[30]

"Daydreaming during prayer is even worse than distraction.

26. Ps 50:19.
27. Episkop Ignatij, *Sočinenija,* 2:168-170: St Isaac the Syrian, Sermon Fifty-
Three.
28. Ibid., p. 170: Fr Athanasius, Recluse of Svensk.
29. Ibid., p. 171.
30. Ibid., p. 172-4.

Distraction makes prayer sterile while daydreaming engenders false fruits, self-delusion and what the Holy Fathers call devilish illusion. . . . Reject seemingly good thoughts and seemingly bright revelations which come to you in time of prayer and take you away from prayer. They come from the province of false reason. They, like horsemen, sit astride vanity. Their dark faces are hidden in order that he who prays may not recognize in them his foes. . . . They are enemies from the Kingdom of the Prince of this world. . . . The fruit of true prayer is a holy peace of soul united with a quiet, silent joy, free of daydreaming, self-esteem and disordered inclinations and movements. . . . Be wise in your prayer. Do not ask in it anything corruptible and vain. Remember the command of the Savior: 'Seek first of all the Kingdom of God and its truth and all that is needed for temporal like will be given to you.' "[31]

"When the Fathers spoke of the practice of the memory of God they meant any short prayer or religious thought which they tried to keep constantly in their mind and memory in the place of other thoughts. This is unceasing prayer. . . . Unceasing prayer destroys cunning by trust in God. It leads to holy simplicity, taking the mind away from a multitude of thoughts. It leads one to give up planning for oneself and others and to keeping the mind always humble and filled with one single thought."[32] The words used in this practice must be said first by the tongue, very quietly and slowly, with complete attention. . . . Gradually the vocal prayer becomes mental and afterwards it passes into the heart. This passing from one stage to another takes many years. It must not be forced. Let the process develop by itself, or rather, let God grant this to you at the time known to him when you will be ready.[33] . . . The gift of God comes by itself. It is necessary first to acquire purity, freedom from bodily passions, solitude, stability and silence. . . . Know that all the passions and the fallen spirits are closely connected and

31. Ibid., pp. 176-178. Mt 6:33.
32. Ibid., p. 127.
33. Ibid., p. 225.

related. This connection, this union is sin. If you become
subject to one passion, you become subject to all the rest. . . .
Prayer is called mental when it is said in the mind with full
attention. It is called prayer of the heart when the mind and
the heart have been united. Ant it is called spiritual when it is
rises from the whole soul with the participation of the
body.[34]. . . When he who prays is taken up in this movement
toward God, he is suddenly united in himself and finds
himself whole, healed by the touch of the finger of God.
Mind and heart, soul and body, until then separated by sin,
are suddenly united and with God. Because this union was
made in God and by God, it results also in the unification of
man himself and in his union with God. After a man has
achieved union with himself, the spiritual gifts become manifest. More correctly, this union itself is a gift of the Spirit.
The first spiritual gift, the one which creates this wonderful
union, is the peace of Christ. The others are, according to the
Apostle, love, joy, longanimity, goodness, mercy, faith,
meekness, and abstinence.[35] The prayer of the healed one,
who is united and reconciled in himself, is free of thought and
dreams of devils. The fiery sword of the fallen cherubim
ceases to hurt; the blood ceases to boil up and cause trouble.
The sea becomes still; the breath of winds, thoughts and
dreams, cease to act upon it. . . . To the elect of the Spirit the
mysteries of Christ are revealed."[36]

"The power of the Prayer of Jesus consists in the Divine
Name of the God-Man, our Lord, Jesus Christ. Because
temptations of the devil are frequent, prayer must be unceasing. The power of the Name of Jesus frees our minds from
indecision, strengthens our wills, and rightly directs our
fervor and the other movements of the soul, our thoughts
and our feelings. This prayer allows only those thoughts and
feelings which belong to the incorrupted nature of man to
remain in the soul. No place remains for alien thoughts and
feelings.[37] . . Among the incomprehensible and wonderful at-

34. Ibid., p. 250.
35. Gal 5:22-23.
36. Episkop Ignatij, *Sočinenija,* 2:252-254.
37. Ibid., p. 282.

tributes of the Name of Jesus is its property and power to exorcize devils. This property is revealed by the Lord himself. He said that those who believe in him will expel devils by his name.[38] It is necessary to pay special attention to this property of the Name of Jesus because it has a great importance for the practice of Prayer of Jesus. We need to say something of the presence of devils in men. This presence is of two kinds. The first presence could be called physical and the second moral. When the physical presence of the devil in a man takes place he enters into the body of the man with his very being and torments the soul and the body alike. One or many devils can inhabit a man in this way. Such a man is then said to be possessed. From the Gospels we know that the Lord used to heal the possessed. The disciples of the Lord did the same, expelling devils by the Name of the Lord. Morally Satan resides in a man when the latter becomes the slave of his will. In this way Satan entered Judas Iscariot, that is, he took possession of his mind and will and became united with him in spirit. All those who do not believe in Christ are in such a state. . . . In this state are also, in various degrees, all those baptized Christian who became separated from him by sins. Thus the Holy Fathers interpret the words of Christ about the return of the devil with seven others worse than himself as applying to the temple of the soul abandoned by the Holy Spirit.[39] . . . The power of Satan remains in man unnoticed and underestimated. When this power hears the Name of the Lord Christ invoked in prayer, it becomes troubled. It excites all human passions and through them troubles man sorely and produces various sicknesses. . . . Passions are demons. Therefore, it is obvious that the beginning of the Prayer of Jesus is accompanied with the boiling up of passions. Gradually the continuous appeals to Christ humble the serpent. The beginning of this exercise is dry and monotonous until the heart answers."[40]

"All Christians may and must practice the Prayer of Jesus for the purpose of repentance and to appeal to the Lord for

38. Ibid., p. 286. Mk 16:17.
39. Ibid.
40. Ibid., p. 287.

help. We must practice this Prayer in the fear of God and with faith, with the utmost attention to the thought and the words of the Prayer, with repentance of spirit. In this way the Prayer of Jesus may and must be practiced not only by monks who live in monasteries and are occupied by obediences but by laymen as well. Such attentive prayer may be called mental prayer and prayer of the heart, because it is expressed with the emotions and with tears on account of warm feelings."[41]

The Bishop discusses at length various methods of practising the Prayer of Jesus. "According to Fr Dorotheus we must at first say the Prayer of Jesus with the voice, that is, the lips, tongue and speech, loud enough for ourselves to hear. When the lips, tongue and feelings become satiated with vocal prayer, the latter ceases and is replaced by another said in a whisper. After this happens, prayer must become mental but still using words. In this way mental prayer and that of heart enter in on their own and start to develop. This prayer can be practiced any time, everywhere, in every work.[42] . . . St Nilus commands us to close up the mind in the heart and, as far as possible, regulate our breathing. This means we must breathe quietly. Generally speaking, all movements must be restrained, keeping the soul and body in quiet state, in a state of stillness, devotion and fear of God. The experience will soon reveal that the regulation of breathing, that is, slow and quiet breathing, considerably helps concentration of mind and makes it less inclined to wander."[43] Describing various Hesychast counsels the bishop quotes at length Nicephoros of Athos: "Thus, sitting down and concentrating the mind, inhale through nostrils; thus breathing reaches the heart. Breathe quietly and force the mind to descend with the inhaled air into the heart. When the mind enters there, all the rest will be for you gaiety and joy. . . . Brother! Train your mind not to leave the heart soon because at the beginning the mind is very depressed by the interior confinement and lack

41. Ibid., p. 303.
42. Ibid., p. 312.
43. Ibid., p. 327.

of space. But when it becomes accustomed to these conditions, it will abandon its wandering because the Kingdom of
Heaven is within us. Contemplating the latter and thirsting
for frequent prayer, the mind will consider everything external disgusting and hateful. If your mind should enter
speedily into your heart, as I have shown you, then thank
God, glorify him, be joyful, and always keep to this practice.
It will teach you things which you do not know. Your mind
finding its place in the heart should not remain there silent
and lazy but should say unceasingly: 'Lord Jesus Christ, Son
of God, have mercy on me, a sinner! ' "[44]

In the same volume Ignatius discusses also the sensible and
spiritual vision of spirits. According to the bishop, because of
our fallen nature we can easily see and know devils. The
angels, on the contrary, are usually seen only by the saints;
rarely by sinners. Devils often pretend to be the souls of dead
men, as Chrysostom says. Our flesh, separating us from the
devils like a wall, saves us from them. After death we enter
the world of spirits and see them. Nevertheless, spirits can
be seen even in this life under certain circumstances. The
bishop quotes many cases from the Scriptures, the lives of
the saints and monastic lore. "Contemplation," the bishop
says, "is common to all men. Everyone can contemplate
when he wants. Vision is peculiar only to those who have
purified themselves by penance. Vision comes not from the
will of man but from the Holy Spirit touching our spirit
according to his all-holy Will."[45] A warm heart is the first
spiritual feeling, then a wholesome sadness, consolation, and
the revelation of incomprehensible things. Those who want
"*Umilenie*"(a warm heart) and spiritual vision, must grow in
humility and self-reproach. The first spiritual vision is the
vision of forgotten and unknown sins. Once all sins become
known, the sinfulness of human nature is fully realized as
well as the origin of the passions and illnesses inspired by
devils. Spiritual vision of spirits is attained by the mind and

44. Ibid., pp. 335-336. *Dobrotoljubie*, 2.
45. Ibid., p. 429.

the heart. The latter feels the presence of spirits. Ideas inspired by devils always trouble the soul and excite pride. The devil may come as an angel of life but he is unable to grant peace and humility. Many pages of this "Sermon on the sensible and spiritual vision of spirits" are worthy of a good psychologist. The bishop's view on the importance of the knowledge of forgotten and unknown sins has been brought out by psychoanalysts. Ignatius Bryanchaninov, although he lived a hundred years ago, is astonishingly modern.

The third volume of the bishop's *Works* is filled with his "Ascetical Sermons." These are profound and interesting but they do not add much to our understanding of the spirituality of Ignatius. He stresses, contrary to the fashion in his age, the need of frequent Communion. He stipulates also that frequent Communion must not degenerate into a routine but always should be preceded by a proper preparation. The last volume of the bishop's *Works* is called "Offering to Contemporary Monks."[46] It contains rules for the external behavior of the monks and spiritual counsels. Ignatius strongly disapproved Western methods of meditation, particularly that of Thomas a Kempis, St Francis of Assisi and St Ignatius Loyola. According to Ignatius the Latins gave far too much importance to the imagination which leads to unhealthy excitement and to delusion. It must be said that the mysticism of the later Middle Ages and of the Counter Reformation was altogether alien to Bishop Ignatius. He advised only the reading of the Bible and the Fathers as well as of those authors who were based on them.

In his last volume Ignatius stresses the need of the continuous memory of death in order for monks to live correctly, and emphasizes the custody of thoughts and the Prayer of Jesus. Ignatius warned monks of the danger of being friendly with women. He writes: "Woman is guided by the feelings of fallen nature and not by sound reason and spiritual wisdom, which are quite alien to her. Her reason is a

46. Ignatius Brianchaninov, *The Arena: An Offering to Contemporary Monasticism*. Trans. from the Russian (Madras, 1970).

servant of her feelings. Seduced by her feelings, she is quickly infected by an attraction for a monk, not necessarily a young or middle-aged one but even for an old one. She makes this monk her idol and later on, very often, becomes herself his idol. Woman sees only perfection in her idol. She tries to persuade him of that and always succeeds. When the monk, because of the dangerous and unceasing suggestions and praises, becomes infected with a high opinion of himself and pride, divine grace leaves him and he, darkened in his mind and heart, is led in his blindness to the most unreasonable behavior and to the fearless breaking of all the divine commandments."[47]

In the fourth volume the bishop discusses once more and at length the fallen angels, how to recognize them and how to fight them. "Clear signs of the coming and of the influence upon us of the fallen spirits are the sudden appearance of sinful and vain thoughts and dreams, sinful feelings, heaviness of body and insistent animal demands, coldness of heart, haughtiness, a peculiar disposition toward earthly occupations, vain thoughts, the rejection of repentance, sadness and forgetfulness of death. The coming of the fallen spirit is always accompanied with trouble, darkening of the mind and indecision."[48] The best way to resist the devil is to open the soul to a staretz and a continuous custody of thoughts. The volume ends with a long meditation: "Lamentations of a monk," arranged in chapters according to the Hebrew alphabet. It gives a good insight into the spirituality of Ignatius. The bishop did much for the Russian monks by his writings. With those of Bishop Theophane the Recluse, and the publications of Athos and Optino, they formed the Russian monks of the last century.

---

47. Episkop Ignatij, *Sočinenija*, 4:282.
48. Ibid., p. 305.

CHAPTER IX

THE STARTZY OF OPTINO

NO RUSSIAN MONASTERY attained such an influence on the Russian élite and people in the nineteenth century as the Monastery of Optino. For this Optino is neither indebted to a magnificent site or buildings, nor to relics or venerated ikons, nor to the learning of its monks or their grandiose liturgy. The greatness of Optino resides entirely in its great startzy, or spiritual directors, of whom Leonide Nagolkin, Macarius Ivanov and Ambrose Grenkov were the most remarkable.

Two abbots of Optino, Moses Putilov and Isaac Antimonov, under whose superiorship the great startzy worked, were hardly less outstanding in their profound mysticism and saintliness than the startzy themselves. Optino produced, also, several remarkable monks: Leonide Kavelin, who was afterwards superior of the Great Laura of Holy Trinity near Moscow; Juvenal Polovtsev, afterwards archbishop of Vilno and Climent Sederholm. Constantin Leontiev, one of the most original Russian thinkers and writers of the nineteenth century, lived for years in Optino. The brothers Kyreevsky, A. S. Khomyakov, and N. Gogol were in close relations with the Staretz Macarius Ivanov and visited Optino. Theodore Dostoevsky, Leo Tolstoy, Vladimir Soloviev and B. Rozanov, powerful Russian writers and thinkers of the second half of the nineteenth century, visited the Staretz Ambrose Grenkov. Dostoevsky indeed described Optino in his greatest and most profound novels, *The Brothers Karama-*

zov. The last four startzy of Optino, although not on the same level as the first three, were, nevertheless, first class spiritual directors. The revival of Optino in the nineteenth century is closely connected with the hermits of the forest of Roslavl to whom belongs Abbot Moses Putilov, and among whom were two profound mystics, Staretz Vasilisk and his pupil, Staretz Zosima Verkhovsky. Finally, the anonymous author of the celebrated *Tales of the Russian Pilgrim,* a Russian spiritual classic, also visited the Staretz Macarius Ivanov for direction. No Russian monastery can show a similar record. In addition, Optino published several collections of the writings of the Fathers.

According to an old tradition the foundation of Optino took place in the fifteenth century.[1] Its supposed founder was Opta, a former robber, who after his conversion, became a hermit and founded a small community. The earliest documentary evidence does not go, however, beyond 1598. The small monastery suffered much during the Russian "Time of Troubles" in the beginning of the seventeenth century. Theodoret was the first superior of the restored monastery. The small monastery vegetated through the seventeenth century. The neighboring nobles often assisted it and made donations. In 1709 the entire community did not number more than sixteen. Peter the Great closed Optino but it was opened again in 1727. Optino survived the secularization of monastic estates in 1764, when so many small monasteries were suppressed; yet the number of its monks was limited to seven which just allowed the monastery to survive. Although Abbot Abraham, appointed by the Metropolitan of Moscow, Plato Levshin, made efforts to stabilize the monastery, it continued to vegetate. Abraham died on January 14, 1817 at fifty-eight years of age. He had been superior for twenty years. According to his will, among the books he left was a three volume set of *Dobrotolyubie.* The ideas of Paisius had reached Optino.

---

1. For the history of Optino see Leonid Kavelin, *Istoričeskoe opisanie Kozelskoj Vedenskoj Optinoj Pustyni* (St Petersburg, 1862).

The prominence, wealth and influence of the monastery begin with its first remarkable abbot, Moses Putilov.[2] He was born on January 15, 1782. John Putilov (1752-1809) a Moscow merchant, was father of three abbots: Moses of Optino, Isaiah of Sarov and Anthony of Maloyaroslavetz. His widowed son-in-law, Cosma Krundishev, also died as a monk in Sarov in 1823. Moses at first was an employee in an important business in Moscow. However, he did not like commercial life and wanted to become a monk. He came into contact with Mother Dosithea, nun of Ivanovsky Convent in Moscow. Her counsels led him to enter religious life.

Mother Dosithea was a mysterious and enigmatic personality. Born in 1749, she was the only daughter of Empress Elisabeth from her morganatic marriage to Field-Marshal Count Alexis Rasumovsky. As Princess Augusta Tarakanov, she lived in Russia until the death of her mother in 1761. She was then sent abroad by her father to keep her safe from the Court intrigues. In 1773, an unknown adventuress adopted the name of the Princess and made a great deal of trouble for Empress Catherine II. The Empress had the adventuress kidnapped and imprisoned. She died in the prison in St Petersburg on December 4, 1775. The great rebellion promoted by Don Cossack Emelian Pugachev, who pretended to be the murdered husband of the Empress, Peter III, and the Moscow disturbances in 1771 led to the Empress' decision to bring Princess Augusta back to Russia. In 1785 Princess Augusta was kidnapped abroad and brought to St Petersburg. Thereupon the Empress ordered her to become a nun in Ivanovsky Monastery. Professed under the name of Dosithea, the Princess was kept locked up like a recluse. Except for the abbess, the confessor and the Metropolitan of Moscow, no one was allowed to visit her. Only after the death of Catherine II was she allowed more freedom She was visited by members of the Imperial Family, aristocrats and merchants. Dosithea died on February 4, 1810. She was buried with all the honors due to

2. Archbishop Juvenal Polovtsev wrote a good life of Abbot Moses: *Žizneopisanie Nastojatelja Koselskoj Vedenskoj Optinoj Pustyni Archimandrita Moiseja* (Moscow, 1882).

her rank by the bishop of Dimitrov. The Moscow Commander-in-chief, Count I. V. Gudovish, whose wife was a
cousin of the Princess, represented the Imperial Family at the
funeral. He was surrounded by senators and aristocrats.
Mother Dosithea was a woman of great virtue and spiritual
insight. She recommended to Timothy Putilov and to his
brother Thomas that they consult Abbot Alexander of
Moscow Novospassky Monastery and the confessor of the
same monastery, Fr Filaret, both of whom were disciples of
Paisius Velichkovsky.

Because Cosmas Krundishev, the young men's brother-
in-law, was already a novice in Sarov, the abbot of Novospassky Monastery recommended that they go there. This they
did and in November, 1805, they arrived at Sarov. They went
without the permission of their father, who was opposed to
their plan. The brothers remained there for two years. Sarov
Monastery was at that period renowned for its three mystics:
St Seraphim of Sarov, Marco the Hermit and Nazarius, the
former abbot of Valaam. The brothers met all three of them
and learned much from them. Thomas remained in Sarov,
where he made his profession. In 1842 he was elected abbot,
an office which he filled until his death in 1860. Timothy,
however, was not satisfied in Sarov. The vast and populous
monastery was too big and noisy for him. In 1808 he left
Sarov for Svensky Monastery in Bryansk, where Fr Seraphim,
a disciple of Staretz Basil Kishkin, was superior. Seraphim
gathered around himself several contemplatives: Fr Athanasius, a monk of Mount Athos and a personal disciple of
Paisius Velichkovsky, Fr Anastasius, a disciple of Staretz
Basil Kishkin, and others. Svensky Monastery, which was
founded in 1288 by the Grand Prince of Chernigov, Roman
Mikhailovich, was a pleasant place near to the great Roslavl
forest, where many hermits lived at that time.[3] Timothy
Putilov hoped to become a monk of Svensky Monastery and
to receive permission to live as hermit in the forest. His ex-
pectations proved false. The Holy Synod, to which Catherine

3. N. Tikhonov, *Brjansky Svensky Monastyr, 1288-1888* (Bryansk, 1888).

II reserved the right to gran permission to become a professed monk, refused to allow Putilov to make monastic profession in Svensky Monastery on the basis of a formality, the
lack of a permit from the merchants' guild. Timothy did
obtain the demanded permit on March 16, 1811, but then he
did not return to Svensky Monastery. Instead he joined the
solitaries of the Roslavl forest. He spent the next ten years
with them.

The hermits of the Roslavl forest represent an exceptionally interesting group in Russian monasticism of the nineteenth
century.[4] The first hermits had lived in the neighboring
Bryansk forest since the eighteenth century. The persecution
of monks by the Imperial Government and severe restrictions
imposed on them forced many aspirants to go to the forest
rather than to the state-controlled monasteries. In the eighteenth century Fr Serapion, Theodore of Sanaksar and
Joasaph of Ploshchan lived in the Bryansk forest. In the
second half of the eighteenth century and in the nineteenth,
the hermits rather favored the Roslavl forest. Over forty of
them lived there during that period. The best known of them
was Fr Adrian, a monk of Ploshchan who settled in the forest
together with Fr Jonas and two novices in 1775. In 1786 a
great Russian mystic, Staretz Zosima Verkhovsky, joined
him. About the same time another mystic, Staretz Vasilisk,
came to Adrian. In due course Adrian left the forest and
accepted the abbacy of Konovetz, where he ruled for ten
years. In 1800 he retired to Simonov Monastery in Moscow.
He died there in 1812. It was on his advice that Timothy
Putilov went to the Roslavl forest.

Staretz Zosima Verkhovsky, the best known disciple of Fr
Adrian, cannot be passed over. Born in 1767, son of the
Governor of Smolensk, Zakhariya Verkhovsky was educated
at home by private tutors. Then, together with his two brothers Philip and Elias, he joined the Imperial Guard. When his
father died, Zakhariya returned home. For a while he in-

4. Orlovsky wrote a monograph on them: *Pustynnikik roslavlskich Iesov* (Smolensk, 1904).

tended to marry and to settle down as a wealthy landowner.
Yet he did not feel attracted to life in the world. Remembering his youth the staretz afterwards wrote: "When I meditated in those days that after marrying I would be obliged to
care for my wife and children and that this wife might turn
out to be quite unpleasant and the children anything but a
consolation, I was depressed. I was depressed still further
when I thought that I would be obliged to worry over the
vast estates and the serfs, who need sometimes to be punished, and that I might very well be involved in troubles with
relatives and neighbors. . . . These thoughts made me often so
depressed that I did not know what to do. I felt that this
manner of life was not for me."[5] However Verkhovsky was
nearly on the point of marrying when he had a strange vision.
"I saw," he remembered, "a maiden standing near my bed.
She was quite unlike the one of whom I thought. She was
dressed in a long white gown with a belt. Her head was
covered with a white veil but so transparent that her face,
shining with celestial beauty, was clearly visible. She stood
before me, amiable, pleasant and friendly. Although her eyes
were looking down, she did look occasionally upon me
humbly and agreeably. When I woke I was filled with a new
and holy admiration. I felt myself renewed, restored. There
was no trace of my confused and sad thoughts. Not only the
love but even the memory of my fiancée were blotted out.
The heavenly maiden had entered my soul This attraction
was not sensible but something pure, ennobling, indescribably
consoling because the soul felt that this was not an earthly
maiden but a heavenly being, the incarnation of purity and
chastity."[6]

Still Zakhariya remained undecided until his mother died.
Then giving his estates to his brother-in-law, and taking only
4,000 rubles, he went to Fr Adrian in the Roslavl forest. He
was only nineteen years old. When Adrian refused to accept
the money, Zakhariya was astonished: "O wonder, there are

5. "Starec Schimonach Zosima," *Žizneopisanija* (Oct. 1909), pp. 606-607.
6. Ibid., p. 607.

yet men on the earth who do not need money because they
have abandoned all temporal things." When Adrian was appointed abbot of Konevetz, Zakhriya followed him there and
was professed receiving the name of Zosima. In Konevetz
Zosima became greatly attached to one of the disciples of
Adrian, Staretz Vasilisk, a peasant from Tver province.
Zosima and Vasilisk began to live as solitaries. When Adrian
retired, the community elected Zosima abbot. He declined
and retired with Staretz Vasilisk to Siberia. They settled in
the virgin forest about forty miles from Kuznetzk. Zosima
spent many years in solitude. He wrote a true panygeric to it.
"How is it possible to describe exactly all those interior,
spiritual feelings which are so sweet that no glorious reign can
give so much joy and serenity as the solitary life! When you
neither see nor hear, nor have contacts with the deluded
world, then you find peace. The mind naturally soars toward
the One God. In solitary life there is nothing to distract you
from divine service. Nothing prevents you from reading Holy
Scripture and from meditation. On the contrary, every happening and object incites you to soar to God. The virgin
forest is around you. It hides the world from you. The only
open and pure way leads you to heaven. The latter attracts
your thoughts and your desire to be worthy to attain its
beatitude. But even if your thoughts are directed to the earth
contemplating nature, your heart is nevertheless excited with
a sweet love for the Creator of everything, with wonder at his
wisdom, with thanks for his goodness. Even the pleasant singing of birds invites you to thanksgiving and to songs of
prayer. All creation assists our eternal spirit to unite with its
Creator. And what joy from this union with God, what fear,
love, consolation, illumination, trembling, warmth of heart,
tears and perfect forgetfulness of everything earthly."[7]

In Siberia the two hermits lived in separate huts just as in
the Roslavl forest. They confessed and received Holy Communion four times a year. After Easter they used to wander
together in the forest for two or three weeks saying the office

7. Ibid., pp. 630-631.

in various places. Zosima was twice assaulted by the devil, once with religious doubts and another time with blasphemy. His most astonishing mystical experience relates to his prayer about sinners. He prayed once: "Lord, let me learn the torments of sinners that I never forget by your great mercy that I am a great sinner. Show me, O Lord, what will be the torments in hell, that I , fearing them always, will always serve you well." Shortly after this prayer, he recounts, "I felt inexplicable suffering in all my being, spiritual, psychical and physical. No words can describe this suffering. My soul understood what are the sufferings of sinners in hell. I saw and heard nothing. Everything in me suffered: trouble of spirit, darkness, sadness, . . . a terrible state. If this were to last a few minutes longer, either my soul would leave the body or I would become a raving lunatic. All here, I say, is nothing compared with that suffering. It was awful, inexplicable! Trembling, I fell in prayer before the Lord but was unable to pronounce anything. I could only shout out loudly: 'Lord, have mercy! ' And he forgave me. Suddenly everything changed. Warm tears of grace streamed out by themselves and in abundance."[8] The two friends remained twenty-four years in Siberia. In 1820 Zosima organized the community of women, which settled in Turinsky Monastery. Within a short period there were forty sisters. Staretz Vasilisk died in Siberia, in Turinsky Monastery in 1824. He left a remarkable description of the effects on him of Hesychast prayer. The manuscript, preserved before the Revolution in Odigitriev Convent near Moscow, has never been printed in full so far as I know. After the death of Vasilisk, Zosima experienced many troubles in Siberia which forced him to return to European Russia. He died on October 24, 1833 in Odigitriev Convent which he had founded.

Zosima left a number of treatises which were partly published. Some of them deserve quotation. To the nuns of the Convent which he founded, he wrote: "Be humble and heaven and earth will be subjected to you. . . . [9]

8. Ibid., pp. 638-639.
9. Ibid., p. 663.

Created things are good but they all pass. Everything says: do not become attached to me —or I leave you. . . . It is impossible to look to heaven with one eye and to the earth with another. Likewise, it is impossible for our soul to cling at once to earthly and to heavenly things. We must select one or the other and cling to it. . . .[10] Why can man never be satisfied? Because his soul is not created for this world. The spirit engenders spirit. To the soul which comes from the divine source by the breath of God, everything temporal is alien. Therefore it can find nothing congenial to it on this earth. It cannot be quieted. Whatever earthly thing you give to the soul, it is unsatisfied. It wants more. God alone can satisfy the soul fully. . . .[11] How must we pray before the crucifix of our Lord Jesus Christ? As soon as you approach him, he at once opens his hands in order to meet and embrace you. He inclines his head to listen to you. He shuts his divine eyes to avoid seeing your sins. He chains his feet in order not to go away and separate himself from the unworthy. He has not merely opened but we can say made wide with the lance the door of his heart of love allowing his mercy and love to pour forth without obstacles on all who prostrate before him, our sweet and merciful Creator and Father. Meditate on a love so boundless that it nailed him to the Cross. Pray like the publican and say humbly and quietly: 'God have pity on me,'[12] or cry out like the woman of Canaan,[13] or remain silent and in tears like the sinful woman at the feet of the Savior,[14] or like the prodigal son hasten to him without fear.[15] He embraces every soul coming to him.''[16]

"He who wants to live without revealing his thoughts suffers much. Many and various vain thoughts and passions are born in him. As a vine left neglected produces many

10. Ibid.
11. Ibid., p. 670.
12. Lk 18:13.
13. Mt 15:22.
14. Lk 7:38.
15. Lk 15:20.
16. "Starec Schimonach Zosima," p. 672.

branches, so too, a novice, if he does not reveal his thoughts and deeds to the staretz to cut them off, grows, develops and strengthens a multitude of thoughts and passions. The enemy, knowing full well how deadly is the custom of keeping everything to oneself, encourages and inspires the ascetic to live on without revealing his thoughts. He who has accepted such a devilish inspiration is deluded, thinking that he lives well and without sin in his relation to the staretz, while he is not frank in hiding his thoughts. Therefore he does not feel peace and consolation in his soul. Because he lives with his Staretz without faith and love he is overcome with murmuring, pride, condemnation of others, dissatisfaction and absence of peace. These spiritual illnesses, fortified by being hidden, make the life with the Staretz intolerable. They go so far as to force this man to leave his Father and the brotherhood. Seduced by his self-will and his own wisdom, such a man abandons the right road approved by the Holy Fathers."[17]

"Those who have met God and are united with others in God, united among themselves by divine grace, must have nothing as their own, neither food, nor clothing, nor any other thing lest, according to St Basil the Great, a diabolical snare appear among them, that is: 'mine' and 'yours.' Moreover, they must try to possess in common not only material things but to consider their salvation and sins as common to all. They should care not merely for their personal salvation and progress but for that of their brethren as well. Virtues become common when no one can take pride considering himself above the rest, or become weak-hearted and hopeless seeing himself behind the rest. Those who labor and perform ascetic exercises must think and believe that all their good deeds and works are carried out with the help of the community's prayers and still more with the prayers and counsel of their Father and teacher. Therefore, they have a common reward. Those who are weary, seeing themselves left behind

---

17. *Žitie i podvigi v Boze počivšago schimonacha Zosimy, ego izečennija i izvleče nija iz ego sočinenij* (Moscow, 1889), part 2, pp. 45-46.

and fallen, not from laziness and neglect, but from weakness and illness, become humble and contrite in heart. True humility is great before God even without deeds. Therefore they are not deprived of the common reward and salvation but like those who received an equal wage for one hour of work, they receive as much as if they worked the entire day. . . ."[18]

In the Roslavl forest Timothy Putilov became a disciple to Father Athanasius, a professed monk of Optino, who had been a hermit in the forest since 1805. There were seven other hermits in the neighborhood. Each hermit lived in his own small hut. The huts of these disciples were relatively near to that of their staretz. Each hermit said all the offices alone in his hut. Only on Sundays and feasts did the hermits come together for services. On Christmas, Easter and some other feasts the parish priest from Luga came to the hermits to give Holy Communion. The hermits copied books and worked for their living on their small plots in the forest. The forest was full of wild beasts but these did not trouble the hermits: however robbers occasionally did. Fr Athanasius received Timothy Putilov's profession, giving him the name of Moses. In 1816 Moses' younger brother, Alexander, joined him. Alexander, who received the name of Anthony at profession, became in due course abbot of Maloyaroslavetz. In 1816 both brothers made a pilgrimage to Kiev. During this journey they met several mystics, disciples of Paisius Velichkovsky or of his friends, Abbot Barlaam of Sofroniev Monastery, Abbot Filaret of Glynsky Monastery and Staretz Basil Kishkin.

Living with Fr Athanasius, Moses quickly absorbed his teaching, particularly on the need of obedience. In one letter Moses wrote to a friend: "Perchance it will be your lot to travel to St Petersburg to see your superior. Do not contradict him, if you want to be happy. Take my own case as an example. What hardships I suffered when I followed my own will. As my dear friend, I tell you plainly, as a commandment of God and not of men, that you should never decline any

18. Ibid., pp. 51-52.

mission entrusted to you, and never impose yourself on others. If you observe this always, you will find happiness in the most trying circumstances and will remember me well. But if you seek something or renounce it according to your own arbitrary will, you will regret it bitterly your whole life. I tell you this not from my wisdom but from my experience. You are a young man. This advice is necessary and useful for you if God would allow you to visit St Petersburg. You may learn many useful things, which at present you are unable to understand because you think you are already perfect."[19]

In 1820 Moses visited Optino, where he met the bishop of Kaluga, Filaret Amfiteatrov, a great lover of monks. The bishop asked Moses and his friends to come to his diocese to start a small skete under the jurisdiction of Optino Monastery. After some hesitation, Moses agreed to do so. His brother, Anthony, and two Roslavl hermits, Hilary and Sabbatius, came with Moses to Optino. Hardly had they begun to construct the skete, when the bishop ordained Moses on Christmas day, 1825, and appointed him confessor of the monastery. In 1826, when he was forty-three years old, Moses was elected superior of Optino. He remained its abbot for thirty-seven years. The abbey witnessed astonishing progress while he was superior. Several of its monks were chosen to be abbots to other monasteries, the number of monks vastly increased, great churches and buildings were erected, the works of the Holy Fathers were published and enormous crowds from all over Russia started to visit Optino seeking the spiritual direction of its Staretz. The first great Staretz of Optino was Leonid Nagolkin, who came to Optino in 1829. Its second great Staretz, Macarius Ivanov, came in 1834. Abbot Moses Putilov was a wise man and extremely charitable to the poor. He died on June 16, 1862 in his eighty-first year.

Alexander Putilov, Moses' brother and disciple, must be mentioned. Born in 1796, Alexander joined his brother in the Roslavl forest in 1816, where at profession he received the

19. *Žizneopisanie nastojatelja Koz. Ved. Pustyni Arkh. Moiseja* (Moscow, 1882), pp. 27-28.

name of Anthony. He went with him to Optino and remained
in the skete there for eighteen years. Chosen abbot of Maloyaroslavetz in 1839, he retired to Optino because of ill health
in 1852. He died there on August 8, 1865.[20] When he still
lived with his elder brother in the Roslavl forest, Anthony
had some mystical experiences similar to those of St Seraphim of Sarov. Once during the autumn season he was sent
very late at night to look after the nets on a river in the
depths of the forest. He went with fear but he returned in a
very different spirit. "Instead of fear he experienced in his
heart a great joy. Suddenly a light appeared around him and
started to increase until the dark night turned into a bright
day. After some time darkness returned, but the heart of
Alexander was filled with an inexplicable joy such as man
rarely experiences on earth. In his joy he went to the Staretz
(Moses) and told him what he had seen. That entire night he
could not sleep. It seemed to him that he was in paradise.
Such was the joy in his soul."[21] Anthony again experienced
the same phenomenon on Easter night.

Anthony left several letters which have been published.
They well express his spirituality. "Peace of soul is acquired
by a perfect surrender to the divine will, without which
nothing happens. . . . He, in whose heart humility and
meekness are reborn, will find true rest for his soul. He will
be satisfied with everything, grateful for everything, peaceful
and full of love for everybody. He will judge none and will
feel no anger. His heart will be filled with divine sweetness,
that is, he will feel in himself the Kingdom of God because
God grants his grace only to the humble."[22] "We must not
try to find out why this happened in this way, and not in
that, but with childlike obedience we must surrender ourselves to the holy will of our heavenly Father and say from

20. There is a life of Anthony which was published in Moscow in 1870: *Žizneopisanie nastojatelija Marojaroslaveckago Monastyrja Igumena Antonija.*
21. "Pustynniki v Roslavlskich Lesach," *Žizneopisanija* (March, 1907), pp.
162-163.
22. *Pisma k raznym Licam Igumena Antonija, byvšago nastojatelja Malojaros-
laveckago Nikolaevskago Monastyrija,* (Moscow, 1869), p. 143.

the depth of our soul: 'Our Father, Thy will be done! ' "[23]
"Whatever troubles come to you, whatever misfortune happens, say only: 'I shall endure this for Christ's sake.' Only say this and you will feel better."[24] "What is the Kingdom of God? The Kingdom of God is the virtuous life in God, in humility, silence and patience. Living in this way, you will find within yourself the peace of God that is the Kingdom of God, and you will find yourself in the Kingdom of God after death."[25]

The first staretz of Optino, Leonid Nagolkin, was born in 1768 in Karachevo, in the province of Orel. He was an able man with a good memory. He obtained a good position with a wealthy Bolkhov merchant, Sokolnikov. He travelled much in Russia on business and gained much experience and a sound knowledge of men. Religious life greatly attracted Leo (his secular name) Nagolkin. In 1797 he entered Optino Monastery together with the future archimandrite of Simonov Monastery in Moscow, Melchisedek. For some reason he did not remain long in Optino but transferred to Beloberezhsky Monastery, the superior of which was the celebrated Staretz Basil Kishkin who had lived a long time on Mount Athos. After his monastic profession Leo, who changed his name to Leonid, was ordained. During his visit to Cholnsky Monastery, Leonid met Fr Theodore, a disciple of Paisius Velichkovsky. This meeting influenced him for life. In 1804 Leonid was made abbot of Belobereshsky Monastery. In 1805 Theodore came to Beloberezhsky from Cholnsky to initiate Leonid in Athonite mysticism. Within a short time Leonid understood that it was impossible to combine the duties of a superior with a contemplative life. In 1808 he resigned his abbacy and in 1811, seeking a more retired place, went to live in a skete in Valaam, a great monastery on an island in Lake Ladoga. Fr Theodore, also, went there to live. Leonid spent six years in Valaam. He soon acquired a great influence over the monks and visiting pilgrims. This did not please the

23. Ibid., p. 147.
24. Ibid., p. 264.
25. Ibid., p. 290.

superior, Abbot Innocent, who reported to the Metropolitan of St Petersburg that Fr Leonid and Fr Theodore were troubling the community and teaching strange doctrines (Hesychasm). The Metropolitan ordered an inquiry which ended in the complete justification and acquital of both of them. Not wishing to antagonize the abbot of Valaam and considering himself a pilgrim on the earth without the abiding city, Leonid left Valaam in 1817 for a still more remote monastery, Svirsky, in the northern province of Olonetz. On April 7, 1822 Theodore died. After the death of his staretz, Leonid wanted to leave Svirsky Monastery for another but the abbot did not want to lose him and his disciples. Only in 1828 did Leonid finally leave Svirsky Monastery. After a pilgrimage to Kiev and a short stay in Ploshchansky Monastery, where he met Fr Macarius Ivanov, who succeeded him in due course as staretz in Optino, Leonid decided to settle for good in Optino Skete.

Leonid arrived at Optino in April of 1829 and remained there the rest of his life. He introduced starchestvo in Optino and led to its being known all over Russia. E. Poselyanin gives a good description of Starchestvo: "The business of saving one's soul is a difficult one. The unceasing struggle with self, that is, the struggle of the spirit with a nature infected with original sin, and a continuous watch over self, necessary for success in this struggle, are not yet enough. A vast knowledge of human nature and its relations with the external world, of the spiritual benefit and harm which may be derived from contact with this world, and of the way by which grace is obtained is needed. To aid the soul in its exercises, and to preserve its balance, continuous guidance is necessary. Such guidance makes uninterrupted progress toward perfection possible, without the spiritual fluctuations and vicissitudes common to people who have no guide. There is needed someone who knows the soul, its dispositions, abilities and sins, a person with spiritual experience and wisdom one who can guide the soul, encouraging it in times of laziness and sadness and restraining it in times of immoderate elation, one who knows how to humble pride, foresee danger and treat sins with penance. Quick and safe is the way of the man who has subjected himself to such guidance because he practices then two great virtues: obedience and humility. Manifestation of conscience which is the condition *sine qua non* of starchestvo, is a powerful means of progress, terrible to the enemy of our salvation. The unrevealed thought troubles and depresses the soul; revealed, it falls away and does no harm."[26]

In practice starchestvo consists in the daily revelation of thoughts, intentions, temptations and so on to the staretz and accepting his counsel, without resistance, in its entirety, As soon as Fr Leonid arrived at Optino, the Abbot Moses entrusted him with the spiritual direction of all the monks, novices and postulants. The abbot himself sought his direction in everything. Gradually Leonid began to receive visitors and pilgrims for spiritual direction. Soon great crowds started to come to Optino. This created great difficulties for Leonid. Many monks were scandalized by this behavior. They could not understand the evening revelation of thoughts which they took for an irregular sacramental confession. The crowds of layfolk, including women, who visited Leonid appeared to them unbecoming and harmful to a regular monastic life. Complaints were sent to the hierarchy. Leonid was transferred to another cell and obliged to go daily to church in spite of his illness. Layfolk were denied access to him. In the end, however, Leonid was allowed to continue his ministry. In 1834, Fr Macarius Ivanov, a monk of Ploshchansky Monastery and a friend and disciple of Leonid, came to Optino to stay and became a close collaborator of the staretz and, finally, his successor. Shortly before the death of Fr Leonid his influence spread to Tikhonov Monastery in Kaluga where his disciple, Fr Gerontius, was appointed abbot and to Maloyaroslavetz Monastery, where Anthony Putilov, another disciple, became abbot. His ideas also penetrated three convents: Troitsky in Sevsk, Borisov in the Kursk Province and Belev in the Tula Province. Staretz Leonid Nagolkin died on

26. E. Poselijanin, *Russkie Podvižniki 19-go veka* (St Petersburg, 1910), pp. 221-222.

October 11, 1841. He was seventy-two years old. Many sayings of Fr Leonid were written down by various people. He
also left replies to questions put to him and a few letters. His
counsels were always very sound. He once visited Fr Theodosius in Sofroniev Monastery. The latter was well known as
a seer and prophet. Leonid asked the recluse how he knew
the future. The recluse answered that the Holy Ghost himself
told him of the future appearing as a dove and speaking with
a human voice. Fr Leonid said that the Holy Fathers warn
against such manifestations which might well be diabolical
delusions. The recluse became angry and said: "I thought you
came to learn from me. Instead you came to teach me." Fr
Leonid, after leaving the recluse, said to the abbot: "Watch
out for your recluse because he is in a grave danger." Within a
couple of days the recluse committed suicide.[27] Fr Leonid
read the thoughts of men easily and answered questions
before they were put to him. He also healed the sick and the
possessed.

To all visitors Leonid recommended a simple way of life.
He said to one monk: " 'Live simply and God will not leave
you'. . . . Leonid always took the last place and never declined
any request of the superior. On the eve of the great feasts
while others hurried to church, Leonid used to be sent to a
grange to collect hay for visitors' horses. Afterwards, dead
tired and without having any food, he went to choir to sing.
He obeyed without resistance. Try to do the same and the
Lord will manifest to you his mercy."[28] The methods of
spiritual direction used by Fr Leonid are of great interest but
it would take pages to describe them adequately. One monk,
a disciple of Fr Leonid, came to him one evening when the
brethren were visiting the staretz for the daily manifestation
of thoughts. When everybody had left, he asked the staretz:
"I have observed this evening how the brethren have been
coming to you and how they have been received by you. One
monk came before everybody but waited longer than anyone
else and came to you the last. Others, arriving, waited a little

---

27. *Pervyj veliky starec Optinsky,* pp. 64-65.
28. Ibid., p. 71.

and then came to you and explained their cases. Some people did not want to wait at all but as soon as they arrived they went forward and demanded to be received at once. Is there some difference? " "There is a difference," the staretz said, "a big difference. Those who, coming to me, do not want to wait and try to come first of all, are unable to retain in their memory what I tell them. They ask again, and again forget. But those who come to ask my advice and wait with patience and humility, allowing all others to come before them, considering others better than themselves, keep my word firmly in their heart. They will remember as long as they live what I said."[29]

Staretz Leonid did not like those who asked to perform heroic deeds and exercises but were deficient in humility and obedience. One monk of Optino often told Leonid that he desired to suffer martyrdom. The staretz told him that this was a dangerous thought. No one should seek martyrdom unless called by the Lord in the appropriate circumstances. The monk, however, continued to insist upon his wish. The staretz then tested him. One stormy and bitterly cold winter night, he called the monk and told the latter that he intended to send him from the skete to the monastery. The monk began to excuse himself, saying that they were in a great forest, the road was difficult and the blizzard was terrible. "Miserable man," the staretz answered. "You wanted martyrdom and here is the opportunity. The wolves would almost certainly kill and devour you. This death would be the crown of martyrdom for holy obedience."[30] The monk was ashamed and never said another word about his desire.

Another monk wanted to wear chains. Fr Leonid disapproved of this custom. He told the monk that salvation did not depend on wearing chains. Finally, the staretz decided to silence him. He called the monastery's smith and told him: "When a certain brother comes to you asking you to make chains for him, tell him: 'What do you want chains for? ' And then strike him hard in the face." After a short time the staretz said to the monk: "All right, go to the smith and ask

29. Ibid., p. 142.
30. Ibid., p. 143.

him to make the chains for you." The monk ran happily to the smith and said to him: "The staretz has given permission for chains to be made for me." The smith, very busy at the moment, said: "What do you want chains for? " and struck him hard in the face. The angry monk struck the smith in his turn and both came to the staretz. Acquitting the smith, the staretz said to the monk: "How can you dare to wear chains when you are unable to endure a mere slap in the face? "[31]

Fr Leonid left written replies to the questions put to him by Paul Tambovtsev, his disciple who died at the age of twenty-five. Paul's father, a wealthy merchant whom he loved much, committed suicide and this greatly depressed the son. Some of the replies of the staretz give a good idea of his spirituality. When Tambotsev asked Leonid why after five years in Optino he did not seem to make any spiritual progress, Leonid answered: "A very few people within such a short time fly on the wings of faith and the virtues to the spiritual heaven and feel in themselves unmistaken signs of hope, a pledge of the future glory. A few after only a little labor mysteriously feel comfort and consolation, as it were the flowering of sincere works for God which promise the gathering of fruits in the garden of Jesus Christ above. Quite a few during their whole life on the earth never will feel this. This is all according to the discretion of our heavenly Protector and God, whose providence for us is the best. We are babies in relation to the Pantokrator. Often we ask from him means which are in themselves salutary, but which we in our ignorance could use to our own hurt. Therefore, the all-loving Father of lights hides from some godly people gifts which could be salutary to one and destructive to another. What would happen if the all-seeing God were to fulfill all our desires? I believe, although it is only an opinion, that all living things would perish. God, although he does not despise the prayer of the elect, nevertheless does not always grant their requests. He does this solely in order to arrange everything better by his Divine Providence. Besides, those who live without due attention to themselves are never

31. Ibid., p. 143-144.

honored with a visit of grace. If by the sole goodness of God they are so honored, it happens only on their deathbed. To see oneself without progress does not mean that there is no progress. Such feelings may well produce in the heart a true humility. But if you are truly convinced that you are deprived of spiritual gifts, then try persistently to turn to God. When we find ourselves deprived of virtues, we have no exalted idea of ourselves. This may attract divine condescension which will strengthen us against the deadly spirit of despair. When we do not make progress in virtue, the means for salvation present to us is humility. Haughtiness is abominable before God, even with virtues, while a humble thought is not forgotten before God.[32]

When another monk, Fr Anthony Bochkov, later abbot of Cheremenetsky Monastery, asked the staretz whether mental prayer is given to all, the latter answered: "When God visits someone with a painful experience, sorrow, loss of a dear one, this man unwillingly will pray with all his heart, thought and mind. Therefore everyone has the source of prayer. But this source opens either gradually by the deepening of attention to self or immediately by God's touch."[33] To the same monk Leonid explained how divine grace is most easily drawn into our hearts. "If you were as simple in heart as the Apostles were, you would not hide your human faults, would not appear very pious and would live without hypocrisy. This way, which appears so easy, is not given or understandable to all. Yet this is the shortest road to salvation and attracts divine grace. The absence of pretences and of cunning, frankness of soul, this is pleasant to the Lord who is humble of heart. Unless you become as little children, you cannot enter the Kingdom of God."[34]

Fr Leonid was succeeded as staretz, or spiritual director, of Optino by the Staretz Macarius Ivanov.[35] Macarius, an Orel nobleman, was born in 1788. His great-grandfather had died

32. Ibid., pp. 162-164.
33. Ibid., p. 185.
34. Ibid., p. 186.
35. For his life see E. Poselihanin, *Russkie podvižniki 19-go veka* (St Petersburg, 1910), pp. 231-248.

as a monk and his grandparents were known as devout people. After finishing school, Ivanov entered the provincial civil service in Lgov; then he succeeded his father as landowner. In 1810 he made a pilgrimage to Ploshchansky Monastery and decided to become a monk. Five years later he made profession, taking the name of Macarius. The monks of Ploshchansky Monastery lived a very austere life but they knew little of Hesychast prayer and nothing of starchestvo. This changed when Fr Athanasius Zakharov, a former Hussar officer and pupil of Paisius Velichkovsky, settled in the monastery. Soon after Fr Seraphim, pupil of the Staretz Seraphim, was appointed abbot of Ploshchansky. Fr Macarius was ordained by this time. In 1828 Macarius met Fr Leonid Naglokin and became greatly attached to him. He wanted to be transferred to Optino but had to wait until 1834. In 1836 Macarius was appointed the confessor of Optino and three years later superior of the skete becoming thereby Staretz of Optino. Macarius reorganized the skete and constructed many buildings.

Macarius was the staretz of Optino until his death in 1861, nineteen years altogether. While Leonid was from a lower middle class, Macarius was a nobleman with a different background. Well educated, devout and mystical, Macarius was a first class spiritual director. Among his lay disciples and correspondents were several eminent Russians among whom the greatest were the Russian author and playwright, Nicholas V. Gogol and philosopher I. V. Kyreevsky. The former, a Russian classicist, second only to Pushkin, wrote the "Meditation on the Divine Liturgy," while the second collaborated with Fr Macarius in the publication of Patristic and mystical writings. They published Slavonic and Russian translations of Greek manuscripts prepared by Paisius Velichkovsky as well as the treatise of St Nilus of Sora. Altogether sixteen volumes were published. The most precious of these publication, to judge by the results achieved, were the treatises of St Isaac the Syrian, Abbot Dorotheus and St Simeon the New Theologian. A copy of all these publications was sent to all bishops, rectors and inspectors of theological academies and seminaries, to all academy and seminary libraries, to monasteries and to Mount Athos. Fr Ambrose Grenkov, who was to become the third staretz of Optino, Fr Juvenal Polovtsev, future archbishop of Vilna, and Fr Leonid Kavelin, future superior of the Laura of Holy Trinity near Moscow, assisted Fr Macarius in this work.

Already in the time of Fr Leonid vast crowds of people from all over Russia started to come to Optino for spiritual direction, exorcising of the possessed and healing of the sick. Macarius was a very successful spiritual director and had an enormous influence on the monks of the monastery. He never experienced any resistance or critism on their part. He was, moreover, spiritual director of three large monasteries for men, Maloyaroslavetz, Meshchov and Tikhonov and over twenty for women, including those of Sevsk, Belev, Kazan, Serpukhov, Kaluga, Eletz and Bryansk. E. Poselyanin describes the working day of the staretz: "The staretz received men in his cell any time from the early morning until the gates were shut. He received women outside the gates or in a room at the gates. After meals, and a half-hour rest on a narrow bed, he used to go to the guesthouse of the monastery. On the path of the skete and everywhere along the way, multitudes of people waited to consult him about their sins and sorrows and hesitations."[36]

Concerning exterior exercises Fr Macarius kept to the middle way. He tasted all the dishes served in the refectory but ate little. He was hardly ever able to attend the evening meal and ate in his cell. The staretz got up at 2 AM for the long office. He began to receive people at 7 AM and after the community meal he attended a long evening service. The staretz practiced unceasing prayer. The hard life and great labors gradually exhausted him. He died on September 7, 1860, seventy-two years old.

Staretz Macarius left a voluminous correspondence to monks, nuns, clergy, and layfolk. This correspondence was published after his death. Although it is quite impossible to

---

36. Ibid., pp. 239-240.

sum up in a few line, or even pages, the correspondence of
the staretz, some extracts may be given al illustrations.

In his letters to monks, Macarius strongly recommended
the study of the Holy Fathers. "You note," he writes to a
bishop, "that monks nowadays neglect reading the Fathers.
This is why they are so weak."[37] Macarius urged monks who
were called to the priesthood and prelacy to accept the offer
but never to intrigue for promotion. To one monk he wrote:
"This is true, Reverend Father. A heavy yoke is put upon
you and you have received your cross. Still you have expressed your obedience to the will of the Almighty and have
embraced him with tears. You offer thanksgiving and have
not failed. . . . You have succeeded well in your beloved solitude and with a true obedience tasted the incorruptible food
from this tree. Divine Providence put you on the candlestick
to illuminate the district to which you are appointed."[38]

To those abbots for whom power was a stumbling stone,
Macarius suggested retirement: "Remember your intention
and your fervor when you entered the cloister," he wrote to
an abbot, "your vows, your concern, under the direction of
the staretz, for the salvation of your own soul. All that was
earned, but where is it now? The time of impoverishment
came. But why? You say because of the rank of superior.
This is true, unquestionably. However, it is not the rank of
superior, strictly speaking, that is to blame, but your own
spiritual weakness and your unconquered passions, especially
love of glory, comfort and wealth."[39] To the same abbot
Macarius wrote: "When one uses power not for his own
benefit, not for easy living but for the salvation of his
neighbors, then it is a thing full of sorrows and troubles. But
if one wants to exercise authority for honor, glory and pleasure, then he himself and all his subjects fall miserably en-
gulfed in a storm of passions: 'Woe to the city where the king

37. *Sobranie pisem blažennyja pamjatim optinskago starca ieroschimonacha
Makarija k Monasestvjiscim* (Moscow, 1861), p. 4. Some of Macarius' Letters of
Direction have been published in English. See Bibliography.

38. Ibid., p. 37.

39. Ibid., p. 81.

is young.' "[40] Macarius disapproved changing from monastery
to monastery or from job to job. And he warned his monks
that no one should move on to practice Hesychast prayer
unless he had mastered his passions and attained pure prayer.

In his letters to people living in the world, he recommended
particularly that they endure with patience and gratitude all
the sorrows of this life because these save us for eternity and
turn us to God. "The narrow gate and the painful way,"
Macarius wrote to a couple of noblemen, "lead to eternal
life."[41] This is particularly true of sickness. "The most important thing during illness is to offer to God patience and
thanksgiving for his merciful visitations. Sickness purifies sins
and gives one time to meditate on the past."[42] Macarius
always urged surrender to Divine Providence. "Men, however
great and powerful" he wrote in a letter, "can do only that
which God allows them to do. They can do nothing more. If
God has allowed something to happen, it means that this was
necessary and for our benefit. . . . Often we consider something useful and we try to obtain it, but God knows better. If it
is not good for us, he does not give it. We worry about our
present passing life while the Lord thinks of our eternal salvation."[43] Salvation and peace of mind come to them who
follow Christ in humility, charity and obedience. "You want
serenity and peace of mind," Macarius writes to a man, "but
you are unable to attain them. O! This is a great gift of God.
The Lord himself has indicated where to look for them:
'Learn from me because I am meek and humble of heart and
you will find peace for your souls.'[44] In order to attain to
this, temptations and sorrows are necessary. The Lord himself, before his death on the cross, suffered and endured great
agony. He was reproached, tormented, humiliated. He left us
the example we must follow. Read sermons seventy-eight and
seventy-nine in the book of St Isaac. You will find that temp-

40. Ibid., p. 85. Eccles 10:16.
41. Ibid., p. 82.
42. Ibid., pp. 225-226.
43. Ibid., p. 117.
44. Mt 11:29.

tations are needed, why they are allowed, and how one can be freed of them. Moreover, interior spiritual temptations are spoken of there, and how to deal with them. If you should find some of these temptations in yourself, do not be dismayed but humble and quiet yourself. I tell you once again peace and serenity are a great gift, but as soldiers receive rewards for deeds and for shedding their blood, so we, spiritual soldiers, must first endure many temptations and sorrows with humility, accusing ourselves and not others. To subjugate our passions in this way is to overcome them, especially pride and haughtiness, anger and irascibility. When they are overcome we shall be rewarded with peace of mind.

Staretz Macarius Ivanov was succeeded by Staretz Ambrose Grenkov. Staretz Ambrose was spiritual director of Optino for thirty-one years, almost as long as his two predecessors put together. In the time of Ambrose, Optino reached the zenith of its renown and influence. Tremendous crowds used to invade the monastery during his lifetime, in search of healing and consolation. Along with the masses, the most eminent Russian thinkers, writers and statesmen of the age used to visit the staretz, including T. Dostoevsky, L. Tolstoy, Leontiev, Rozanov, V. Soloviev and T. Filippov. Staretz Ambrose and his life in Optino are described by Dostoevsky in his greatest novel, *The Brothers Karamazov*. Vl. Soloviev remembered him as Staretz John in *Three Conversations*. The sister of Leo Tolstoy became a nun of Shamardino, founded by the staretz. The great author died on his way to see her, apparently to die reconciled with the Church.

Alexander Grenkov (the secular name of Staretz Ambrose) was born on November 23, 1812 in a village in the province of Tambov. His father, Michael Grenkov, was the village sacristan. He and his wife had eight children of whom Alexander was the sixth. He was a gay and boisterous boy. When he was twelve he was sent to the Tambov Clerical School and in 1830 he entered the Tambov Seminary. He was a bright student and finished among the first in his class. He liked theology, history and literature. In the seminary he was an active young man who never thought of the cloister. He was, however, very devout. Toward the end of his years in the seminary he fell gravely ill and made a vow to become a monk if he recovered. Healed, he hesitated for four years to fulfill his vow. He spent a year and a half as the tutor in the family of a landowner and then he became a teacher in Lipetzk Clerical School. He even thought of becoming an officer in the army. In the summer of 1839 Alexander Grenkov and his friend P. Pokrovsky visited Hilarion the Recluse in Troekurovo. Hilarion said to Grenkov: "Go to Optino, you are needed there."

This advice Grenkov took as divine guidance and on October 8, 1839 he arrived at Optino where he at once became a disciple of Staretz Leonid Nagolkin. On April 2, 1840 Alexander was received as novice. He served the staretz and was also employed in the kitchen and in the fields. On the eve of his death, Staretz Leonid called Fr Macarius Ivanov, who was to succeed him, and entrusted to Macarius the spiritual formation of Grenkov, saying: "He will be useful to you." In 1842 Alexander Grenkov was professed as a monk with the name of Ambrose and in 1845 he was ordained. In 1846 he again fell dangerously ill. He survived but his health became so delicate that he was freed from all obligations and allowed to live in retirement. He was only thirty-six years old at the time. Apparently his monastic career was over and the only future for him was to vegetate in the infirmary. Remembering that time later on, Staretz Ambrose used to say: "The Lord begins to manifest his strength when he sees that all human means to help the suffering man are exhausted."[45] Although Ambrose's health gradually improved he remained an invalid for the rest of his life. Yet he lived to be nearly eighty and had an exceedingly laborious life as staretz.

At first he began to assist Staretz Macarius in the publication of patristic writings. The latter began also to associate

45. Archimandrite Agapit, *Žizneopisanie v Boze počivsago Optinskago starca ieroshimonacha Amvrosija*, 2 vols. (Moscow, 1900), 1:45. John B. Dunlop has just published a study of Ambrose including many passages from his writings: *Staretz Amvrosy* (Belmont, Mass.: Nordland, 1972).

Ambrose with himself in the spiritual direction of some of the monks, nuns and layfolk. On September 7, 1860 Macarius died and Ambrose carried on his work. In 1862 the abbot of Optino, Moses Putilov, died and was succeeded by Isaac Antimonov, a faithful disciple of Staretz Ambrose. Ivan Antimonov, the son of a very wealthy Kursk merchant, was born in 1809. He was a very able merchant and could have enjoyed life in the world but he was inclined toward the cloister. Still it took him seven years to make the final decision. In 1847 Ivan came to Optino and became a disciple of Staretz Macarius. Professed with the name of Isaac in 1854, Antimonov was ordained in 1858. In 1862 Abbot Moses died and Fr Paphnutius was elected his successor. Staretz Ambrose opposed this election on the grounds that Staretz Macarius had designated Fr Isaac as the next abbot. The election was annulled and the abbot-elect was appointed superior of Maloyaroslavetz Monastery while Fr Isaac was appointed abbot of Optino. He was a very good and fatherly abbot. In his relations with Staretz Ambrose, he remained a lifelong pupil. He did nothing without his blessing. He survived the staretz by three years, dying in 1894, eighty-five years old.[46]

On account of the great multitude which daily visited the staretz, Ambrose had three monks at his disposal to assist him. The office was sung at 4 AM in the special house which he occupied. The staretz used to spend the entire day listening to people who came to him, and giving advice. People lived for weeks in the vast monastic guesthouse before they could get to see the staretz. He received men first and then women, including nuns. At noon he had a simple meal. It took but fifteen minutes. After lunch the staretz again received people and then rested until 3 PM. He received people again until 8 PM when he had a simple dinner. In the evening he received the monks of Optino for direction and attended the evening prayers. He went to sleep at 11 PM or at midnight. The staretz used to give his counsels in a few words, often in

46. His life has been written: *Očerk Zizni nastojatelja Optinoj pustyni Archimandrita Isaakija* (Moscow, 1899).

verses. When he was asked how to live, he answered: "One must live without sadness, judge no one, trouble no one and revere everybody." Another time he said: "We must live without hypocrisy and give a good example. In that case our affairs will go on well but not otherwise." To those who asked him if one could live well in the world, he answered:— "One can live in the world, but not conspicuously, he must live quietly."[47]

"In order to live in the monastery," the staretz said, "one must not have merely one wagonload of patience but a caravan of it. . . . If anyone offend you, tell no one except the staretz and you shall be at peace. Revere everybody and take no notice whether people reciprocate or not. We must humble ourselves before everyone considering ourselves the worst of all. If we have not committed the crimes committed by others, this may be merely because we have had no opportunity, our milieu and circumstances were different. In everybody there is good and bad. We usually see in other people only faults but not their good side."[48] When asked once how the just live according to the will of God and remain humble, the staretz answered: "They do not know what end awaits them. Our salvation must be achieved with fear and hope. No one in any circumstances must let himself despair but it is equally bad to have too much hope." "Once," the staretz said, "a visitor came to Abbot Moses and not finding him at home went to his brother, Abbot Anthony, and asked him: 'Tell me, Father, what Rule do you observe.' And Fr Anthony answered: 'I have observed many Rules. I have lived as a solitary and in various monasteries and they all had different Rules but now I know only one, that of the publican: 'God, have mercy upon me, a sinner.' "[49]

"When you are troubled by others, never ask why and for what cause. There is nothing about this in the Scripture. On the contrary, it says: 'If anyone strike you on the right

47. Agapit, *Žizneopisanie,* 1:97.
48. Ibid., p. 98.
49. Ibid., pp. 98-99.

cheek, turn to him the left as well.' To be struck on the right cheek is indeed unpleasant. This may be understood in this sense: if anyone begins to tell lies about you or molests you without provocation, this is a blow on the right cheek. Do not murmur but endure this blow with patience, turning the left cheek, that is, remember your own unjust deeds. And even if at the moment you are fautless, you have sinned much in the past. You will quickly realize that you merit this punishment."[50]

"Love covers everything. If anyone does good to his neighbor out of affection and not merely out of duty, the devil will not disturb such a man; but where good is done merely out of duty, he tries to make trouble. God has mercy on him who labors, but sends his consolation to the one who loves. Love is, of course, above everything. If you find that you have no love but desire to have it, do the works of love and the Lord will see your desire and effort and will put love in your heart. Take care, when you notice that you have sinned against love, to reveal this to the staretz. Some times it may be from a bad heart and some times from the devil. You cannot distinguish this yourself but when you reveal this to the staretz, the enemy leaves you. A man who has a evil heart must not despair because with the help of God he can correct his heart. We must only observe ourselves closely and miss no opportunity to assist our neighbor, often reveal our state to the staretz and give alms when possible. This, of course, cannot be done at once but the Lord is patient. He terminates the life of man only when sees he is ready for eternity or when there is not hope for his correction."[51]

"Although the Lord forgives the sins of the penitent, every sin demands a purifying punishment. The Lord himself said to the good thief: 'You will be today with me in paradise.' Yet after these words, his legs were broken. How painful it was to hang on the cross with broken legs for three hours. The robber needed this purifying suffering. Sinners who die immediately after

50. Ibid., p. 100.
51. Ibid., p. 101.

repenting are purified by the prayers of the Church and of those who pray for them. But those who are still alive are purified by correcting their lives and giving alms which cover sins. God does not create the cross for man (that is, purifying suffering of body and soul). However heavy is the cross which man carries in his lifetime, its wood is always produced from the ground of his own heart. . . . When man walks on the right road, he has no cross; but when he leaves the straight road and starts to go about on one side or another, then various circumstances arise·which push him back toward the right road. This pushing back creates a cross for man. These crosses differ according to the needs of each one. Go where you are ordered; see what is granted to you and say always: 'Thy will be done.' "

The staretz always said that those who asked his advice must accept it at once as the will of God. If they resist there will be no benefit for the soul. The staretz read thoughts and possessed supernatural powers. Those who rejected his advice always paid by suffering and misfortunes. The staretz also healed the sick and the possessed. The cases are so numerous that long books have been written about them.

Poselyanin describes the external appearance of Fr Ambrose which explains a good deal of his interior life: "The older the Father became, the more kindly and joyous he appeared. He can not be pictured without the compassionate smile which made people happy, good and warmhearted, without his kindly regard which said that something very good is reserved for you. He was always lively in movements, and in his fiery eyes. He listened with attention and you realized that at that moment he lived with you and that he was nearer to you than your very self."[52]

The staretz also founded the great Convent of Shamordino. Nine years after its foundation the convent had five hundred sisters. He died during a visit to the convent on October 10, 1891.

The staretz continued the publication of Patristic writings

52. Poselihanin, *Russkie*, p. 350.

as well as those of the Russian mystics. His letters to monks and nuns were published in two volumes after his death.[53] They are interesting and instructive. The first volume contains explanations and interpretations of various sacred and liturgical texts as well as instructions. The second volume contains only instructions. In contrast to the Staretz Macarius, Staretz Ambrose willingly recommended to religious the Prayer of Jesus, including Hesychast prayer. In one of his letters to nuns, Ambrose wrote: "*Question*: What is better, to read the usual office or to practice the Prayer of Jesus? *Answer:* The best thing is to observe both practices because this was done by such great men as Anthony the Great and St Zosima who saw Mary the Egyptian. While in church we must listen with attention to the reading and singing. Those who are able should continue at the same time the Prayer of Jesus, especially when the reading cannot be heard well. The Prayer of Jesus, according to the Fathers, is always suitable. Whether a man walks, sits, or lies down, eats, drinks, talks, or works, he should say the Prayer of Jesus with humility. He must not give it up. If he does, he must reproach himself and repent humbly but not be dismayed, because dismay, whatever its nature, always shows the secret pride and inexperience of the one concerned."[54] In another letter Ambrose writes: "Among the ancients, the experienced Staretz Basil said, he who observes a long rule of prayer, when he fulfills it, tends to become vain and when he fails, tends to be dismayed. While he who continually practices the Prayer of Jesus, remains always in humility and serenity as one who does little and cannot take pride."[55] In the second volume Ambrose writes more about the Prayer of Jesus and mentions the anonymous writer of the Russian spiritual classic, *Tales of the Russian Pilgrim.* About this author and Staretz Ambrose's view of him, we shall say something later. Generally, in his letters Staretz Ambrose advises surrender to

53. *Sobranie pisem optinskago starca ieroschimonacha Amvrosija monasestvjuscim,* 2 vols. (Sergiev Posad, 1909).

54. Ibid., 1:83.

55. Ibid., p. 177.

Divine Providence, the patient enduring of sorrows and sickness and the exact fulfillment of duties. Staretz Ambrose died on October 10, 1891 in Shamordino Convent. He was buried on October 15 in Optino by Vitalius, bishop of Kaluga, in the presence of a great multitude. This service was more like a canonization than a burial.

Staretz Ambrose was succeeded as staretz by Anatoly, Joseph, Barsanuthius and finally Nectarius, who died in 1928 exiled from Optino which was closed by the Soviet Government some time before. The last four startzy of Optino although they were very saintly men and experienced spiritual directors, never reached the same renown and influence as the first three and, particularly, as Staretz Ambrose.

Even today when no religious literature is available in Russia for the general reader, millions read about and know Fr Ambrose through Dostoevsky's great novel *The Brothers Karamazov.* Indeed, he is known all over the world through the various translations of this novel. The startzy of Optino, as spiritual directors, were practical men. They were not theoreticians of mysticism. The theoretician of this tradition was the last and greatest Russian spiritual writer, Bishop Theophane the Recluse.

CHAPTER X

BISHOP THEOPHANE THE RECLUSE

BISHOP THEOPHANE THE RECLUSE is the greatest Russian writer on mystical subjects not only in the
nineteenth century but throughout Russian history.
Theophane was not only a theoretician of mysticism but also
a man with a profound and varied mystical experience. In
this sense he is quite unique.[1] Bishop Theophane, in the
world George Govorov, was born on January 10, 1815 in the
village of Chernavsk, in the province of Orel. The bishop's
father, Basil Govorov, was rector of Chernavsk and rural
dean. He was a man of great piety and ability. The bishop's
mother was kindly and compassionate, as well as deeply religious. The childhood of the bishop was very happy. He grew
up in Christian surroundings. Well prepared at home, in 1823
George Govorov entered the Clerical School in Livny where
he was one of the best pupils. In 1829 he went on to the
flourishing seminary in Orel. The rector, Archimandrite
Isidore Nikolsky, was afterwards to become the Russian
Primate and Metropolitan of St Petersburg. One of the professors, Fr Plato, became in due course Metropolitan of Kiev.
Govorov was influenced most of all by Mr Ostromuislensky, a
professor of philosophy.

1. There are several lives of Theophane. The best are: P. A. Smirnov, *Žizn i
učenie Preosvjačšennago Feofana, Vyženskago Zatvornika,* (Šack, 1908) and I. A.
Krutikov, *Svjatitel Feofan Zatvornik i Podvižnik Vyšenskoj Pustyni* (Moscow,
1899).

Philosophy and psychology greatly interested Govorov. In 1837 when he finished the seminary with highest honors he was sent to the Kiev Ecclesiastical Academy. In Kiev Govorov was as brilliant a student as he was in Orel. The rector of the Academy, Bishop Innocent, afterwards archbishop of Kherson, and the inspector, Archimandrite Dimitry Muretov, afterwards successor of Innocent in Kherson, were good men and outstanding professors. Two other professors, T. Skvortsov, professor of philosophy, and J. Amfiteatrov, professor of homiletics, greatly influenced Govorov. He was already manifesting an inclination to religious life and often visited the Laura of Kiev, which made a strong impression on him. Finally, he decided to become a monk. He was professed on February 15, 1841 in Kiev. At the same time another student, M. Bulgakov, who would become a Russian Church historian and dogmatic theologian and eventually Metropolitan of Moscow, was also professed. After profession the young monks visited the renowned Kiev mystic, Fr Parthenius, who said to them: "You, learned monks, have much learning, but remember that the most important work is prayer, pray unceasingly to God with mind and heart united. This you must attain."[2] Govorov remembered the advice well!

In 1841 Fr Theophane was appointed headmaster of the Kiev Clerical School; then in 1842, professor of logic and psychology, and inspector of Novgorod Seminary. Two years later Theophane became a professor in the St Petersburg Ecclesiastical Academy. In 1855 he was named rector of Olonetz Seminary, and then he became rector of St Petersburg Academy in 1857. As a professor, Theophane was clear and interesting. He inspired enthusiasm in his pupils. He was specially good in moral theology and in the theory and practice of education. While he was a professor in St Petersburg in 1847 the Russian Government decided to send an ecclesiastical delegation to Jerusalem to study the state of

2. Smirnov, *Žizn i učenie*, p. 19.

Orthodoxy in the Middle East and to establish a permanent
Russian mission in Palestine. The learned archimandrite,
Porphirius Uspensky, was appointed the head of the mission,
and Theophane was a member. The mission was based in
Jerusalem but its members travelled far and wide, to Syria,
Egypt, Sinai, Mt Athos, and so forth, visiting libraries, study-
ing manuscripts, and so on. Theophane worked particularly
in the library of St Sabas Monastery in Palestine and in St
Catherine's Monastery, Mt Sinai. He also visited Coptic monasteries. Unfortunately he was unable to visit Mt Athos,
which the head of the mission reserved for himself. Theophane entered into a close contact with the Orthodox clergy
of these lands. He soon realized that they were very poor and
ignorant, and yet quite haughty. The custom of the Palestinian clergy, eating meat, smoking, and the like, quite scandalized him at first. Theophane also studied the work of the
Catholic and Protestant missions in the Holy Land. During
these years he learned French, Greek, Arabic and Hebrew.
The Crimean War caused the delegation to return to Russia in
1855. En route they spent some considerable time in Italy
and Germany. Theophane particularly liked Florence,
Venice, and Rome. Pius IX received the delegation and complained to them about the conduct of Nicholas I, who, dis-
regarding the Holy See, translated Roman Catholic bishops
from one See to another, and appointed and dismissed them
and other Catholic clergy as he liked. "This," the Pope said,
"is an unheard of thing not only in Europe but elsewhere."[3]
In 1857 Theophane was appointed to represent the Russian
Church in Constantinople during the Bulgarian controversy.
Theophane decided that the Bulgarians had every right to
have their own bishops and clergy and to celebrate in Slavonic as they demanded. The Russian Synod agreed with him.
It was upon his return to Russia from this mission that
Theophane became rector of St Petersburg Ecclesiastical
Academy. He remained there for two years.

---

3. Bishop Porfiri Uspensky described the work of the mission including the talk
with Pius IX in *Kniga bytija moego,* 8 vols. (St Petersburg, 1894-1909).

On June 1, 1859 Archimandrite Theophane was consecrated bishop in the Laura of St Alexander Nevsky in St
Petersburg. He was appointed to the See of Tambov, where
he remained for four years; then he was translated to the
wealthy and important diocese of Vladimir. He remained
there only three years. The episcopate of Theophane coincided with the period of the liberal reforms of Alexander II.
With some of them he sympathized. In his dioceses he
opened a diocesan boarding schools for girls and many parish
schools. He founded diocesan magazines in Tambov and
Vladimir. Theophane did his best to improve the standard of
preaching of the clergy and established special courses for
preachers. The bishop himself was a first class preacher. He
tried to teach people the way of salvation and, in particular,
how to pray. In the diocese of Vladimir, where the so-called
Old Ritualists were numerous and the conversion of Orthodox to them common, the bishop was obliged to preach
against them from time to time. Theophane was a most fatherly bishop and helped his people as much as he could in
cases of fires, accidents, and the like. He himself lived very
simply. He dressed simply and ate only once a day. Toward
his clergy he was very kind and friendly. Although Theophane was an able administrator he did not like to act as
judge. The duty of attending church tribunals was painful to
him. In the last year of his life in Vladimir he left to a priest
of the Cathedral the duty to reprimand and to punish delin-
quents among the clergy. Inclined since his seminary days to
solitude and to prayer, the bishop became more and more
tired of life as an administrator. Like St Tikhon Zadonsky
and Bishop Ignatius Bryanchaninov, he decided, finally, to
resign his see and to become a contemplative monk.

In the spring of 1866 Bishop Theophane requested permission from the Holy Synod to retire to Vysha Monastery in
the diocese of Tambov. On June 17, 1866 the Synod accepted the request and allowed him to retire, appointing him
abbot of Vysha. On June 24 Theophane pontificated for the
last time in his splendid Cathedral. An enormous crowd attended the service and the clergy presented him with a part-

ing address. The bishop, answering the clergy, delivered a
remarkable "testament and will." "Do not reproach me, for
the Lord's sake," Theophane said, "that I leave you. I leave
you not because I am forced to do so. Your kindness would
not allow me to exchange you for another flock. But, as one
who is led, I go to a place which is free of worries, looking
and hoping for the best as it is natural to us. How this intention was formed I cannot explain. I can only say that, besides
external circumstances which influence our deeds, there are
also interior changes which lead to certain resolutions. There is,
besides external necessity, an interior need which conscience
listens to and the heart does not seriously contradict. Finding
myself in such a state, I ask from your love one thing only,
abandoning discussion and condemnation of the step I have
taken, pray for me with insistence that the Lord may not
confound my hope and may grant me, after my labor, to find
what I seek."[4]

Theophane arrived at Vysha on August 3, 1866. He remained there until his death twenty-eight years later. Vysha,
a large and well organized monastery with a hundred monks,
was hidden in the great pine forests. Two rivers, the Tsna and
the Vysha, ran by it. The site was beautiful and remote,
suitable for a contemplative monastery. In his letter to the
Russian Primate, Theophane wrote: "The solitude promises
rest. The monastic regulations here are fine and the community is good. Services are long but one can become accustomed to them. Matins begin at 3 am. Immediately after
them the early Liturgy is celebrated. The late Liturgy takes
place at 8 am Vespers are at 4 pm. At 7 pm we recite compline.
We have some strong men of prayer who stand up throughout
the service and never sit down. They are even offended if
someone ask them to sit down. The monastery is in the
forest."[5] The bishop was lodged in the upper story of a small
house. He had several rooms: a bedroom, living room, chapel

4. Smirnov, *Žizn i učenie*, p. 82.
5. Krutikov, *Svjatitel Feofan*, p. 120.

and a library with a workshop. The bishop was a good ikon painter and worked on wood. His library was very large and well selected. On the whole his style of living was rather like that of the Carthusians in the West.

The first six years of his life in the monastery the bishop used to attend all the offices as well as the early Liturgy. In church he stood motionless, never leaning on anything, with his eyes closed in order not be distracted. It happened occasionally that he did not notice for several minutes that the antidoron had been brought to him. On feast days he himself usually celebrated. During these six years Theophane received visitors and even acted in the beginning as abbot. However on Easter day, 1872, Theophane became a recluse. He ceased to leave his house and receive people, except the abbot of Vysha, his confessor and a monk who served him. Even they came only when he called them. Theophane ceased to go to the monastic church and said his offices alone in his chapel. The first nine years of his reclusion he said Mass every Sunday and feast day. The last eleven years he said Mass daily, always alone, sometimes silently, sometimes singing. Very little is really known about the details of Theophane's life in reclusion. After the services Theophane used to meditate and then, after having a cup of tea, work on his books until dinner. During his seclusion the bishop wrote a good many books, a whole library in fact. His dinner, served at 2 pm, outside the fasts consisted of two eggs and a glass of milk with a piece of bread. After manual work in his workshop the bishop drank two glasses of tea at 4 pm and then went to his chapel to read Vespers and to prepare for the next day's Liturgy. The evening Theophane spent in reading books or answering letters. He received from twenty to forty each day. The bishop received nobody but he was always ready to answer by letter people who asked his counsel in the spiritual life. Theophane never supped. His whole daily food consisted of three cups of tea, a glass of milk, a piece of bread and one or two eggs. During the fasts he took no eggs or milk. In Lent on certain days he took nothing, yet he lived to be nearly eighty, in almost perfect health to the last. Only his eyesight bothered him in the end. Although a recluse, Theophane was well known all over Russia, thanks to his writings and correspondence. He was made an Honorary Fellow of all Russian Ecclesiastical Academies and a Doctor of Divinity. He was once invited to return to the active life. Apparently the Metropolitan See of Kiev was offered to him. Theophane, however, declined the offer.

Although Theophane was a strong and healthy man and quiet life in Vysha suited him well, his astonishing scholarly and literary output, along with severe asceticism and age, gradually wore him down. Twice, in 1878 and in 1879, Theophane left Vysha for treatment of cataracts in his eyes but without result. In 1888 he became blind in one eye, but he continued his work. The Bishop did not change his manner of life until the end. Only five days before his death were some changes made in his time table. Professor P. A. Smirnov thus described his last days: "On the eve of his death, January 5, his Lordship, feeling weak, asked for help to walk. The keleinik (the monk who served the bishop) assisted Bishop Theophane for a few turns around the room. But his Lordship, quickly becoming tired, sent the keleinik away and went to bed. On the day of Theophane's death the keleinik, hearing no accustomed knock, looked into the study of the bishop at 1 pm. The bishop was sitting and writing something. . . . After half an hour there was a slight knock. During the meal the bishop consumed half of the egg and drank half of the glass of milk. Hearing no knock for tea the keleinik looked in at 4:30 pm. The bishop was lying in bed . . . dead. His left hand rested on his breast while the right was formed as for the episcopal blessing. When the bishop was pontifically vested a smile clearly appeard on his face."[6] The bishop died four days before his eightieth birthday. He had no long sickness and no agony. The bishop of Tambov buried Theophane in the presence of a vast multitude.

During his twenty-eight years in Vysha, Theophane wrote a

6. Smirnov, *Žizn i učenie*, p. 325.

great deal. He left a veritable library. His works on the spiritual and mystical life are the most important. They include:
1. *Letters on Spiritual Life;* 2. *Letters on Christian Life;* 3. *Letters to Various People on Various Subjects of Faith and Life;* 4. *What is the Spiritual Life and How to Lead It;* 5. *The Way of Salvation;* 6. *On Penance, Communion and Reformation of Life;* 7. *On Prayer and Vigilance.* The bishop also wrote commentaries on nearly all the Epistles of St Paul and on Psalms 33 and 118. He translated and edited the *Dobrotolyubie, Ancient Monastic Rules,* the *Spiritual Combat* of Lorenzo Scupoli and the *Sermons* of St Symeon the New Theologian.

The most important work of Theophane is the *Way of Salvation.*[7] It sums up rather well the spirituality of the Recluse. According to the *Way* the purpose of Christian life is union with God. The way to this union lies through faith and life according to commandments of God. The Christian is saved by the grace of the Holy Spirit, which is given freely because of the redeeming merits of the God-Man. The Christian achieves his salvation under the guidance of the Church. In order to attain the age of Christ the sinner must cleanse himself first with external ascetical exercises and then with interior purification. There are three states: the beginning of Christian life, growth and strengthening in it, and, finally, perfection. In other terms the first stage is conversion, the second, purification, and the third, consecration. In the first stage man turns from sin to the light of Christian truth and virtues, in the second he prepares himself for the reception of the Lord by being cleansed from interior impurities and in the last the Lord comes and dwells in the heart of man. Christian life begins with baptism and develops in the Christian family with the proper education of the children which determines their future. People, however, generally lose the grace of baptism through sin and fall into a spiritual torpor which manifests itself in worries about a multitude of things, worldly interests and business and indifference to and neglect

7. *Put ko spaseniju (Kratkij Očerk Askitiky)* (Moscow, 1908[9]).

of the spiritual life. A few only awake from this spiritual
torpor, under the action of divine grace, either through a
sudden and complete conversion, as in the case of St Paul or
St Mary the Egyptian, or through a gradual change in their
life. In the latter case a thought comes to a man to live
better, in a more Christlike manner. Usually such a thought,
although welcomed, does not lead to a radical change. Conversion is ordinarily postponed to some future date when
there will be "more opportunities." The bishop advises
against the postponement of conversion to some future date
and opportunities; they may never come. The beginning of
conversion is the mastery of the body. This is attained with
ascetical exercises. But they are merely the beginning. There
are two far more formidable obstacles: worries and incon-
stancy of mind. "Worries," the bishop writes, "do not leave
one time to take care of oneself. With them there is one
business at hand and dozens in the head. In this way, worries
push a man forward all the time leaving him no opportunity
to consider his position. Therefore, put aside, for a time, all
cares, without any exception. You can take them up in due
course but for the time being cast them out altogether. But
even then, when worrying and anxiety are given up, confusion reigns for a long time in the head. Thoughts race
through, one after another, and contradict each other. The
soul is distracted. The mind sometimes leans to one side and
sometime to another, preventing the establishment of something permanent and firm."[8] It is impossible, according to
Theophane, to attain any modicum of spiritual stability
without retiring into solitude. The best place to retire is a
monastery, the remoter the better, and the best time is Lent.
In solitude man gradually comes to himself and acknowledges
his sinfulness and corruption. He then comes to a desire to
reform his life. He hears the interior voice which says: "Stop,
to where have you come? " A fear is born from contemplation of one's vices, passions and faults. When grace has awak-
ened his soul, man realizes his dependency on God and the

8. Ibid., pp. 108-109.

horror of sin. His conscience starts to trouble him and he understands the sweetness of life in God as the safest and happiest refuge from all troubles. But hardly does a man make the resolution to change his life when all his habits, customs and manners revolt at the sacrifice imposed on them. Only divine grace and a firm resolution can save him.

Spiritual consolations and good intentions, according to Theophane, may keep a man from backsliding but they are unable to make him progress. For this, divine grace is needed. The first thing to do is to find out the root of sin. Softness toward self, sensuality, fear of men and "earthliness" are the chief features of the sinful heart. We all are apt to look on ourselves like a loving mother on her children, excusing ourselves in every possible way and regretting our sad fate brought on, it is supposed, by unhappy circumstances and the intrigues of others. Sensual passions of every kind keep us in bonds. We are afraid to do right things in order not to disturb public opinion however wrong it may be. Finally, we are so attached to material things, comfort, money, goods and so on that the spiritual world hardly exists for us. We must be merciless to self, indifferent to sensuality and public opinion and consider ourselves pilgrims on the earth. We must say within ourselves: "I rise up and come." The first movement of the sinner is toward self and the second to God. When man, abandoning sin, comes to the border of light and is ready to ascend, the devil comes and whispers: "One day more and then," suggesting the postponement of the spiritual struggle. The soul, already tired from the previous struggle, wants a rest. It does not resist good but only asks for less tension. If the concession is granted, everything is lost and the old habits and customs come back strengthened. The sole way out is to march forward without surrender.

Starting the Christian life, we must dedicate it to God. The Christian must do good not only for its own sake and because it is demanded by the moral dignity of man but because it is a sacrifice pleasing to God. The Lord gave to man moral freedom in order that man might return this gift to God as the supreme sacrifice. The first thing to do is to repent truly, so strive for the fullest possible confession. This purification is to be followed by Holy Communion which strengthens a man for a new life. Conversion is a pledge of new life, confession and absolution are the assertion of it, Communion is union with Christ. From the moment it is received grace begins to flow. As food is necessary to preserve the body, so Communion is necessary for spiritual life. Offering to God our freedom, we return to him as runaway slaves. In order that God would receive us, we must acknowledge our sins, repent and promise to sin no more. We must imitate the prodigal son who on his return to the father asked to be received as a servant. Sin leaves its traces everywhere in us and around us. To live in Christ is to have an intense Eucharistic life.

From entering into new life to living in union with God, the distance is great. The long road must be filled with ascetical exercises and interior purification. According to Theophane, there are three kinds of union with God: the first is mental, existing during the period of conversion, and other two are factual, but one of them is hidden, invisible to others and unknown to self, while the second is visible to everyone.[9] Success depends greatly on initial fervor. Those who want to preserve an intense fervor must live within themselves, contemplate the new world and cultivate thoughts and feelings proper to a new life. The term *Vnutr-prebuivanie*, staying within, means strictly speaking a conscious centering in the heart, an intensive gathering thereto of all the forces of soul and body, using the essential means, the exercises of the spiritual life. He, who abides within the heart, is recollected, and he who is recollected, is in the heart. Around the consciousness in the heart all forces, mind, will and feelings must be gathered. The gathering of the mind in the heart is attention, the gathering of will, readiness and the gathering of the feelings, watchfulness. Attention, readiness and watchfulness are three interior works which affect the gathering of self and, signify the staying within (recollection). He, who has all

9. Ibid., p. 177.

things, without exception, within himself is within, while he, who lacks even one of them, is outside. Therefore, all the work of staying within, through self-gathering, consists in the following:

"In the first moment after awakening, as soon as you come to yourself, descend into the heart, and then call, appeal, force thereto all the forces of the body and soul, by the attention of the mind, by turning the eyes thereto, by readiness of will with a certain tensing of the muscles, and by watchfulness over the feelings. Repress feelings of pleasure, especially of the flesh, and do this until consciousness has firmly established itself in the heart as on a throne. Remain there all the time while you still have consciousness. Repeat often this exercise because self-gathering needs continuous renewal and strengthening."[10] Every spiritual work requires great concentration. The Kingdom of God is within us and in order to find it we must, according to the Savior, enter into the room of our heart. He who enters the heart and gathers there all his forces is a flaming spirit.

He who enters into his heart is on the threshold of the new world and life. He must impress the structure of the spiritual world on his consciousness and receive it in his feelings. The bishop describes the structure of this invisible and spiritual world in these words: "The one God, worshipped in Trinity, who created and maintains everything, guides all of us in our Lord Jesus Christ through the Holy Ghost, who acts in the Holy Church and translates the faithful, when they are perfect, into another world. This will continue until the time of fulfillment or the end of the world comes. Then, after resurrection and judgment, everyone shall receive according to his deeds. Some will fall into hell while others will go to paradise and God will be all in all."[11] We must meditate on these subjects one after another in order to understand their complexity. Some subjects are proper for meditation on certain days while others are good for a part of each day.

10. Ibid., pp. 205-206.
11. Ibid., p. 210.

Theophane then gives various counsels on meditation. Those who have entered a new life must necessarily change their manner of living. They must give up manners and habits contrary to the Spirit of Christ and oust passions, replacing them by purity. Monastic life is the best condition for this work. Virtues are acquired first through ascetical exercises and then through the interior cleansing of heart. The necessary ascetical exercises are fasting, manual labor, vigils, solitude, prayer, reading Holy Scripture and the Fathers, retreats and works of charity, material and spiritual. Depending on one's past, the character of the exercises changes. There is a hunger for unceasing prayer, long fasts, frequent Communion.

To form the heart means to educate it in the desire for everything holy and in indifference and disgust to every passing thing. When the mink contemplates the spiritual world and the heart rejoices in it, the soul, dead to sin, awakens. Nothing helps as much to cultivate the heart as worship, private and public, and a prayerful spirit. Participation in the liturgy revives the soul and introduces it to a new world. The bishop advises attendance at all Church services, matins, Liturgy and vespers, as often as possible. The Church is paradise. While we must cultivate private prayer, the great Church solemnities should not be neglected. All this is important and helpful if a prayerful spirit is to be preserved. When fervor subsides, retreats, confessions and Communion are indicated. Finally the entire life becomes a continuous retreat. Every sin which troubles the conscience must be immediately confessed. Neglected it leads to indifference in religion, but confessed it leads to warm tears of repentance. The bishop advised the daily examination of conscience, continuous watchfulness over thoughts, and spiritual direction by a staretz.

The last pages of the book are devoted to rules for the struggle with the passions and the progress of man toward union with God. In his description of the struggle with the passions, the bishop follows the Fathers, especially St Nilus of Sora. His method of dealing with thoughts is the same as we described when speaking of St Nilus. When the struggle with the passions is over, man is on the threshold of living in union with God. The first sign is the abandonment of all worry about oneself and complete surrender to the Divine Will. "He who surrenders himself to God or is honored with this gift, begins to be moved by him and lives in him. Freedom is not destroyed but exists because self-surrender is not a final, confirmed act but one continually repeated. Man surrenders himself to God and God takes him and acts in him or through his faculties. In this consists the true divine life of our spirit. He who surrenders himself into the divine hands receives from God and acts with what he has received. This is a living union, life in God."[12] Those who have attained perfect surrender to God and unceasing prayer are ripe to enter solitude. "He who has tasted divine sweetness hungers insatiably after solitude in order to be filled with it without any obstacles. He continually engenders in himself fire with fire, effort with effort, desire with desire. Therefore, the solitary is the earthly image of the angel. . . . Those who love blessed solitude live as angels and imitate their manner of life. The angels will never be sated with glorifying the Creator, neither will those who ascended to the heaven of solitude."[13] "Impassibility is the final crown." The impassible man is indifferent to all objects which inspire and feed on passions. They produce no impression on him even if they are before him. This is because he is united with God. . . . He who is honored with such a state even here, in the flesh, becomes a temple of the Living God, who guides and instructs him in all his words, deeds and thoughts. . . . Those who reached this state are friends of God and their state is the same as that of the Apostles because they, too, recognize the Divine Will in everything. . . . Because the apostolic state is the fruit of solitude when it is well lived, not all solitaries are left by God in solitude forever. Those who have attained to impassibility through solitude and are honored with true divine union and the habitation of God within are often taken for the service

12. Ibid., pp. 306-307.
13. Ibid., pp. 308-309.

of those who look for salvation. Such a holy man serves, teaching, guiding, working miracles."[14] "We know nothing here on the earth above the state of apostles. Here is the end of the survey of the God-pleasing-life."[15] Theophane ends his book with these words.

The letters of Bishop Theophane give deep insight into his spirituality and are full of precious counsels and instructions. They illustrate his *Way to Salvation*. In one letter Theophane gives a real treatise on prayer. "Prayer," he writes, "is the elevation of the mind and heart to God in praise, thanksgiving and petition for the spiritual and material goods we need." The essence of prayer, therefore, is the ascent of the mind from the heart to God. The mind stands up in the heart, in full consciousness, before God and, filled with proper devotion, begins to open to him its heart. This is mental prayer. But every prayer must be like that. External prayer, in church or at home, merely gives to prayer words and form but the soul or the substance of prayer everyone has in his mind and heart. All our order of church prayer, all prayers composed for home use, are full of the mind's appeal to God. He who uses them, even with little attention, cannot avoid this mental appeal to God unless he is altogether neglectful of what he does. No one can go without this prayer of the mind. We cannot avoid ascending to God in prayer. Our spiritual nature demands this. We cannot ascend to God in any other way but mentally because God is a spirit. It is true there is prayer of the mind, going together with vocal or external prayer, in church or at home, and there is mental prayer as such without any exterior form or bodily posture. But the substance of the work is the same in both cases. In both forms it is obligatory for laymen as well.[16]

"The Savior commanded us to enter into our inner room and there to pray to God the Father in secret. According to St Demetrius of Rostov, the room means the heart. Conse-

14. Ibid., pp. 312-314.
15. Ibid., p. 314.
16. *Pisma k raznym licam o raznych predmetach very i žizni* (Moscow, 1892²), pp. 381-382.

quently, the commandment of the Lord obliges us to pray mentally in our heart to God. This commandment extends to all Christians. The Apostle Paul commands the same, saying that we must pray in spirit always.[17] He commands mental or spiritual prayer to all Christians without exception. He also orders all Christians to pray unceasingly.[18] To pray unceasingly is possible only in the heart. Therefore, it is impossible to contest the fact that mental prayer is compulsory for all Christians, and if it is obligatory, it is also possible because God does not command the impossible. That this prayer is difficult is true. However it is not impossible. But, generally speaking, every good is difficult. Prayer is necessarily still more so because it is the source of all good and its surest mainstay.

"If someone should ask: how am I to pray? , the answer is very simple: fear God. Experience of the fear of God arouses attention and consciousness in the heart and forces it to stand with devotion before God. This is a mental 'standing before God' —mental prayer. So long as fear of God remains in the heart, so long mental standing before God will not disappear from the heart. Here is an all-powerful help in mental prayer. If someone should say: business distracts me, we answer that you have not the fear of God. Business is not an obstacle to mental standing before God nor to the memory of God, but an empty and evil life. Oust every empty and evil thing from your life, leaving only duty according to the commandments of the Gospel, and you will see that the fulfillment of your obligations does not separate you from God. On the contrary, it attracts your mind and heart to him. Deeds and prayer prescribed by the Gospels are the same and demand the same regime of the soul. Whatever you shall do in this sphere, you should always turn to God, asking his assistance and dedicating your deeds to his glory. Rising up in the morning, stand firmly before God in your heart during your morning prayer and afterwards go to the job appointed

17. Eph 6:18.
18. 1 Thess 5:17.

to you by God, remaining with him in your feelings and consciousness. You will then accomplish your work with your bodily and spiritual faculties, while remaining in God in mind and heart.[19]

"Those who suppose that to practice mental prayer we must sit secretly somewhere and in this way contemplate God do not understand mental prayer. We do not need any hidden place but our heart. We must stand there and contemplate God before us as if he were on our right hand, as St David did. People say that for the cultivation of mental prayer solitude helps much, and for laymen this is impossible. They live in unceasing business and conflicts. Therefore, they have no time for mental prayer. It is true that for mental prayer solitude is needful but there are two kinds of solitude. The first is complete and permanent, when people retire to a desert to live alone and the second, partial and temporary. The first undoubtedly, is unsuitable for laymen but the second is possible for them, too, and they have it. Everybody has some moments in the day when he is alone, even if he did not try to arrange for himself a few hours of solitude. This time he can employ in the development and strengthening of his mental prayer. Consequently, no one can excuse himself by saying he has no time to practice mental prayer. Find an hour and look into yourself. Give up all worries, stand mentally in your heart before God and open to him your soul.

"Besides external solitude there is also interior solitude. Outside there can be the usual stream of human affairs and at the same time, in the midst of them there can be one who stands in the heart taking no notice of what is going on about. Everybody knows that when one is preoccupied with sorrow he neither sees nor hears even in the gayest and noisiest of crowds. He is alone in his heart with his sorrow. Everybody knows that from personal experience. If this is so in ordinary life, the same can happen in the spiritual life. When one begins to be sorrowful in heart, he will be able to fix his consciousness in his heart. Therefore, it is enough to strive for this interior state in order to be solitary every-

19. *Pisma kraznym*, pp. 382-383.

where. This is not so difficult. Revive the fear of God and you will soon be sorrowful and contrite, fixing your attention on the one thing needful: how we must appear before the face of God. This is solitude. One more difficulty: in the practice of mental prayer a guide is needed. Where can a layman find one? "There where he is, in the world." It is true that fewer and fewer are the people to whom one can turn safely for advice in the spiritual life. But they exist and will continue to be there. He who wants them can always find them with the grace of God. Spiritual life is divine life. God has a special providence for those who seek it. Only desire and you will find everything needful around you."[20]

In one letter Theophane writes on the Prayer of Jesus said vocally, mentally and in the heart. Speaking of the first prayer he says: "In the shortened form this prayer is said as follows: 'Lord Jesus Christ, have mercy on me, a sinner.' In full the prayer is said thus: 'Lord, Jesus Christ, Son of God, have mercy on me, a sinner! ' In the beginning this prayer is said in most cases with compulsion and unwillingly. After some practice and self-compulsion, if there is a firm intention to master our many passions by means of prayer and divine assistance, this prayer, because of practice and the decrease of passions, will gradually become easier, pleasanter and more lifegiving. In vocal prayer every effort must be made to fix the mind on the words of prayer, to speak slowly, turning our whole attention to the ideas expressed in the words. When the mind turns to alien thoughts we must, without dismay, fix it again on the words of our prayer. The absence of distractions is given to the mind only after a long time, and not when we want it, but when we are humbled and God grants it to us.

"From attentive vocal prayer we pass to mental prayer. The latter takes place when we ascend mentally to God and see him. Practicing mental prayer, we must keep our attention in our heart before the Lord. According to our effort and humble perseverance in prayer, God grants to our mind the first gift: integration and concentration in prayer. When attention to

20. Ibid., pp. 383-385.

the Lord becomes permanent, this is the grace of attention. Our own attention is always accompanied with an effort. From mental prayer we pass to interior prayer of the heart, if only there is an experienced teacher. When the feelings of our heart abide with God and the love of him fills our heart, then our prayer is called the prayer of the heart.

"It is said in the Gospel: 'If anyone wants to come to me, let him renounce himself and take up his cross.'[21] If we apply these words to prayer, they mean this: he who wants to exercise himself in prayer must first renounce his own will and his own judgments and take up his cross. This is that bodily and spiritual labor which is essential for this exercise. Surrendering ourselves altogether to the ever watchful Divine Providence, we must humbly and willingly endure labor for the sake of the true good which is given in due course by God to the fervent man of prayer, when God, by his grace, sets limits to our mind and establishes it unmoved in the memory of God in the heart. When such a state of mind becomes natural and permanent, it is called by the Fathers the union of the heart with the mind. In this state the mind has no more desire to wander outside the heart. On the contrary, if by circumstances or conversations the mind is retained outside the attention of the heart, it will experience an overpowering desire to return within itself, thirsting spiritually and burning with desire to continue the construction of its interior mansion. In this centering in the heart everything in man descends from the head to the heart. Then some mental light illuminates the interior man. Everything that he does, says and thinks is done in full consciousness and attention. Man is able then to see crystal clear the ideas, intentions and desires that come to him. He willingly forces his mind, heart and will in obedience to Christ to observe every divine commandment. With feelings of repentance of heart and contrition he rules out of his life every breach of the commandments. Filled with sincere and humble regret, he painfully prostrates before God, begging for assistance for his frailty. God, seeing

21. Mt 16:29.

such humility, does not deprive man of his grace. Know also that before the destruction of the passions there is one prayer and afterwards when the heart is freed from the passions another. The first prayer is a help during the purification from passion, while the second is like some spiritual gauge of future beatitude."[22]

In his letter to Mother Magdalen, Megaloschema (a nun who has received the great "angelic" habit) of Znamensky Eletsky Convent, Theophane wrote of the highest state of prayer which he himself experienced: "In the beginning, when someone turns to the Lord, prayer is the first exercise. He starts to go to church and to pray at home either with a prayerbook or without one. But his thoughts wander all the time. It is impossible to control them. But with exercise in prayer his thoughts begin to settle down and prayer becomes purer. Nevertheless, the atmosphere of the soul remains un-purified until a spiritual flame appears in his heart. This little flame is the work of divine grace which is common to all and is nothing special. This flame appears as the result of a certain measure of purity in the moral life of the man who is making progress. When this little flame appears or when a continuous warmth is formed in heart, then the whirling of thoughts stops. The same thing happens to the soul as happened to the woman who experienced the loss of blood: 'The issue of her blood stopped.'[23] In this state prayer becomes more or less unceasing. The prayer of Jesus serves as an intermediary. This is the limit which prayer practiced by man can attain without special grace. I believe that all this is clear to you. Later on in that state infused prayer which is not the work of man comes as a gift. A prayerful spirit comes and summons one down into the heart, just as one person might take another by the hand and draw him forcibly from one room into another. The soul is bound by an external force and remains willingly within while the prayerful spirit is with it.

"I know two degrees of this infused prayer. In the first

22. *Sobranie Pisem Svjatitel Feofana,* 6 vols. (Moscow, 1899), 5:226-228.
23. Lk 8:44.

degree a soul sees everything and has a consciousness of self
and of the external world. It can judge and rule itself. It may
bring this state to an end if it wants to. This, too, must be
understandable to you. The Holy Fathers, particularly St
Isaac the Syrian, indicated a second degree of gratuitously
given or infused prayer. Beyond the prayer which I have just
described, St Isaac mentions another prayer which he calls
ecstasy or rapture. Here, too, a prayerful spirit comes, but
the soul led by it enters into such contemplation that it
forgets its external location. It does not meditate but contemplates. It has no more power over itself and is unable to
end this state at will. Remember what is written in the *Paterikon*, how someone stood for prayer before his evening meal
and came to himself only in the morning. This is the prayer of
rapture or contemplation. In some people this prayer has
been accompanied with a luminous radiance of the countenance and all around the person; in other people, it is accompanied by levitation. St Paul the Apostle in this state was
taken to paradise. The holy prophets were in this state when
the spirit carried them away."[24]

Theophane was familiar with Western Catholic mysticism
and, on the whole, was favorable to it, in contrast to Bishop
Ignatius Bryanchaninov who severely condemned it for its
unrestrained use of imagination in prayer. Ignatius wrote on
The Imitation of Thomas a Kempis: "It leads its reader
straight to union with God without the preliminary purification
by penance. Therefore, this book inspires pleasure and sympathy in those who are not prepared and warned by the doctrine of the Holy Fathers of the Orthodox Church, and who
are not familiar with the way of penance. *The Imitation* is
particularly liked by people who are slaves to their senses.
One can take pleasure in what it speaks of without giving up
sensuality."[25]

Ignatius was even harder on St Ignatius Loyola and
St Francis of Assisi whom he took for deluded men.
Abbot Anthony Putilov, a monk of Optino and superior of

24. Ibid., 4:241.
25. Episkop Ignatij, *Sočinenija*, 1:157.

Maloyaroslavetz, was more favorable to Thomas a Kempis. In
one of his letter to the people whom he directed he advised
them to read it. He also quoted form St Catherine of Siena.
Theophane translated *The Spiritual Combat* of Lorenzo
Scupoli but modified it considerably. He used the Greek
translation of Scupoli made by St Nicodemus the Hagiorite,
who himself had edited the text. I have been told by Western
contemplatives that Theophane's text of *The Spiritual Combat* is far superior to the original.

In one of his letters to a lady, Theophane wrote: "Take for
translation *The Introduction to the Devout Life* by Francis
de Sales. I have this book. It has an appendix with many
letter, chiefly those written to console and warn laymen. . . .
These letters could form a separate volume and *The Introduction* another. . . . I finished the translation of *Spiritual Combat*. I am now translating something from the French, similar to *The Introduction* of Francis but a bit more refined
and contemplative. When Duzhepolesnoe Chtenie finishes the
printing of *The Spiritual Combat* I shall ask them to print
what I am now translating."[26] A short time later the bishop
wrote: "I informed you that I had started to translate something. I reached the chapters on prayer. What obscurity and
confusion! I have stopped. . . . The Latins do not understand
mental prayer as we do. With them it is meditation concluded
with a prayer. Although meditation is a very fruitful exercise,
it is not prayer. Prayer and meditation are different exercises.
I devoted twenty-two chapters to this alone. I do not know
whether I shall have any desire to rewrite the book. In *The
Spiritual Combat,* which is also the translation of a Catholic
book, I have many changes."[27] Returning to the same subject
Theophane wrote: "Try to translate Francis. We shall see.
Why did I give him up? Because it will be necessary to make
changes. In *The Spiritual Combat* I recast several chapters.
That book is written by a Catholic and the Catholics do not
judge mental prayer and other ascetical exercises as we do.

26. *Sobranie Pisem,* 6:111.
27. Ibid., p. 115.

Staretz Nicodemus made some corrections but not enough. I have completed the work of correction. Remember, I wrote to you that I was translating a book similar to the *The Spiritual Combat?* I reached the part on prayer and stopped. The author says: 'I shall now speak of mental prayer,' and he speaks all the time on meditation and more meditation. Twenty chapters and more on it. And everything is so complicated! It is hardly possible to correct. I have given it up until I recover my courage. In this bout of displeasure with the book I was translating I even became displeased with Francis . . . although he is much simpler. . . . All right, translate. We shall clean up Francis and straighten things out so much that no one will recognize him."[28] In a last letter on the subject, Theophane writes: "Finally, Francis de Sales. . . . How to begin? Make an abstract from his life, very short, in ten lines, at most one printed page, giving the most important points. . . . Afterwards, the conclusion—and do not worry. There is no need to be a slave of the letter. You should translate in such a way that it comes forth as words of your own from your own heart . . . straight, clear, balanced warm. In one place you may add something, in the other place you may shorten, in a third place you may change. You should have in view edification and adaptability to life. *The Spiritual Combat* is hardly ever translated word for word. Several chapters have been rewritten. Everything on prayer is rewritten. You can do the same. We shall call it a free translation."[29]

Let us conclude our study of Theophane with a few quotations from his letters which give a good idea of his spirituality. "Christian faith is not a doctrinal system but a way of restoration of fallen man through the death of the God-Man and the grace of the Holy Spirit. Take anyone who has followed the Lord and you will see that little by little he grows in spirit and becomes great in spite of all his insignificance. Fr Seraphim is an example. He was a simple, unlearned man and

28. Ibid., p. 117.
29. Ibid., p. 123.

yet to what heights he attained! He closed the mouth of erudite unbelievers with a single word. This is strength. And his life and his manners? Grace remakes in this way all those who submit to it."[30]

"In the spiritual life there is the city of Light and many roads lead to it . . . and everyone can reach it. But if one starts to change roads, even on the advice of an experienced man, he might very well never reach that city. . . . Marital life does not close the gate of heaven. It need not create obstacles to spiritual perfection. Perfection lies not in any external regime but in interior dispositions, feelings and intentions. Try to plant them in your heart. Read the Gospels and the Epistles and consider how a Christian should live, then do the same."[31] "Is writing a service to the Church or not? If it is so, and is fitting and necessary for the Church, why should you seek or desire another service."[32]

"If you believe in a Divine Providence which determines the earthly fate of everyone and the way by which he is to be saved, you must also believe that the disposition of your life is the most suitable for you in working out your salvation. As I see it, it gives you complete freedom to be preoccupied with your soul. This is a great privilege. Realizing this, thank God for everything pleasant and otherwise. Enduring cheerfully unpleasant things, you approach a bit to the martyrs. But if you murmur, you will not only lose that 'part' but will be responsible for your murmuring besides. Be cheerful."[33]

"God brings about the salvation of everyone in this way. Those who are disposed he attracts to the Son. The Son accepts each as he comes, and each is then transfigured by the grace of the Holy Spirit. This is the first, preliminary period. It lasts from the initial conversion until the time when the voice in the heart says: 'God does everything in all.' Complete abandonment to Divine Providence then comes to birth and God begins to act in man but through man's own

30. Ibid., 1:148.
31. Ibid., pp. 118-120.
32. Ibid., 6:11.
33. Ibid., p. 348.

forces. This is the second period—God-manhood. The third
period is rest in God. The true place for this rest is in the
world to come, but the beginning of it we have here. Most
people are in the first period, some are in the second, only a
few reach the third, but in heaven all the saints are in this
period, yet each according to his own proper rank. This is
eternal beatitude."[34]

"The ultimate end of the world process we may describe as
the spiritualization of reasonable creatures through moral
order and the rest in some related order. St Paul gives us
reason to think so, when he says that our body in the world
to come will be not only incorruptible but somehow ethereal
or even spiritual. Because even then the body will not be
separated from the entire concert of being, but will remain in
essential connection with it, we may conclude that everything will be related to it, becoming not only incorruptible
but spiritualized. This spiritualization we see in progress in
reasonable creatures through the mystery of the incarnation.
We can suppose that spiritualization is in progress, for the
same reason, in the material world, but only invisible. At
the end of the world the invisible shall become visible. Everything will be spiritualized: 'There will be a new heaven and a
new earth.' Their present appearance will wear out and disappear.[35]

"The Triune God guides the world to its last destination.
Because the salvation of men is the condition *sine qua non* of
the completeness of the world's existence, Divine Providence
is centered now on this. It cares only to convert sinners and
to purify and spiritualize the converts. The Incarnation, the
angels and saints, all serve this purpose. All the forces are
directed to it by divine order. Nevertheless, not everybody is
saved. This is so because God does not force men. What is the
proportion of those who want to be saved? Everybody can
judge by the proportion of the perfect in every generation."[36]

"All heaven is boundless light. The Tri-hypostatic, Tri-
illuminated Deity is hidden by the impassable divine light

34. *Pisma k raznym licam,* p. 445.
35. Ibid., p. 464.
36. Ibid., p. 465.

which can only be mentally contemplated. But God the Incarnate Word, although he shines with light of an intensity which created light never possessed, yet his light is accessible to the created eyes and is received according to the perfection of the creature who looks on him. Our Lady, the Theotokos, is nearest. Farther away are the Apostles and the Prophets, who were God-enlightened even here on the earth. After them come the secondary depositories of Divine Revelation. Then all the saints in their various degrees: martyrs, ascetics, just men from all states and conditions of life. All are inundated with light coming out from the Face of our Lord and Savior, a light beyond all description. Below the saints are those who repented but had no time to purify themselves and who are purified by the action of the grace of penance and the prayer of the Church of the saints perfected and glorified in heaven. The light here is received according to the degree of purification, from a hardly noticeable twilight to the full light."[37]

With this vision of Theophane we close our chapter on him. He wrote so much and so profoundly that even a huge book could not do full justice to him. Theophane had a great influence on Russian monks, clergy and laymen, through his translation of *Dobrotolyubie,* through his numerous books, and his even more numerous letters. In the Library of St Panteleimon's Monastery on Mount Athos, nearly all his printed works are preserved in manuscript. I saw several of them during my stay there. At the same time I found some other interesting mystical manuscripts. It may be that some unpublished works of Theophane still remain in St Panteleimon's. The latter possesses not only a fine library but copious archives where priceless manuscripts are still not yet even classified. I barely began to survey them.

Theophane died at the very end of the nineteenth century. Russian monasticism was then in full swing. The next century promised, it appeared, a wonderful harvest. A harvest there certainly was, but a harvest of martyrdom, persecution and spoliation. To the study of this we shall now turn.

37. Ibid., p. 456.

CHAPTER XI

RUSSIAN MONASTICISM IN THE
TWENTIETH CENTURY

AT THE BEGINNING OF 1902, according to *Vedomost Muzhskim i Zhenskim Monastuiryam i Obshchinam Za 1901 god*, there were 783 monasteries in the Russian Empire, excluding bishop's houses and fifty-seven monastic annexes. Out of the 783 monasteries there were 423 monasteries for men and 303 monasteries and fifty-seven communities for women. According to their relation to the state there were 368 *Statny* monasteries, that is, subsidized by the state, and 415 non-*Statny*. According to their manner of life 466 monasteries were cenobitic.[1] By 1907 the number of monasteries reached 970; 522 for men and 448 for women. There were 24,444 monks and novices and 65,959 nuns and novices. By 1914 the number of monasteries rose to 1025; 550 for men and 475 for women. The number of monks and novices was 11,845 and 9,485 respectively, while that of nuns was 17,283, with 56,016 novices. While the number of monks began to decrease, that of the nuns was rapidly increasing.[2]

A study of *Vedomost* shows that monasteries of men although more numerous than those of women were far less populous. Except the great Lauras and a few monasteries their membership varied from thirty to fifty. The stricter the

1. *Vedomost mužskim i ženskim monastyrjam i obščinam za 1901 god, Supplement*, p. 15.
2. J. Smolitsch, *Russian Mönchtum. Entstehung, Entwicklung und Wesen. 988-1917* (Würzburg, 1953), p. 538.

monastery was and the more renowned were its spiritual directors, the larger it was. Sarov Monastery had in 1901 seventy professed monks and 240 novices; Optino Monastery, 133 monks and 130 novices; Valaam, 191 monks and 591 novices; Solovetzky, 147 monks and 77 novices; Glynsky, 129 monks, 45 novices and 286 postulants. The women's communities were much more populous. Diveev Convent, founded by St Serafim of Sorov, had ninety-nine nuns and 791 novices; Shamordino Convent, founded by Staretz Ambrose of Optino had 540 sisters. Convents with 150 to 300 sisters were common. The diocese of Nizhni-Novgorod and of Samara were particularly renowned for their vast convents of over 300 sisters and more. The dioceses of Kiev and Moscow were richer in monasteries and convents than others but the vast and wealthy dioceses of Novgorod, Vladimir, and Volyn, were also well provided for. The Volga dioceses provided the largest number of big convents. There were special missionary monasteries in Eastern Russia, Siberia and abroad.

Among the latter monasteries those of Mount Athos were most remarkable and numerous. The largest and most renowned of the Russian monasteries on Mount Athos was that of St Panteleimon.[3] The Russians visited Mount Athos from the eleventh century onwards. St Anthony of Kiev received his monastic formation there before 1051. In 1030 Theotokos of Xylourgou was founded. The Russians in that monastery became so numerous that in 1169 they received from the Athonite government St Panteleimon's Monastery, then in ruins, to restore it and to take it over. This they did, turning Xylourgou into a dependency. At the end of the twelfth century Prince Rastko, afterwards St Sabas, archbishop of Serbia, became a monk of St Panteleimon. In 1309 the Catalan pirates sacked the monastery and burned it down. All the Imperial Chrysobulls perished but the Emperor Andronicos II Paleologos renewed them in 1312. The Russians almost stopped coming to Mount Athos in the fourteenth and fif-

3. See D. A. van Ruijven, "Le 'Rossikon' ou monastère russe de S. Panteleimon au Mont Athos," *Irenikon* 30 (1957): 44-59; also A Soloviev, "Histoire du monastère Russe au Mont Athos," *Byzantium* 8 (1933): 231-233.

teenth centuries on account of their wars with the Turks and
the Lithuanians. The monastery became practically Serbian.
In 1347 King Stephen Dushan, of Serbia, became Protector
of the monastery. In 1349 he granted to St Panteleimon's
several estates. From 1500 the communications between
Athos and Russia improved. Ivan III, his son Basil III (himself
half Greek through his mother, the niece of the last Byzantine Emperor), Ivan IV, and Theodore, his son, made donations to the Mount Athos' monasteries. The civil wars in
Russia in the beginnings of the seventeenth century, followed
by long wars with the Poles, the Swedes and the Turks, again
created obstacles for the Russians coming to Mount Athos. In
1705, in the reign of Peter the Great, the entire community
of St Panteleimon numbered only four monks, two Russians
and two Bulgarians. Some time afterwards the monastery became insolvent and was taken over by the Athonite Monastic
Government. Finally it was abandoned. Some time between
1725 and 1744 Greek monks restored the abandoned monastery and it became entirely Greek. When Paisius Velichkovsky stayed on Mount Athos, St Panteleimon, then entirely
Greek, did not attract his attention. He looked to other monasteries for inspiration.[4]

The new Greek monks of St Panteleimon, wretchedly poor,
found their new protectors in the Phanariote Princes of Valakhia and Moldavia. These Rumanian Principalities were ruled
at this period by Princes nominated by the Turkish Sultans,
overlords of Rumania, from among the Greek aristocracy
which resided mostly in Phanar, a district of Constantinople,
where the Ecumenical Patriarchate now stands. In 1765 the
Greeks transferred the monastery from the mountains to the
seacoast. Prince Skarlatos Kallimachos was their chief benefactor. There were then twelve monks. During the long war
for Greek independence Prince Skarlatos Kallimachos was
executed by the Turks for treason and the monastery was
again abandoned in 1821. In 1839 the Greek monks returned

4. As mentioned above, Emmanuel Amand de Mendieta's book on Mount Athos
is best of the more recent books on the subject.

but they were faced with a debt of 800,000 piastres owed to the Jewish usurers of Salonica. They invited Russians to come to the monastery to assist them in paying the debt. The Russians accepted the invitation and within a short time the enormous debt was paid off and the mortgaged estates redeemed.

Abbot Gerasim who received the Russians into St Panteleimon's was a Slavonic-speaking Macedonian. In the middle of the nineteenth century, when the well-known ecclesiastical traveler, the hieromonk Parthenius, afterwards abbot of Guslitsui in Russia, visited St Panteleimon, he found there 200 monks.[5] At the time Fr Arsenius was confessor and spiritual director of all the Russian monks on the Holy Mountain. Fr Arsenius was a remarkable man and a mystic. A native of Balakhna, in the province of Nizhni Novgorod, he left his home as a youth in search of perfection. After visiting several Russian monasteries he entered the celebrated Pesnoshsky Monastery near Moscow and remained there for three years. The proximity of the capital and the numerous visitors displeased him so he went to Moldavia accompanied by his friend from Tula, Nicetas. In Moldavia, in the austere Balashev Skete, the two friends were professed, and Arsenius, then called Abel, was ordained. Balashev Skete did not satisfy the friends who were seeking true solitude. They decided to move to Mount Athos. They arrived during the Greek War of Independence when the Turks garrisoned the Holy Mountain and most of the monasteries were either abandoned or barely surviving. The friends came first to Iveron Monastery. When the situation improved and monks began to come back, the friends started to dwell in an hermitage, making wooden spoons and selling them for a living.

Parthenius tells one story which well describes the personality of Abel. Once the two monks saved 2,000 levas from their work in order to buy some badly needed things. Meanwhile a Greek from Chios visited. He told them that the Turks had

5. Pathenius left a remarkable description of his travels in Russia and the East: *Skazanie o stranstvii i putešestvii Rossii, Moldavii, Turcii i Svjatoj Zemle,* 4 vols. (Moscow, 1855).

carried away his wife and children into captivity and demanded
a ransom of 5,000 levas for their return. Although he had
collected 3,000 levas, he still needed 2,000. He was visiting
the Holy Mountain, asking for prayers and small alms. At
once Abel gave the man the 2,000 levas which astonished and
delighted the unfortunate man. When the visitor left, Nicetas,
now called Nicander started to reproach Abel: "Father, what
did you do? Why did you give him all the money? We
worked for it for four years and thought it would satisfy
some of our urgent needs and now we will be in trouble
again." Abel answered him: "Oh, Father Nicander! When
shall we become true monks? The Lord has already preserved us amid all these tribulations. You are still weak. The
Lord fed us in the most difficult times. Is he unable to feed
us now? At present, thanks be to God, our products sell. We
shall again work and sell and deposit all the surplus with God.
Why keep money which is not ours? This money detaches us
from God. We begin to pray but our mind clings to money.
The Lord said: 'Where your treasure is, there also will be
your heart.'[6] Let our money remain with God and we shall
keep our heart there as well." Nicander, very much touched,
prostrated before him, wept, and asked forgiveness.[7]

Abel and Nicander became in due course Megaloschemoi
Arsenius and Nicholas. After living ten years in the Skete of
St John the Forerunner of Iveron Monastery, they went to
the remote Hermitage of St John Chrysostom to live in complete solitude. They repaired the chapel there, in which
Abbot Parthenius himself was professed in due course. They
rose at midnight for their office which was very long. When
they had wine and bread, they celebrated the Liturgy. They
each made ten wooden spoons daily and spent the rest of the
time in prayer and meditation. Parthenius was much impressed with the manner of their celebration of the Liturgy.
"One, standing in the sanctuary before the Throne of the
Lord," he wrote "weeps copiously and can hardly pronounce

6. Mt 6:21.
7. Pathenius, *Skazanie,* 4:206-207.

the words for tears, while the second, standing before the lectern also sobs."[8] In 1836, Fr Anikita (Prince Shikhmatov) enabled them to go on pilgrimage to the Holy Land. Nicholas died in 1841; Arsenius in 1846.

The true restorer of Russian monasticism on the Holy Mountain was Fr Jerome Solomentsev, a great mystic.[9] Born on June 28, 1803 in Starui Oskol, in the province of Kursk, John Solomentsev was the son of the wealthy merchant, Paul Solomentsev, and his wife, Martha. Afterwards this good woman became a nun and a recluse. John's oldest brother was a monk and his sister, Margaret, an abbess. She died in 1886. Altogether fifteen monks and nuns, including abbots, abbesses, recluses and startzi came from the family of Solomentsev. John early decided to become a monk but was obliged to remain in the world until he was twenty-seven because his eldest brother and sister went to the cloister and his youngest brother was too young to assist his father in business. After some years of living in Russian monasteries as oblates, John Solomentsev and his friend, Nicholas, left for Athos in 1836 and joined Fr Arsenius. The latter professed them as Joanniky and Nikita. Both friends became solitaries, the second dying shortly afterwards as megaloschemos Nicodemus. Joanniky began to receive disciples. Fr Arsenius used to visit him and his disciples and to celebrate the Liturgy for them. In 1836 Fr Anikita (Prince Shikhmatov) tried to settle Russian monks on Athos but failed. The Russians settled in the Skete of St Elias, founded by Paisius Velichkovsky, but the Great Russians and the Ukrainians could not get on together, and the former were obliged to leave St Elias. The Russians lived dispersed all over Mount Athos until 1839, when the abbot of St Panteleimon, Gerasim, invited them to come to settle in his monastery. The Russians were allowed to have their own chapel and use Slavonic. They were also permitted to have as their confessor, Fr Paul, former abbot of the Skete of St Elias. Gerasim was to be the common abbot

8. Ibid., p. 210.
9. See *Žisneopisanija* (Moscow, July-December, 1919).

of all, Greeks and Russians. The Russians, with the blessing
of Fr Arsenius, accepted the invitation, and moved in on
November 20, 1834. Paul died on August 2, 1840. On
November 23, 1840 Joanniky was ordained and appointed
confessor to the Russian Community of St Panteleimon. In
1841 he became megaloschemos with the name of Jerome. Fr
Jerome attracted to St Panteleimon many Russian benefactors and crowds of postulants. A Russian monk, Seraphim
Svyatogoretz, wrote his celebrated letters about the life on
the Holy Mountain which became very popular in Russia and
produced a veritable invasion of Athos by Russian postulants.[10] Under Fr Jerome St Panteleimon began its vast pub-
lishing activity. It published nearly all the works of Theophane the Recluse and many other texts. Jerome founded the
magnificent New Athos Monastery in the Caucasus. He helped the poor on a grand scale. He continued as confessor for
the Russian monks for forty-five years, until his death on
November 14, 1885.

During my stay at St Panteleimon in the spring of 1957 I
looked through the voluminous correspondence of Fr Jerome. His letters are worthy of publication and demonstrate his
spirituality and his great influence on monks and visitors. In
the library of St Panteleimon among unpublished Russian
manuscripts, I found a manuscript copy of the celebrated
Russian spiritual classic, *Tales of the Russian Pilgrim*. This
copy is longer than the existing printed version, including five
additional episodes. It also contains a postscript. The history
of the *Tales* is full of mysteries. In 1884 a short book was
published in Kazan, *Sincere Tales of a Pilgrim to his Spiritual
Father.*[11] According to the introduction, this book is the
reproduction of a manuscript which Paisius, abbot of St
Michael of the Cheremissi, found and copied on Mount
Athos. Paisius died in 1883. The book became very popular

10. Ieroschimaonach Serafim: (Vesnin), *Sobranie Sočinenij i Pisem Svjatogorca,*
4 vols. (St Petersburg, 1865).

11. *Otkrovennye rasskazy strannika* (Kazan 1884). The *Tales* have had many
editions and translations. The latest English translation is R. M. French, *The Way
of a Pilgrim* and *The Pilgrim Continues his Way* (New York: Seabury, 1965).

in Russia. Later it was translated into German, French, English, Japanese and Greek. It contains four tales. The story is told by the pilgrim himself.

In the first tale the pilgrim tells how, upon entering a church on one occasion and hearing the advice of St Paul to pray unceasingly,[12] he was curious to learn how one might do this. He asked for an explanation from the clergy, theologians, and educated laymen, but could find no satisfactory answer. Finally, he found a skhimnik who gave him *Dobrotolyubie* to read. The monk afterwards ordered the pilgrim to say the Prayer of Jesus 3,000 times a day. Within a few days the pilgrim managed to say that number. The monk ordered him thereupon to say it 6,000 times a day. Within ten days the pilgrim mastered 6,000 prayers a day. The skhimnik then prescribed 12,000 prayers a day. Finally, the pilgrim prayed without counting, associating his prayer with his breathing and the beating of his heart, in Hesychast fashion.[13] With his progress in prayer his psychology began to change. "During the day," the pilgrim writes, "if I met some people, they all, without exception, appeared to me as my dear relations even if I did not talk to them. My thoughts became calm and I thought of nothing but the Prayer to which my mind began to incline while my heart began to feel occasionally warmth and a peculiar pleasantness. When I came to church, the long monastic office seemed to me short and ceased to be tiring as before. My solitary hut seemed to me a magnificent palace and I did not know how to thank God that he had sent to me, a reprobate sinner, such a salutary staretz and teacher."[14] After the death of his staretz the pilgrim bought *Dobrotolyubie* and continued his study of prayer. His mystical experiences increased: "I walk sometimes forty miles and more a day and do not feel that I have walked a great deal. I only feel that I pray. When severe cold assaults me, I begin to pray with more fervor and soon I am warm. If hunger troubles me, I appeal to Jesus Christ oftener and forget that I want to eat.

12. 1 Thess 5:16.
13. French, *The Way*, pp. 1-16.
14. Ibid., p. 16. There is a very informative book on the Prayer of Jesus published by the Benedictines of Chevetogne in "Collection Irenikon": *La Prière de Jésus*, by a monk of the Eastern Church (1951); trans. *The Prayer of Jesus* (New York: Desclée, 1967).

When I become ill and feel pains in the back and in the legs, I listen to the prayer with more attention and experience pain no more. If someone offends me, I merely remember how sweet is the Prayer of Jesus and all offence and anger pass off and I forget all that."[15]

In the second tale the pilgrim describes how he decided to settle down in order to study *Dobrotolyubie* in earnest. He went to Siberia where those great Russian mystics, staretzy Zosima, Vasilisk and Daniel flourished in the first half of the nineteenth century. During this journey "I felt," the pilgrim writes, "that the Prayer, on its own accord, began to pass to my heart, that is, my heart in its usual beatings began, it seemed, to pronounce within itself, with every beat, first Lord, second, Jesus, third, Christ, and so on. I ceased to pronounce the prayer with my lips and began to listen to how my heart prays. Then I began to look within my heart, according to the advice of my late staretz. This was very pleasant. Afterwards I began to feel in my heart a slight pain and in my mind such a love for Jesus Christ that it seemed to me that if I would see him, I would at once prostrate myself at his feet, without leaving them, kissing them, and thanking him with tears."[16] During his Siberian journey the pilgrim was robbed of his books but found them again. He also met some very interesting people. "During this time," the pilgrim writes, "I also read my Bible. I realized that I began to understand it better, not like before, when many things appeared to me incomprehensible and I often doubted. The Holy Fathers are right when they say that *Dobrotolyubie* is the key to the mysteries of the Sacred Scriptures. With my present guidance I began partly to understand the hidden meaning of the Word of God. I began to realize who is the interior, hidden, man of heart, what is true prayer, what is spiritual worship, what is the interior Kingdom, what is the indescribable prayer of the all-merciful Holy Spirit, what is the meaning of: "You will be in me;" "Give me your heart;" what it means to be clothed in Christ; what is the meaning of spiritual espous-

15. Ibid., pp. 17-18.
16. Ibid., p. 20.

als in our hearts; what is the cry of the heart: "Abba! Father! " When I prayed in my heart at the time, all the surroundings used to take on a wonderful appearance: trees, grass, birds, earth, air, light, everything. It seemed to me that they existed for man and testified to the love of God for man. Everything prays and glorifies God. I understood from this what *Dobrotolyubie* calls the understanding of the words of all creatures and I found the way to talk to creatures of God."[17]

During this journey the pilgrim met a woodsman, who, after listening to a sermon on the Last Judgment, left his trade for solitude in order to repent. He began afterwards to be assaulted by the thought that, perhaps, there is no hell at all and that hell was invented by the clergy and gentry in order to keep people in subjection while it would really be wiser to spend this short life in pleasure. The pilgrim told the woodsman that the abstinence from sin merely from the fear of torments is sterile and unsuccessful. The soul cannot free itself from mental sins except by custody of the mind and purity of heart. All this is acquired by interior prayer but not for fear's sake or even for the desire to enter the Kingdom of Heaven, which is, according to the Fathers, the way of a mercenary. The Fathers say that the fear of pain is the way of a slave and the desire of reward is the way of a mercenary, but God desires that we come to him by the way of sons who have lived well and honestly for love of him and desire to serve him and take pleasure in a saving union with him in soul and heart. Whatever ascetical exercises one undertakes and however he wears out his body, if he does not always have God within him and the unceasing Prayer of Jesus in his heart he will never be able to master his thoughts and will always be inclined to sin even at the smallest provocation."[18] The pilgrim remained with the woodsman in his hut for a few months. He had a vision of his late staretz who indicated to him what parts of *Dobrotolyubie* to read most arduously: Nicephoros the Monk, Gregory Sinaite, St Simeon the New Theologian, Callixtus and Ignatius.

17. Ibid., pp. 31-32.
18. Ibid., p. 36.

The pilgrim describes his mystical experiences after he mastered the Hesychast method. "Closing my eyes, I looked with my mind, that is, with my imagination, at my heart, wanting to picture it as it is in the left side of the breast and listening to its beating. At the beginning I experimented with this for half an hour several times a day. At first, I experienced nothing except darkness. Soon enough, however, I began to see the heart and its movements. Then I began to bring into the heart and out again, the Prayer of Jesus, synchronizing it with my breathing, according to the instructions of St Gregory of Sinai, Callixtus and Ignatius. Inhaling air and mentally looking into my heart I imagined and pronounced: 'Lord Jesus Christ,' then exhaling: 'have pity on me.' I experimented at first for an hour or two a day, then more and more, until I spent nearly the entire day in this practice. When I was attacked by heaviness. laziness or doubts, I started to read at once those places in *Dobrotolyubie* which spoke of the work of the heart, and I felt again desire and fervor for prayer. Within three weeks, I began to feel a pain in my heart and then a most pleasant heat, along with joy and serenity. This excited me and attracted me more and more to this practice so that all my thoughts were occupied with it, and I felt a great joy. I was so light, so free, so full of consolation that I was completely transformed with joy. From this time I began to feel various passing sensations in my heart and mind. I sometimes felt a flaming love for Jesus Christ and all the divine creation; sometimes sweet tears of thanks to the Lord, who had forgiven me, a reprobate sinner, streamed out of my eyes; sometimes my former foolish misunderstandings became illuminated and I understood easily and meditated on subjects of which previously I could not even think. Occasionally the sweet heat of the heart spread all over my body, and I experienced, with an inexpressible sensation, the omnipresence of God. Sometimes I felt within me the greatest joy from calling on the name of Jesus and I understood the meaning of the words: 'The Kingdom of God is within you.'[19] Experiencing these and similar consolations, I ob-

19. Lk 17:21.

served that the results of prayer of the heart reveal themselves in three ways: in spirit, in feelings and in revelations. In spirit, for instance, I experienced the sweetness of divine love, interior rest, rapture of mind, purity of thoughts, the sweet memory of God. In feelings I experienced a pleasant warmth in the heart, sweetness all over the body, a joyful boiling in the heart, lightness and freshness, pleasantness of living, insensibility to sickness and sorrows. In revelations I experienced illumination of mind, understanding of the Sacred Scriptures, understanding of the language of animals, detachment from vanity and realization of the sweetness of the interior life, certainty of the nearness of God and his love for us."[20] There are few pages in the whole of Russian mystical literature which equal or surpass these lines. The rest of the tale is filled with the description of various happenings and meetings during the journey.

There is, however, one more remarkable mystical experience. "Thus, I again went," the pilgrim writes, "on my solitary journey. I felt such a lightness that it seemed as if a mountain had fallen off my shoulders. Prayer more and more consoled me to such a degree that sometimes my heart boiled with boundless love for Jesus Christ. From this sweet boiling something like comforting streams spread all over my body. The memory of Jesus Christ became so impressed on my mind that when I meditated on the events of the Gospel I saw them, it seemed, with my own eyes. I was exceedingly moved by them and cried. Sometimes I felt in my heart such a joy that I cannot describe it. It happened occasionally that for three days I did not enter any human habitation. Enraptured, I felt that I was the only man on the earth, a reprobate sinner, before the merciful and man-loving God. This solitude comforted me and the sweetness of prayer was greater there than in populous cities."[21]

Arriving in Irkutsk the pilgrim met a merchant who suggested that he visit Jerusalem and offered to help pay his way.

The third tale gives the autobiography of the pilgrim. He

20. French, *The Way*, pp. 40-42.
21. Ibid., pp. 64-65.

was a peasant from the province of Orel. An orphan, he was brought up with his brother by their grandfather, a devout old man who kept an inn. The elder brother started to drink and broke the left hand of the younger who became semi-invalid. The grandfather liked the pilgrim and taught him to read and to write and left all his fortune to him. The pilgrim married a good girl and they just started to live happily together when the elder brother burned the house down, and they lost everything. Within two years the pilgrim's wife died and he became a pilgrim, a tramp like St Benoit Labre in the West. When he left for Jerusalem he was thirty-three. The last tale describes various adventures of the pilgrim during his journey. It is rich in mystical descriptions. When the pilgrim was with people he felt a great hunger for solitude.

"I felt," he writes, "a hunger for prayer, a strong need to open my soul prayerfull to God, a need for solitude and silence, which I had been without for more than twenty-four hours. I felt in my heart something like floods which wanted to break through and inundate all my members. But because I restrained this I felt a strong pain in my heart, albeit pleasant, begging for solitary rest and nourishment by prayer. I understood then why true Hesychasts run away from men and hide themselves in the desert. I understood also why St Hesychius called even the most spiritual and useful talk vain speaking. St Ephrem the Syrian also said: 'good speech is silver but silence is pure gold'."[22] Describing the psychical phenomenon to a blind man, the pilgrim said: "The human soul up to a point, is neither bound by matter nor by space. It can see in darkness and it can see distant events as though they were happening before it. We do not allow this capacity of the soul to develop but repress it either by the chains of our coarse body or by the confusion of our thoughts and dissipation. But when we concentrate in ourselves and become detached from our surroundings and refined in our mind, the soul comes into its own and acts in a higher way. This is natural. I heard from my late staretz that some people, either predisposed to this or sickly, can see in the darkest

22. Ibid., p. 98.

room the light radiated by things therein, distinguish objects, feel their own double and read the thoughts of others. But things which happen during prayer of the heart come directly from divine grace. They are so pleasant that no language can describe them. They cannot be likened to anything material. Everything sensible is too insignificant in comparison with the sensation of grace in heart."[23]

We shall close our account of the *Tales* with one more quotation: "Prayer of the heart so comforted me that I could not imagine anyone happier that I on the earth. I could not understand what could be a greater and better pleasure in the Kingdom of Heaven. I did not merely feel all that within me but everything external appeared to me wonderful. Everything urged me on to the love of God and to thanksgiving: people, trees, plants and animals. They all were to me like members of my own family. In everything I used to find the impress of the name of Jesus Christ. Often I felt a lightness as if I had no body and did not walk but joyfully floated in the air. Sometimes I entered altogether into myself and saw clearly all my interior, admiring the wisdom of the construction of the human body. Sometimes I felt as joyous as a newly-crowned king. With all these consolations, I wanted God to allow me to die soon in order to empty myself in thanksgiving before his throne in the world of spirits."[24]

The manuscript which I studied on Mount Athos is longer than the printed text. It could reliably be supposed that Abbot Paisius copied his printed text from the Athos manuscript. Why he omitted five episodes, I cannot say. Perhaps they seemed to him unsuitable either because they implied some criticism of the learned clergy for their neglect of prayer of the heart or because they touched on sexuality. The omitted episodes are very important, particularly the one which shows that unceasing prayer of the heart cannot continue during sexual excitement. I did not study in detail the voluminous correspondence of Fr Jerome Solomentsev but it seems to me that the pilgrim visited Mount Athos and wrote or dictated his story for Fr Jerome.

23. Ibid., pp. 104-105.
24. Ibid., pp. 105-106.

We do not know much about the pilgrim except what he tells us of himself in the *Tales*. I found, nevertheless, some new information about him from two letters of Staretz Ambrose of Optino to a nun who was a prioress of a convent and who had read the manuscript of the *Tales* before it was printed. I seems that the manuscript of the *Tales* was frequently copied in Russia before it was printed in Kazan. In his letter Staretz Ambrose writes: "You write that you came across a manuscript which indicates a simple method to learn the Prayer of Jesus, vocal, mental, and of heart. This manuscript was written by a peasant from the province of Orel who was taught the Prayer of Jesus by an unknown staretz. You write that the manuscript of this peasant ends in 1859. Shortly before that time we heard from our late staretz, Father Macarius, that he was visited by a layman who had attained to such a high degree of spiritual prayer that Fr Macarius did not know what to tell him. This layman, in order to receive advice, described to our staretz various states of prayer. Fr Macarius could only tell him: "Be humble, be humble.' Afterwards he told us about this experience with astonishment. I thought at the time that this concerned the Orel merchant Neumuitov who was a great man of prayer, but I think now that he might well be that peasant of whom you write. In the forties of this century, a skhimnik of Mount Athos, Fr Athanasius, used to live in Bryansk Monastery in the province of Orel. He practiced the prayer of mind and heart. Still earlier, a hiero-skhimnik, Basil, who called himself a tramp used to live in various monasteries in the provinces of Kursk and Orel. He taught many people to practice the Prayer of Jesus, all those who wanted to learn it. You write that this peasant was so attached to the Prayer of Jesus that he was hardly able to read morning prayers. But according to the sermon of Gregory of Sinai in *Dobrotolyubie* this prayer is suitable only to very simple folk and to solitaries. To those who live in monasteries, this prayer is not so well adapted. If St Anthony the Great read the ninth hour, and St Zosima, who found Mary the Egyptian, observed his rule of prayer even while walking in the desert, so much more we, who are so frail, must not give up our usual prayer as long as we are able to continue it."[25] In the second letter Ambrose writes: "I shall tell you in a few words of the manuscript of the pilgrim. There is nothing objectionable in it. The pilgrim lived as a pilgrim. He was a wanderer, free from cares and worries. He could freely practice prayer when he wanted. But you lead the life of a prioress and, besides, you are sickly, hardened with monastic duties. Therefore practice prayer as much as you are free to, and the rest will be made up for by obedience which also has its importance."[26]

There is only one Athanasius we know of who corresponds to the description of Staretz Ambrose. He is Skhimnik Athanasius, disciple of Staretz Basil Kishkin, whom Ambrose mentions above. Athanasius lived with Staretz Basil on Mount Athos. He retired afterwards to Svensky Monastery in Bryansk but died in 1844 in Beloberezhsky Monastery. In the materials which I had before me on Mt Athos he is called a holy man who trained many people in the Prayer of Jesus.

In 1852 there were already eighty Russians in St Panteleimon. In 1866 Slavonic reading was introduced in the refectory on alternate days. The Greeks protested and did not want to come to the refectory. In 1870 Gerasim declared the Russian monk, Macarius, his successor. The Greeks complained to the Athonite Government which declared the nomination of Macarius invalid and prescribed that the abbots must always be Greeks and the Russian monks always a minority. Yet in 1874 there were already 300 Russians and only 200 Greeks. Gerasim died in 1875 leaving a community of 400 Russians and 180 Greeks. The Russian majority elected Macarius abbot. After long negotiations, the Patriarch of Constantinople confirmed the election. In 1887 St Panteleimon had 1,000 monks and in 1900 over 2,000, of whom only twenty-five were Greeks.[27] By 1903 there were on Mount Athos, in all monasteries, 3,496 Russian monks and 3,276 Greeks. In 1914 as a result of the Imyabozhniki Movement, about 500

25. *Sobranie pisem Optinskago Starca ieroschimonacha Amvrosija k monašestvujuščim* (Sergiev Posad, 1908), pp. 119-210.
26. Ibid., p. 121.
27. The library of St Panteleimon contains the chronicle of the monastery for this period. It includes several volumes and all are written in a beautiful hand.

monks were obliged to leave St Panteleimon. 450 more
monks were mobilized in the First World War, besides the
postulants. Only twenty-two novices came between 1917 and
1928 and hardly any after that. In 1924 there were 625
monks; 1934, 450; 1944, 234; 1954, 88; and 1956, 70.[28]
When I visited the great monastery for the second time in
1957, there were only sixty old monks, of whom the youngest was over fifty. Although no postulants are yet allowed to
enter from the Soviet Union, a few from the Russian diaspora
can be admitted. Whether St Panteleimon will survive or die
out is still uncertain. In 1907 there were in the Monastic
Republic altogether seventy-nine Russian monastic institutions,
including St Panteleimon and four big Sketes: St Andrew, St
Elias, Khromitsa and New Thebais.[29] St Andrew's Skete was
reputed to have 800 monks, novices and postulants and the
Skete of St Elias about 600. In 1957 there were perhaps
eighteen old men in the first monastery and sixteen in the
second. The smaller Russian communities have nearly all disappeared.

A still worse fate awaited Russian monasteries at home.
According to the best study of Russian monasticism before
the Revolution by L. T. Denisov, on December 1, 1907 there
were in the Empire altogether 1,105 monastic institutions, of
which 540 were communities of men, 34 were podvories or
priories and 75 were Episcopal Residences, all of which possessed a small monastic community because all Russian
bishops are monks. The total number of the institutions for
women was 448, among which there were 367 monasteries, 61
communities and 20 podvories. The total number in all these
communities was 90,403, of whom 24,444 were men and
65,959 women. There were five monasteries for men for
every four for women but there were eleven nuns for every
four monks. The communities of men declined in membership while those for women increased. Only five dioceses had
more than 1,000 monks, Kiev (2,805), Moscow (2,219),
Kursk (1,265), Viborg (1,052) and Kharkov (1,033); but 25

28. Van Ruijven, "Le 'Rossikon'," pp. 58-59.
29. According to *Putevoditel po Afonu*, 1913.

dioceses had more than 1,000 nuns, including Nizhni-Novgorod (5,541), Moscow (3,878), Orel (3,799), Tambov (3,354), Perm (2,644), Samara (2,694), Kiev (2,308), Saratov (2,262) and Orenburg (2,076). A good many of these monasteries possessed magnificent buildings, ikons, libraries, vestments and relics. Several communities maintained guesthouses, schools, old folk homes, hospitals and printing presses.[30]

The Soviet Revolution changed all that. Very soon after the Soviet Government came to power on January 23, 1918, it published a decree which separated Church and state and took the schools from the Church. At that time the landed estates of the Church comprised about nineteen million acres. It possessed also many houses and commercial enterprises. Its annual income was estimated to be over a hundred million dollars. The bank deposits of the Church reach nearly two billion dollars.[31] All this disappeared over night. The monasteries suffered as much as other Church institutions. Besides nationalizing Church property, the decree deprived the Church of corporate juridical rights, closed all theological academies and seminaries and prohibited religious instruction in all schools. I have already described the story of the Russian Church during the revolution in two different books.[32] Here I shall tell only what happened to the monasteries.

In order to escape suppression, many communities registered themselves as labor communities according to Soviet law. To counteract this the Soviet Government prohibited people formerly known as monks or nuns to join labor communities. Meanwhile the closing of monasteries went on. Several great monasteries like Solovetzky and Sarov were turned into prisons.[33] The Lauras of Kiev and of St Sergius became muse-

30. L. T. Denisov, *Pravoslavnye Monastryi Rossijskoj Imperii* (Moscow, 1908), pp. ix - xii.

31. S. Bolshakoff, *The Christian Church and the Soviet State* (London, 1942), p. 1.

32. In addition to the book just cited, see also by the same author, *Russian Nonconformity*.

33. See I. M. Kontzevitch, "Father Nicholas Zagorovsky (in Monasticism Hieromonk Seraphim)," *Orthodox Word* 8 (1972): 178-187; and also in the same issue, the anonymous account of the fate of Solovetzky Monastery.

ums, hospitals and schools. By 1930 not a single monastery survived openly in the Soviet Union. The efforts to found secret monasteries did not produce much fruit because of the severe punishment inflicted on those who joined them. The only Russian monasteries which survived those years were those abroad; three monasteries in Finland, two in Estonia, two in Latvia, several in Poland (former Western Russian provinces) and in Rumania (Bessarabia). A few monasteries survived, also, in China and the United States, while some new ones were founded in Manchuria, the United States, Canada and Czechoslavakia.[34]

The Second World War again changed the situation. The Baltic Republics, the Eastern provinces of Poland and Bessarabia were occupied by the Soviet Army. The Soviet Union also annexed Galicia, Sub-Carpathian Ruthenia and Bukovina. Nearly all those provinces possessed Orthodox monasteries. they were not closed but allowed to continue in existence. Moreover, during German and Rumanian occupation of the Ukraine a number of monasteries were reopened. They too have been permitted to continue. Finally, the Soviet Government has allowed the reopening of the celebrated Russian sanctuary of the Laura of the Holy Trinity, founded by St Sergius of Radonezh in the nineteenth century. It is supposed that there are now about forty Orthodox monasteries in the Soviet Union with, perhaps, 2,000 monks and nuns or more.[35] There are no reliable statistics. The information is often contradictory. Nevertheless, a number of the large monasteries certainly exist. Two Russian Lauras survived until 1963, those of Pochaev and Zagorsk. That of Kiev is now closed. The Zagorsk Laura has over 100 monks and is the show place of the Soviet Union. Besides great masses of pilgrims from all over Russia, nearly all foreign visitors to Moscow visit Zagorsk. The Laura is beautifully restored and gives a good impression. As in the past, it houses the Moscow

---

34. Beginning with 1926 *Irenikon* (Chevetogne) contains much useful information about these matters.

35. Since 1939 we have tried to publish what information is available in *Church and World* and *New Missionary Review* (Oxford).

Theological Academy and Seminary. The Patriarch of Russia himself is the abbot. The relics of St Sergius and of other saints rest again in their shrines. A fourth Russian Laura, that of St Alexander Nevsky in Leningrad, although it houses the Metropolitan of Leningrad and the Theological Academy and Seminary and has several monks on the staff and among the students, so far has no regular monastic community.

Other known surviving monasteries are Pskovo-Pechersky, near Pskov, with about seventy monks, Uspensky in Odessa, Zhirovitsi in White Russia and Glinsky in the Ukraine. There are also several convents, mostly in the Ukraine and White Russia. Some of them have as many as 250 nuns. Pokrovsky and Florovsky Convents in Kiev, the convent of Odessa and Pukhtitsi in Estonia, with a community of 100 nuns, are often visited.[36] The great and celebrated monasteries like Solovetzky, Sarov, Optino and Vysha for men or Diveev and Shamordino for women remain closed. What future awaits these communities it is difficult to say. The growing dechristianization of the young by the Marxist-inspired schools so far does not prevent the inflow of postulants into the monasteries. Those that are open certainly do not suffer from the lack of vocations. It is rather unlikely that the painful happenings of the stormy years of the Revolution will be repeated but the growing secularization might affect adversely the recruitment of the monasteries in the long run.

Outside of the Soviet Union and Mount Athos Russian monastic communities exist in Finland, the Holy Land, the United States, Canada and Western Europe, and there are the beginnings of new ones in Australia, England and South America. On the other hand, the Russian monastic communities in China, Manchuria, Czechoslavakia and Yugoslavia have disappeared. The most illustrious among the Russian monastic communities abroad is that of Valaam. This great monastery, existing since the twelfth century on the islands of the greatest European lake, Ladoga, had a very stormy history, being in the territory of the Russo-Swedish wars. It was

36. *Žurnal Moskovskoj Patriarchii,* published in Moscow since 1943, occasionally gives interesting information on Russian monasteries in the Soviet Union.

sacked and destroyed many times. In 1717 it became
Russian. With the proclamation of the independence of Finland, it became Finnish. During the Second World War the
Valaam Archipelago was occupied by Soviet troops and afterwards annexed to the Soviet Union. The community moved
to Central Finland, where it established itself in Uusi Valamo.
In 1907 the Valaam community had 199 monks and 591
novices and postulants. When I visited Uusi Valamo in 1954,
the community numbered about seventy. The Orthodox
Church in Finland is very small, about 80,000 people. It
cannot provide enough novices to maintain the community in
reasonable strength. Valaam was always supplied with postulants from Russia. Cut off from its recruiting grounds, Valaam like Russian Athos can hardly continue. Valaam was a
great Russian spiritual center and even lately it has produced
great mystics of whom more will be said in the next chapter.

The largest Russian monastery abroad is that of the Holy
Trinity in Jordanville, N.Y., in the United States.[37] Founded
between the two World Wars, it now has over fifty monks
and houses a seminary. It tries to continue the publication
works of Optino and other Russian monasteries. Jordanville
Monastery belongs to that group of Russian exiles abroad
who do not accept the Russian Patriarch in Moscow, convinced that the latter is under the control of the Soviet
Government. This group has its own ecclesiastical organization which is temporary, awaiting the day when the Church
in Russia will be really free. Their situation is very similar to
that of the so-called Petite Eglise of the French Revolution,
which refused to accept the Concordat of Pius VII with
Napoleon under the pretext that no cooperation could exist
between the Church and the Revolution, represented by the
First Consul. The remnants of that group still survive.

Instead of more than 1,000 Russian monasteries before the
Soviet Revolution, hardly 50 exist now in Russia and abroad,
less than five percent of those of the Imperial period. The

37. Holy Trinity Monastery publishes two reviews, one in Russian and one in
English. Related to this monastery, though actually independent from it, is the
very flourishing skete in Brookline, Massachusetts, Holy Transfiguration, which is
actually dependent on St Paul's Monastery on Mount Athos.

same happened in Western Europe after the French Revolution and the mass closing of monasteries by the anti-clericals of the nineteenth century. What happened to the numerous and glorious monasteries of Egypt, Syria, the Holy Land, Messopotamia and Asia Minor, after the Moslem conquest was repeated later in Western Europe under Protestantism, the Enlightenment, the French Revolution and Anti-clericalism. Yet the great spiritual experience of those monasteries which produced so many saints and mystics has not been lost but lives enshrined in the Church and in culture. The same is true of the Russian monasteries.

CHAPTER XII

RUSSIAN MYSTICS IN THE
TWENTIETH CENTURY

THE TWENTIETH CENTURY has so far been a stormy period in Russian history. Its first half has been spent in wars, revolutions, invasions and troubles of all kinds. Such times do not favor the flowering of mystical life which demands serenity, peace, and retirement. Troubled times are the times that produce martyrs and confessors of the faith. The Russian Church has produced many: bishops, clergy, monks, nuns and lay folk of both sexes and of every age, class, and occupation. No one but God knows the names and numbers of all the martyrs and confessors of the faith.[1] It is quite probable that their number has been greater than that of all the martyrs and confessors in the Roman Empire up to the edict of Milan in 315. So much blood shed can hardly be in vain. The Russian Church has survived the storm, albeit much reduced. Monasteries have survived, also.

Even in such stormy period the Russian Church has not failed to produce mystics. Perhaps they are only a few, but they are of a very high quality indeed. These mystics flourished outside Russia, on Mount Athos and at Valaam, where they could have a relative peace and tranquility. The last of the Optino startzy, Joseph, who died in 1911, Barsanuthius (Varsanofy), who died in 1913, and Nectarius, who died in 1928, to whom Anatolius (d. 1922) is usually joined, were good spiritual directors but they were merely shadows of the

---

1. See M. Polsky, *Novuie Mucheniki Rossiiskie,* 2 vols. (Jordanville: Holy Trinity, 1949-1957).

first three startzy. They never had the same influence and power. Neither Sarov, nor Vysha, nor the Laura of Kiev were able to produce anyone remotely similar to St Seraphim, Bishop Theophane the Recluse or staretz Parthenius.

Although Mount Athos and Valaam produced some outstanding mystics in the twentieth century, they suffered, too, from interior stresses and external troubles due to wars and revolutions. Russian Mount Athos was much upset at the beginning of the century with the Onomolaters Movement. The origins of this movement are rather obscure. In the library of St Panteleimon's I found a manuscript entitled, "True Happening in the Mountains of the Caucasus."[2] This manuscript was the root of the trouble. Its author, Skimnik Hilarion, came to St Panteleimons from Russia in 1872. After being professed receiving the name Januarius, he was sent to New Athos Monastery in the Caucasus to teach in the school attached to that monastery. This was around 1892. Professed as a skhimnik with the name Hilarion, Januarius retired to live in the solitude of the Caucasian Mountains, where he spent over twenty years. He was a great lover of solitude. Hilarion described his experiences in solitude in the manuscript mentioned above, which he sent to St Panteleimon with the following note: "I beg you most obediently to have this work read over by the startzy, Fathers Macarius and Theodosius, to correct the errors, to explain the doubtful and to strike out the harmful. If it is approved, I shall begin, with the assistance of God, to develop this manuscript to the full. Here only the principal features are outlined while details are left for the future." The note is dated by June 10, 1904.[3] The manuscript was received by Fr Vladimir on Mount Athos in 1905 and published in *Dushepolesnoe Chtenie* under the title "True Happenings in the Mountains of the Caucasuss in 1903."

The manuscript describes how the author accompanied by his disciple met in a desert place a hermit from Aksubai, who had spent ten years in solitude after previously living twenty

---

2. Ms 428/1908: *Dejstvitelnoe proizšestvie v gorach Kavkaza.* (1903).
3. Ibid., p. 85.

years in a monastery. The hermit described how he attained to the highest degree of the Prayer of Jesus, that of the heart. The manuscript with additions was published as *In the Mountains of the Caucasus:* The talk of two startzy-hermits about the interior union of our hearts with God through the Prayer of Jesus Christ, or the spiritual activity of modern hermits."[4] The book contains a large number of chapters and some very fine descriptions. It opens with a wonderful description of the Naked Mountains at the source of the river of Urup: "Everywhere around us dead stillness and perfect silence reigned supreme. Every worldly agitation was absent. Nature here, far away from all disturbance enjoyed its rest and manifested the mystery of the world to come. To speak simply, this was the kingdom of the spiritual world and of peace, the new world incomparably better than that where men live. This produced a liberation of soul from everything material, earthly, carnal. This was the freedom of the spirit, the life proper to its immaterial nature. This was the temple of the Living God, not made by man. Chains of snow-capped mountains lit by the sun and all aflame lined the horizon. The wide space, like a shoreless sea extending in all directions, struck us with its splendor and carried us away beyond the limits of everything temporal. . . . The silence of the mountains and valleys engendered a new sensation: the feeling of indescribable stillness and rest.[5] The second chapter describes Hilarion's meeting with a hermit who was returning from Zelenchukov Monastery to his hermitage in Aksubai. This hermit explained how he had attained to the highest degree of the Prayer of Jesus. (He who attains this degree, becomes united with Christ and enters eternal life.) The third chapter treats of the Divine Name. According to it, God himself is present in the Divine Name.

"When man, moved by the divine call, perseveringly and with every effort, regretting not the labor and time, at every work, day and night, calls on the Divine Name, mentally or vocally, by the sacred Prayer of Jesus: "Lord Jesus Christ, Son of God, have mercy upon me, a sinner," fulfilling at the

---

4. *Na gorach Kavkaza Schimonach Ilarion* (Batalpašinsk, 1910²).
5. Ibid., pp. 5-6.

same time, as far as possible, all the other Gospel precepts, and persevering in humility acknowledging his sinful state and need of divine assistance, then after a longer or shorter time, according as he who knows hearts judges fit, some wonderful and supernatural change takes place in him. The Name of the Lord Jesus Christ, if we may so speak, becomes incarnate. The man clearly feels it with the interior sentiments of his soul. The Lord himself is the Divine Name. This feeling of the Lord himself and his Name unites them together in such a way that they can not be distinguished one from another." [6] The fourth chapter tries to show from the Bible that God does not separate his Name from his essence. The sixth chapter describes the fruits of prayer: disappearance of all impure thoughts, establishment in the heart of an indescribable love for God and neighbor, detachment from everything earthly, and understanding of the Sacred Scriptures.

In his talk the hermit of Aksubai described his life. In the world he was called Demetrius. In his youth he lived a depraved life and was an atheist who mocked the Gospel, blasphemed and did not go to Communion. When he entered the seminary, he was far from being good, but a dangerous illness overcame him. He left the seminary and, after two years as a village teacher, entered a monastery and made his profession, apparently in Pokrovsky Skete. He received the name of Desiderius. After twenty years in the monastery Desiderius became a hermit. He spent two weeks with Hilarion relating to him his experiences and views.

Hilarion's book contains many splendid pages which give deep insight into his spirituality. For instance the description of the mountains after a thunderstorm is splendid. "Prayer comforted me. My heart became gay and I joyfully looked around me. Everything was solemn, still, splendid and silent. Silent nature, in perfect serenity, listened to the terrible presence of Almighty God and did not dare to break silence even with the slight whisper of leaves. I entered into the depths of my spirit and mysteriously contemplated the Divine Being, participating in those blessed moments in the higher life, and

6. Ibid., p. 12.

tasting the joy of salvation, although, of course, only in the spiritual betrothal. I was alone, nature sweetly embraced me, full of spiritual peace and deep feeling. And I, as a child at the breast of his mother, drank from nature the living streams of true life, participating in a lively sense of the Deity, who is always sought by our soul as the only true grace, eternal life and beatitude. This ennobling state of soul is impossible in the world sunk in vanity and worldly cares. This belongs to the state detached from everything earthly."[7]

Discussing the solitary life, Hilarion says: "Speaking of the desert and life in it I address myself not to all but only to those who have in their heart the seed of solitary life, that is, an inborn inclination to solitude, silence and separation from men. I speak to those who possess an inclination to recollection and interior life. This is, as everyone knows, a particular group of people rather unlike others. The majority of men live in dreams while wise hermits remain within themselves, keeping the thoughts of their mind and the sacred feelings of their heart pure. They stand before their God and see him in their hearts as the holy prophet Elijah says of himself: "The Lord of hosts lives, before whom I am standing today."[8] In order to live in solitude with profit, it is necessary to be trained first in all the details of monastic life, to know all the rules and statutes, say the office and be experienced in every aspect of monastic life and behavior. But all this is still only external, as a wall around a church, because it is even more necessary to be well tried in spiritual warfare and to know how to fight thoughts inspired by the enemy. The Prayer of Jesus is the potent arm to defeat the enemy. Prayer should be mastered, at least in part, before one retires into solitude."[9]

Hilarion was much in love with solitude. His hymn to the desert reminds one greatly of the celebrated eulogy of Staretz Zosima Verkhovskoy. The latter wrote at the end of his life in Odigitrievsky Monastery:—"O solitude, solitude, my beloved solitude! I bid you farewell as a beloved mother. It

7. Ibid., p. 150.
8, 1 Kings 18:15.
9. Ibid., p. 163.

seems that because of my unworthiness, I have lost you."
The sisters told him: "Father, you shall have a greater reward
if you save all of us than you would if you save only yourself
in the desert." "I do not despair of my salvation," he said,
"and do not oppose the ways of God but that sweetness of
heart, that spiritual consolation, that indescribable interior
joy can be experienced nowhere but in solitude. Sisters, let
me go."[10] Hilarion writes the same in chapter thirty-five:
"When I lost my solitude, leaving for Russia, I understood its
heavenly dignity, its incomparable beauty and the hidden
fullness of the true life which streams through it with full-
flooded rivers of the purest joys—in the sublime feelings of
the heart and in the holy thoughts of the mind. After this
loss, solitude appeared to me as a divine habitation, a garden
of paradise."[11]

"When I walked in the streets of the town or was driven in
a carriage, the sea of vanity surrounded me. Every feeling of
soul was struck and dumbfounded as by the strokes of a
terrible hammer. Everything moved, hurried forward, speedily and unrestrainedly streamed on. A deathlike burial veil was
spread on all this movement of the people. This veil froze the
soul and all its forces with its icy cold, its inescapable sensation of mortality. Certainly there was an absence of rationali-
ty and still more of spirituality. This was the kingdom of
vanity and the life of this world. In that depressing atmosphere my spirit felt itself bound with iron chains. I truly
experienced the torments of hell because my every movement toward God was repressed by the multitude of the
voices of triumphant vanity just as water extinguishs fire! "[12]

In solitude one cannot live without a perfect trust in Divine
Providence. According to Hilarion, there are two kinds of
faith, dogmatic or abstract and active or faith of the heart.
The latter is the undoubting hope of receiving what we ask
from God. It exists when a man has not the least doubt that
he will receive from God what he asks. There is only one

10. *Žizneopisanija* (Moscow, October, 1909), p. 680.
11. *Na gorach . . . Ilarion*, p. 165.
12. Ibid., p. 166. See a description of a comparable experience in Bolshakaff,
"Journey to Solitude," *Church Times* (London, 1956).

undivided faith. Active faith is based on dogmatic truth as on its foundations. It cannot exist without it. Faith in its proper development, according to its degrees, comes to real experience of divine things. At that stage it is called contemplative faith, while before it was faith from hearing."[13]

The book contains a remarkable description of the death of Staretz Desiderius. "The godly and sacred choir virtues, like a light-bearing cloud, hid the approaching end of life, impressing on the body the interior beauty of his soul with all its brightness, joy and rapture of heart. . . . Profound silence reigned in the room. Wonderful, splendid silence! Silence above word! Although to the fleshly eye nothing was seen, to the spiritual eye the corpse was a limitless open world. The sacrament of death, just administered, was still present with all its substances and contents. What happened not only brought us the liveliest sensation of the other world, whereto the soul of the staretz passed, but we, ourselves, it seemed, were there with all our spiritual being. The veil which separates the visible world from the invisible disappeared. We sensed the presence in the room of the heavenly host and their intimate communion with us, which blotted out from our mind everything earthly, visible and temporary, putting us into the state of spiritual, wonderful, enrapturing contemplation. We understood clearly the mystery of our earthly life. We saw all the splendor of the soul of man, when it fulfilled, according to its strength, its earthly destiny."[14]

Although the work of Hilarion was approved by the spiritual directors of St Panteleimon and thrice received the *Imprimatur* of the Russian Church authorities, it contained some ambiguous expressions, as Hilarion himself was well aware as is clear from his letter to Fr Vladimir. These expressions attracted the attention of skhimnik from the Skete of St Elias, Chrysanthus, who wrote a review of the book accusing Hilarion of pantheism. Against Chrysanthus, another skhimnik, Martinian, wrote a strong letter defending Hilarion. Later on two monks, both noblemen and well educated,

13. *Na gorach . . . Ilarion,* p. 186. Rom 10:17.
14. Ibid., p. 219.

Alexis Kyreevsky and Anthony Bulatovich, entered into the conflict, the first attacking and the second defending the book. Russian Athos was in turmoil.[15] Joachim III, of Constantinople, condemned the book. The Russian Synod accepted this condemnation. Those who persisted in adhering to the view that the name of Jesus expressed the essence of Divinity or was the Deity were ordered to leave Athos. About 1,000 Russian monks left Athos for Russia in 1913. The Movement died out in Athos soon after, while in Russia the so-called onomolaters rapidly submitted to the Synod. Hilarion died before all these troubles spread. His expressions were often ambiguous; he himself realized this but he found no one to correct him in time. He was accused, therefore, of pantheistic tendencies, as in the West the great Flemish mystic, Ruysbroek, was in his own time. The Onomolaters Movement was merely a passing stage in a long history of Mount Athos. It touched only the Russians and only two monasteries, St Panteleimon and the Skete of St Andrew. In St Panteleimon there were in the first half of the present century at least two mystics. The first of them was Staretz Silouan, whose life and teaching are described by his disciple. Archimandrite Sophrony Sakharov, in his book *Staretz Silouan.*[16] The staretz was born to a peasant family named Antonov in a village of the province of Tambov in 1866 and was given the name of Symeon. After spending his youth in the village, he went to the Russian Imperial Gurard in St Petersburg for military service. Completing his term of service, Symeon went in 1892 to St Panteleimon on Mount Athos to test his monastic vocation. In 1896 he was professed and in 1911 he became skhimnik Silouan. He died on September 24, 1938.

Staretz Silouan left after him a number of short meditations and notes which well express his spirituality. Some them are worth quoting: "How do you know whether you

---

15. Details on the movement can be found in E. Vychodcev, *Istorija Afonskoj Smuty* (St Petersburg, 1917) and S. Troicky, *Ob Imenach Božijch* (St Petersburg, 1914).

16. Ieromonkh Sofrony, *Staretz Silouane* (Paris: Union, 1952); tr. (partial) Rosemary M. Edmonds, *The Undistorted Image: Staretz Silouan, 1866-1938* (London, 1958).

are living according to the will of God or not? Here is the sign: If you are sorrowful about something, it means that you have still not surrendered yourself altogether to the will of God, although it seems to you that you have done so. He who lives according to the will of God does not worry about anything. If something is necessary to him, he surrenders himself and that thing to God; and if he does not receive the needed thing, he nevertheless remains in peace as if he had it. The soul which has altogether given itself up to the will of God fears nothing, neither thunderstorms, nor robbers, nor anything else. If anything happens to him he says: 'God has willed this.' If he is ill, he thinks: 'Sickness is necessary for me, otherwise God would not send it to me.' In this way peace is preserved in his soul and body. . . . He who worries about himself is unable to surrender himself to the will of God. The humble soul lives before God in fear and love; in fear, lest it offend God in some way, in love for the soul has learned how the Lord loves us. . . . The best thing is to surrender oneself to God and to endure sorrows with hope. The Lord seeing our sorrows never adds more. If sorrows seem to us overwhelming, it means that we have not surrendered ourselves to the divine will."[17]

"If you think evil of men, it means that an evil spirit lives in you and inspires you with those thoughts. And if anyone does not repent and dies without forgiving his brother, his soul will go where the evil spirit who took possession of his soul resides. We live under this law: if you forgive people, it means that you are forgiven by God; but if you do not forgive your brother, you sin remains with you. The Lord wants us to love our neighbor. If you think this of him, that the Lord loves him, it means that the love of the Lord is with you. And if you think this, that the Lord dearly loves his creation, and you yourself love your enemies and consider yourself worst of all people, this means that the grace of the Holy Spirit is with you."[18]

---

17. Ibid., p. 141. (References are to the original French since the English edition contains only about half of the original.)
18. Ibid., p. 147.

"The soul cannot have peace if it will not pray for its enemies. The soul taught how to pray by divine grace, loves and is sympathetic with every creature and, especially, with man for whom the Lord suffered on the cross. He felt anguish in his soul for all of us. The Lord taught me to love my enemies. We cannot love our enemies without divine grace, but the Holy Spirit teaches us to love so that we shall be sorry even for the devils because they have fallen from good and have lost their humility and their love of God. I beg you, try this. Pray to the Lord for those who offend and dishonor you or rob you, or persecute the Church, saying: 'Lord, we all are your creation, be merciful to your servants and convert them to repentance! ' You will then experience grace. . . . If you pray for your enemies, peace will come to you. And when you love your enemies, take for certain that great divine grace dwells in you. I shall not say that it is perfection but it is adequate for salvation."[19]

"I know a boy. He looked like an angel, humble, conscientious and meek. He had a white, rosy face, and bright blue eyes, tranquil and friendly. But when he grew up he began to live impurely and lost divine grace. And when he was thirty he became more of a devil than a man. He was a beast and an animal. And his air was terrible and disgusting. But I have also seen the contrary. I have seen men who came to the cloister with faces disfigured by sins and passions, but with repentance and a devout life they changed and became very comely. The Lord granted me to see in the Old Russik, during confession, the visage of Christ. He stood in the confessional, shining exceedingly, and although he was white with age his face was beautiful and fresh like that of a boy. I saw one bishop in the same transfigured state during the Liturgy. I also saw the face of Father John of Kronstadt, which was by nature quite ordinary, transfigured by divine grace into the face of an angel. It was pleasant to look at him. Thus, sin disfigures man while grace beautifies him."[20]

19. Ibid., p. 156.
20. Ibid., pp. 160-161.

"All men seek rest and joy but only a few know where to find these blessings, and what is needed to acquire them. For thirty-five years I have known a monk who is always gay at heart and in his face is joyful, even though he is old. The reason is that he loves obedience and his soul has surrendered itself to the divine will. He never worries. His soul loves God and contemplates him. He who has within him even a little grace, submits with joy to all superiors. He knows that God rules in heaven and on the earth and in hell. God rules over man and his works and over everything in the world. Therefore, such a man is always at rest. He who is obedient has surrendered himself to the divine will and does not fear death because his soul is accustomed to live with God and it loves him. Such a man cuts off his own will and, therefore, neither in soul nor in body does he ever have the struggles which torment the unruly and selfwilled."[21]

"On July 1, 1932" Staretz Silouan writes, "Father Panteleimon came to me from the Old Russik. I asked him how he was getting on and he answered with his face full of joy: 'I am very happy.'—'But why are you so happy? ' I asked him. —'Because the brethren love me.'— 'But for what special reason do they love you? —'Because I obey everyone when they send me somewhere,' he answered. And I thought: 'The way to the Kingdom of God is easy.' He found his peace through obedience for God's sake. Therefore his soul is so joyful."[22]

Twice I stayed at St Panteleimon, in 1954 and in 1957. Fr Ilian, the confessor of the monastery, was the last representative of the long line of St Panteleimon's mystics and ascetics. There are, of course, many good monks in St Panteleimon as there are in other monasteries, but true mystics are rare, exceedingly rare. It is said that if a monastery in a thousand years can produce one mystic, it has justified its existence. There is, no doubt, some difficulty in defining who is a mystic and who is not. I consider mystics those people who have reached union with God, through unceasing prayer of the

21. Ibid., p. 174.
22. Ibid., p. 197.

heart, custody of the thoughts and complete surrender to the divine will. Some mystics have left writings. Others we know only from accounts written about them by their contemporaries. Many mystics have acquired special gifts from God like reading the thoughts of others, prophecy, the healing of the sick and the possessed, levitation, transfiguration, and so on. However, these gifts, although not to be underestimated, are not essential to the mystic as are those mentioned above.

I had many talks with Fr Ilian which I have described in several articles.[23] There are, in fact, three Mount Athos. The first, the Mount Athos of tourists, is described in many books and articles in dozens of languages. The second, the Mount Athos of scholars and artists, is also well-known and there are a great many learned studies on the history, sociology, art and literature of the Mount. The third, the Mount Athos of mystics, is very little known and well-nigh impenetrable. The mystics avoid publicity as a plague and do not reveal themselves to everybody but only to those who, according to their judgment, are apt to benefit from their sayings. Fr Ilian, a native of Rostov on the upper Volga, spent his childhood and youth in St Petersburg, the Imperial Capital. His father was a merchant. Very early he decided to become a monk. After being a novice for some time in the great Glynsky Monastery in the province of Kursk he came to Mount Athos.

During the Onomolaters controversy, Fr Ilian was stationed in Constantinople in St Panteleimon's Priory. Thus he escaped that painful period in the history of St Panteliemon. In due course he was ordained and became the confessor to the monastery, deputy to the abbot and librarion, and finally in 1958, abbot of St Panteleimon.

I worked in St Panteleimon's library under his guidance. It has about 1,000 ancient Greek manuscripts, several hundred old Slavonic manuscripts and a large number of Russian manuscripts. The latter deal chiefly with the mystical life. Besides the two Russian manuscripts which I have mentioned above, I looked through a most interesting manuscript:

---

23. In the *Church Times* (London, 1956) and in the *FROC Journal* (New York, 1957).

"Razskaz Svyatogortsa iero-monakha Selevkiya o svoey zhizni i o stranstvovanii po svyatuim mestam Russkim, Palestinskim i afonskim." (The Tale of the Agiorite, Skhimnik Selevkios, his Life and Journey to the Holy Places of Russia, Palestine and Athos).[24] Another interesting manuscript was that of Mother Panteleimona, who died on May 7, 1888 in Pokrosky Convent in Moscow. In the world she was Dariya Kolokolova, the widow of a minor court official. She was paralyzed eleven years but was instantly healed on September 11, 1867 by a relic of St Panteleimon brought on a visit to Russia. While several Athonite monasteries have much better collections of manuscripts none has a library as well selected as the 30,000 volumes of St Panteleimon. As far as Russian books are concerned only the library of the Pontifical Oriental Institute in Rome and the Slavonic Library of Helsinki University in Finland can rival it in Western Europe. For Russian manuscripts on mysticism it is altogether unique.

Fr Ilian, being confessor for many years in a great monastery and the spiritual director of several megaloschemoi, knew the human soul well. He had the same disconcerting habit of giving answers to your questions before you formulated them. He explained to me the meaning of *uverenie* or the divine guidance of the heart by giving me, for study, the life of Staretz Daniel of Acminsk and the case of Abbess Susanna which I quoted above. He told me of cases of *uverenie* in his own life and indicated others in my life as well. In regard to the Prayer of Jesus Fr Ilian advised against the practice of the Hesychast method without an experienced staretz and then only after the passions have been mastered.

The best and safest way to perfection according to Fr Ilian, is humility, simplicity and surrender to God. Toward external exercises he was tolerant. They are necessary to keep the body in subjection, but to give them preeminence is unwise. Fr Ilian illustrated his points either with the lives of the saints or with cases from the history of the monastery. He shared the view of Staretz Ambrose that sins, although absolved,

24. Ms 327/80.

need to be punished by expiatory suffering. Those who rebel against such suffering perish forever. Fr Ilian used to exorcise the possessed and to give absolution in the case of terrible sins. He described to me how this affects the confessor. Some of his experiences were very much the same as those of the well-known Curé of Ars.

Like Staretz Silouan Fr Ilian was very devoted to the celebrated Russian priest, Fr John of Kronstadt. [25] Fr John Sergiev was born on October 18, 1829 in Sura in the Russian Arctic province of Arkhangelsk. His father was a psalmist and choir director of the village. The family lived in great poverty. In 1839 John was sent to Arkhangelsk, first to the clerical school and afterwards to the seminary. In 1851 he entered St Petersburg Ecclesiastical Academy which he finished in 1855. While in the Academy John wanted to become a missionary but finally decided that there was much to do in Russia itself. On November 12, 1855 he was ordained and appointed to St Andrew's Collegiate Church in Kronstadt, the Russian naval fortress protecting St Petersburg. John remained on the staff of this church till his death on December 20, 1908.

Fr John was an excellent parish priest and quickly experienced great success in his parish activity. He organized all kinds of charitable and cultural activities. His "House of Labor" became a true city and was occupied in 1902 by 7,281 residents. The House of Labor included workshops, schools, libraries, orphanages and old peoples homes. Fr John founded and assisted convents and built churches in all parts of Russia. For his works and foundations he needed a great deal of money. Like his contemporaries in the West, St John Benedict Cottolengo and St John Bosco, he always found what he needed.

Fr John was a true liturgist, who loved liturgy and celebrated it daily for great crowds and always with the utmost of devotion. He was even more renowned as a confessor. Daily he heard the confessions of 150 to 300 people, and

25. The most recent and well documented life of Fr John of Kronstadt is A. Semenon Tyan-Sansky, *Otetz Joann Kronstadsky* (New York, 1955).

during Lent from 5,000 to 6,000 people a day. As he was quite unable to hear all these people individually, Fr John was obliged to employ a general absolution. He would read two prayers and comment on them. Then he named various sins and commented on them. Then he asked all those present to repent. A witness has described the scene. "Some people wept. Some people cried loudly. Many confessed their sins before all present. . . . Fr John was very moved and over-whelmed by it all. His lips moved in prayer. His eyes were turned to heaven. He stood with his hands crossed on his breast. Big tears fell from his eyes."[26] Finally he read the prayer of absolution. The Communions of the penitents which took place at the liturgy following the general confession lasted over two hours. Father celebrated the Liturgy in such a way that the priests who concelebrated with him hardly dared to look on him. His face was full of light.

Fr John left a number of writings among which the most important is his autobiography, "My Life in Christ."[27] This book is not a theological study but a monument to theological experience. Like all Russian mystics Fr John believed that a proper ordering of the heart will lead man to salvation and perfection. He did not approve of preocupation with the intellect, ignoring heart. He had a very strong sense of Church, its vitality and its unity. According to him the Church of God is a great holy family. Fr John had a profound understanding of the part of Our Lady in the economy of salvation. His ideas on evil and on the struggle with it are very original. The way to overcome evil is by prayer and the name of God which is all-powerful. Consequently Fr John practiced the Prayer of Jesus himself and recommended it to others. However, he considered liturgical prayer superior to private prayer. The center of Christian life is the Liturgy, the Eucharist. Like Nicholas Cabasilas, a Byzantine mystic of the fourteenth century, Fr John of Kronstadt was essentially a liturgical mystic.

26. Ibid., pp. 76-77.
27. English trans., London, 1897.

As Fr John became more renowned greater crowds flocked to Kronstadt. Finally they became so enormous that he was obliged to visit the provinces. His journeys, which began in 1888, were incredible. Any place where he stopped, he was at once surrounded by crowds. When he stayed at one estate near Kharkov 100,000 people visited the estate. When he sang the Liturgy in Kharkov Cathedral the crowd was so great that neither the clergy nor the choir were able to leave the sanctuary during the service. 60,000 people attended his short service in the Cathedral square.[28] The same crowds came to see Fr John in Kiev on the Volga and other places. In 1894 he was present at the death bed of Alexander III in the palace in the Crimea. As a miracleworker Father John of Kronstadt was exceptional. Cases of people whom he healed from all kinds of illnesses are so numerous that they can fill a thick book. He was always gay and cheerful. His mysticism was rather like that of St Seraphim of Sarov, a mysticism of light and resurrection. Fr John was a secular priest and his mysticism was very different from that of monks, hermits and pilgrims. I mention him because he had a great influence on several of the monks of his time. Fr John was conservative in his outlook and a monarchist. He clearly foresaw the end of the Empire and the coming of the atheistic state. He died in 1908 and was buried with Royal honors in the convent which he founded in St Petersburg. The Soviet regime eliminated as much as possible all the souvenirs of this priest with whom it has nothing in common.

Besides Mount Athos another center of Russian mysticism of the twentieth century was the great Valaam Monastery. The spiritual preeminence of this monastery begins with Abbot Nazarius in the eighteenth century. Nicholas Anosov was born in 1735 in the province of Tambov, the son of a sacristan.[29] When he was seventeen years old, Nicholas came to Sarov Monastery, where he was professed, receiving the

28. Semenon, *Otetz Joann Kronstadsky*, pp. 266-267.
29. A good biography of Nicholas can be found in *Valaamsky monastyr i ego podvižniki* (St Petersburg, 1903³).

name of Nazarius. Ordained a priest in 1776, Nazarius was
called in 1781 by the Russian Primate, Gabrie Petrov, Metropolitan of St Petersburg, to reorganize Valaam Monastery.
The abbot of Sarov did not want to lose Nazarius and informed the Primate that Nazarius was not clever enough for
the job. The Metropolitan answered that he already had more
than enough clever monks. Nazarius quickly restored the
monastery. There are many tales told of him which demonstrate his spirituality. Two are particularly characteristic of
him:

Once in the reign of Alexander I, Nazarius visited the
capital and found one of his friends, an aristrocrat and statesman, quite ill. This man had been dismissed on account of
court intrigues. His wife asked the prayers of Nazarius. "Well,"
Nazarius said, "we should pray earnestly to the Lord that
he might change the mind of the Emperor, but we must also
ask his friends." The lady, thinking that Nazarius was speaking of great dignitaries, answered: "We have already asked
everybody but there is little hope that they will intercede."
"But you do not ask the people who really matter," Nazarius
answered, "and you do not ask them in the right way. Give
me some money." The lady brought several gold coins. "No,"
Nazarius said, "these coins are of no use to me. Give me
copper and small silver coins." A whole sack of them was
brought to Nazarius. The latter went out and spent the entire
day looking for beggars and poor people, distributing money
to them and asking their prayers for his intention. Nazarius
returned, empty handed, late in the evening and said: "Glory
be to God! All the court of the Sovereign promised to pray
for us." The lady of the house, very happy, went to her sick
husband and told him the good news. The statesman asked
the abbot into his sick room to thank him. Hardly had
Nazarius left the house when a messenger came from the
Court with a decree of the Sovereign reinstating the sick man
to all his honors and positions. The reinstated statesman
immediately sent for Nazarius in order to ask the abbot
whom he asked to intercede before the Emperor and who
was the most responsive. "I asked," Nazarius said, "the most

powerful courtiers in the city, the beggars and the poor. They make up the Court of the Sovereign of heaven and earth."[30]

The second tale, which stresses still more the great faith of Nazarius in the power of prayer, is even more striking. Nazarius resigned his abbacy in Valaam in 1804 in order to return to Sarov. Before he settled for good in Sarov, Nazarius decided to visit various monasteries in Southern Russia. On his journey he was accompanied by another monk, Fr Hilarion. One day both monks stopped overnight in the house of a parish priest in the countryside. It was Saturday. The parish priest welcomed the monks. They were astonished, however, that he made no preparations to sing the evening service. Nazarius inquired the reason. The rector replied that he did not intend to sing the service, adding that he rarely celebrated even the Liturgy. "My parish, Father Abbot," the rector said, "is large, and we have no sects here, but the people are indifferent. They rarely come to church. I do not see any reason to celebrate frequently in an empty church." "Father," the distressed abbot answered, "if your parishioners neglect their most important duties, you, their pastor, must not neglect yours. The temple of God is never empty. Since it was consecrated, it has its own guardian angel. If your people neglect their duties, their guardian angels do not. They fill the temple. When you celebrate, the angels celebrate with you. You must celebrate regularly and pray to God that he might convert your people to prayer and penitence. The Lord will order their guardian angels to persuade them to come. You are responsible not only for your own soul, but also for those of your flock. You must realize that."

The rector, very much moved, asked the monks to help him. Nazarius told him to ring the bell for the evening service and went himself with Fr Hilarion to the parish church. When the service began, the church was empty. Gradually ten old people came in. After the Gospel was read, the abbot preached a short sermon stressing the need and the benefit of

30. Ibid., pp. 149-150.

regular churchgoing. There were already thirty people in the church, mostly curious villagers who came to find out why the service was sung. The abbot preached again at the end of the service. A large number of people came for the Sunday Liturgy. In the evening the abbot noticed many people gathering near the church. "Why do they come here, Father? " the abbot asked the rector. "They come to sing and to dance," the rector answered. "We shall go there, too," the abbot suggested, taking with him the "Lives" of the saints. Coming to the churchyard the abbot sat on the bench and started to read the life of the saint of the day to a few old women gathered there. In due course a few old men joined them. The abbot received everybody with great kindness. Reading the life of the saint, Nazarius commented on various passages. Still more people came to them. The next day the abbot again celebrated Liturgy and Vespers, preaching at both. He continued to do so every day. After a fortnight of these services people began to come to the church from neighboring villages as well. Gradually the church became crowded. The rector himself became a disciple of the abbot and obeyed him as his staretz.

After a long stay the abbot went away to continue his journey very pleased with the results. Returning to Sarov by the same route, after a considerable time, the abbot and Fr Hilarion arrived one Sunday morning at the same village just before the Liturgy. A vast crowd surrounded the Church. Recognizing Nazarius the people, overjoyed, brought him to the church carrying him shoulder high. The rector was just about to begin Liturgy. Deeply moved Nazarius thanked God for such a transformation in a decaying parish. Crowds surrounded the abbot imploring his blessing. After the Liturgy the Rector preached one of the best sermons of his life, telling the congregation that this vast crowd was the direct result of the prayer of the abbot. The crowds became so large that only a small portion of them could be accommodated in the church, the remainder were standing outside listening under the open windows. Nazarius tarried again for a while in the village. When he left, several thousand people, men, women, and childred, led by the rector, all in tears, accompanied him for some miles. The rector remained under the spiritual direction of Nazarius until the abbot's death.[31]

Nazarius once said to his monks: "I do not know how you feel, but I consider myself indebted to all and at fault before all. How is it possible for us to be offended by anybody? We love but three or four people. How insignificant? It is far better to love everybody with a gracious simplicity. I open the gates of my heart to everyone. If someone is not happy to see me, I am nonetheless happy to see him. Once for three years I felt no sorrow and exercised myself in incredible fasting and mortification of the flesh. I thought that all virtue is in that. But three sisters suddenly came to me: heaviness of spirit, ennui and sadness. When I met them, I did not know how to receive them. I was quite exhausted. But in due course I learned what to do. I told my visitors: 'Welcome, my dear guests, I shall entertain you to the best of my ability. I shall light a candle and we shall pray, weep, sing and shout: "God, be merciful to me a sinner; you who created me, have mercy on me. I have sinned beyond counting, forgive me. How can I look to your mercy? How shall I start my confession? Lady Theotokos, remember your servant!' " My guests started to run away but I begged them: 'Forgive me! ' But they were no more, there was no trace of them. Let us pray in spirit and in mind. Consider the words of the Apostle Paul: 'I would prefer to speak five words with my mind than ten thousand in a tongue.'[32] I cannot describe to you how we are able to pronounce these five words. What a joy! Lord, Jesus Christ, forgive me."[33] Nazarius died in Sarov on February 23, 1809.

Among the successors of Nazarius the most remarkable were Barlaam and Damaskin. The first was professed in Valaam in 1798 and became its abbot in 1830. Nine years later he resigned and retired to Optino, where he gave good counsel to Staretz Ambrose. When someone begged Barlaam to be allowed to accompany him on a walk, he answered: "Well, come along, but on one condition only. We shall walk

31. Ibid., pp. 151-154.
32. 1 Cor 14:15, 19.
33. Ibid., pp. 155-156.

in silence." He also said: "Remember St Arsenius the Great who said: 'Love everybody and run away from everybody.'" Once Barlaam said: "Two thoughts continually assail man: the condemnation of others for their evil living and exalted ideas about himself because of his own successes." Barlaam died in 1849 in Optino. Abbot Damaskin, a Tver peasant, born in 1795, was a remarkable man. He was powerfully inclined toward solitude and early became a hermit. He became known for his mystical experiences and was only forty-four when he was elected abbot. He accepted only in obedience. He was a remarkable abbot, an excellent administrator and a practical man, showing once more that mystics can also be good business men. He died in 1881, eighty-six years of age. The Valaam monks usually live to a very advanced age, keeping all their faculties to the end. Valaam allowed for three degrees of monastic life. The majority lived in a great central monastery as strict cenobites. Those who were able and willing, after several years in the monastery, went to various sketes dependent on the monastery, to live a semi-hermitical life. Those who proved themselves able to live well in a skete, were allowed in due course to retire to a hermitage to live as a solitary. All the sketes and hermitages were situated on various islands of the Valaam archipelago in the lake of Ladoga. In 1902 the community of Valaam, postulants and oblates (trudniks) included, numbered 1,079 monks. Khariton, abbot of Varlaam between the World Wars, was interested in publications. He was a good poet himself. He published during the last war a short but good book on ascetism and before 1939 two books on the Prayer of Jesus in collaboration with Archpriest S. Chetverikov.[34] These two books were based on the teaching of various Russian mystics on the Prayer of Jesus and consist largely of quotations from them. The second book is largely the work of Fr Chetverikov and has some strange affinities with the second, apocryphal part of the *Tales* of the Russian pilgrim.

Father Michael, the Recluse of Uusi Valamo who died in

---

34. *Sbornik o molitve Iisusovoj* (Serdobol, 1936) and *Besedy o molitve Iisusonoj* (Serdobol, 1938).

1962, was the latest representative of the Valaam mystical tradition I visited him personally in 1954 and described my talks with him in various articles and finally in a short book entitled, "Father Michael, Recluse of Uusi Valamo."[35] Fr Michael, a native of Western Russia, entered Valaam at the beginning of this century. He was for a time attached to Valaam Priory in St Petersburg. Otherwise, he spent all his time in Valaam itself. In the early twenties, when there were divisions in the Valaam community concerning which calendar to observe, the Julian or the Gregorian, he sided with the first group but the second came into power. Thereupon he retired, first to a skete and then to an hermitage on Smolensky Island. During the Second World War the Valaam community was transferred to Central Finland to Uusi Valamo. Unable to continue his eremitical life in the new surroundings, Fr Michael became a recluse. Some years ago, Dr Nicholas Yarushevich, Metropolitan of Krutitsi, the second most important prelate of the Russian Church, visited Valaam. He asked Fr Jerome, then abbot of Uusi Valamo, to recommend a monk to him for spiritual guidance, the one whom he considered best. The abbot recommended Fr Michael. The Metropolitan spent a long time talking with the recluse. Returning to the abbot, the prelate expressed his wonder and his admiration for the recluse. The Metropolitan asked the abbot to allow people, particularly the clergy, to visit Fr Michael for spiritual conversation. Since that time an ever increasing number of people from all over the world have come to Uusi Valamo to obtain the advice or direction of Fr Michael in all kinds of difficulties. This ever-increasing stream of visitors began to tire Fr Michael, who was essentially a contemplative. He found himself at eighty years of age in a position not very different from that of the great startzy of Optino. In 1957, when some of the outstanding difficulties which separated the Russian Patriarchate from the Orthodox Church in Finland were overcome, the Metropolitan of Krutitsi once more visited Valamo. He invited Fr Michael to come to Russia, where monks like him are badly needed. Fr

35. Oxford, 1956.

Michael accepted the invitation and on October 15, 1957 he went to Moscow accompanied by seven of his closest friends and disciples, all priest-monks of Uusi Valamo: Fr Luke, Fr Sergius, Fr Gennadius, and four others. The Russian Patriarch gave Fr Michael and his disciples the ancient and beautiful Pskovo-Pechersky Monastery near Pskov in Western Russia. On the eve of his departure to the Soviet Union Fr Michael sent me his last letter of direction. He announced his decision to return to the life of a recluse: "I will give no more direction. The Lord has commanded me to pray fervently for everyone and to lead a hidden life, but not to teach. As St Arsenius the Great, I love everyone and run away from all."

Fr Michael belongs to the school of Paisius Velichkovsky. A disciple of the latter, Theodore, lived in Valaam together with Leo Nagolkin, the first great staretz of Optino. They trained Barlaam, later abbot of Valaam, and Fr Euthemius, the confessor of the community. The latter had as his disciples, Damaskin, who became abbot of Valaam and Fr Agathangel, who became its confessor. The latter trained Maurice, another abbot of Valaam, the teacher and spiritual director of Fr Michael. I had altogether five long talks with Fr Michael. A peculiarity of Fr Michael was that before you could ask him something, he already answered you. He knew what you wanted from him. This was, of course, the case with many other Startzy. In our first conversation we discussed prayer for the dead. Sometime before my meeting with Fr Michael, I had lost someone dear to me and wanted to ask Fr Michael about prayer for the dead. Before I could ask him he took a leaflet from his table and handed it to me. It was entitled, "On Commemoration of the Dead." This leaflet, apparently a sermon he delivered on November 23, 1947, was one of the best vindications of prayer for the dead which I have ever read. The leaflet stressed the need not only for prayer for the dead but also for their commemoration during Liturgy. "We should continue to truly love our dear dead. When we shall die, they shall remember us at death's hour with the same love with which we commemorate them now. This shall help us. While we bid them farewell here with tears and prayers, they shall meet us with joy and good tidings. The dead know everything about us and what we do. They see and hear perfectly when we pray for them. Therefore, if you want to help your dead loved one wholeheartedly and do everything commanded by the Holy Church, never allow yourself any doubt about his or her ultimate salvation. Such doubt is a suggestion of the evil spirit. And why? Because if the dead were unworthy of salvation, God would not allow you to pray for them. As St John Damascene says: 'God moves no one to pray for those dead who are unworthy of salvation, neither their parents, nor a wife, nor a husband, nor any relatives or friends.' The following prophecy is fulfilled in them: 'miserable are those among the dead for whom none among the living prays.' . . . [36] When I finished reading the paper I looked in wonder at the staretz. His astonishing eyes, bright and clear, looked at me. I realized at once that Fr Michael read my thoughts and knew my past. "Father," I asked him, "what do you think of death? " "There is no death," he answered, "there is merely a passing from one state to another. To me personally, the life of the other world is much more real than my life here. . . . The more the Christian lives the interior life, the more he is detached from this world, and imperceptibly he approaches the other world. When the end comes it is easy; the thin veil simply dissolves. . . . Prayers for the dead are needful not only for them but for us as well."[37] During this first talk we also discussed Divine Providence, the interior life, prayer and repentance.

During my second talk with Fr Michael, on August 12, 1954, I wanted to ask him why a tragedy which I experienced in 1951 had happened. When I came to the staretz, before I could ask him anything, he silently gave me another leaflet to read. When I took it I read: "It Came From Me." "Happiness and misfortune, rise and fall, health and sickness, glory and dishonor, wealth and poverty—everything, comes from me and must be accepted as such. Those who entrust themselves to me and accept all the trials which I send to them will not be ashamed in the Day of Judgment. They will realize even here in this world why their life took this course

36. Ibid., pp. 15-16.
37. Ibid., pp. 16-17.

and not another. I send to everyone that which is best for him."[38] During the second talk we discussed many subjects, including miracles, heroic virtues, confession, daily services and mystical states. According to the staretz love is the greatest virtue. "Never judge anyone," he said, "have no foes, revere everyone. In life avoid anything which makes you proud and which disturbs your serenity of mind. The best prayer is, as you said yourself: 'Thy will be done.' True repentance covers all sins. Remember always that all troubles in this life are designed to make us more detached in this world. Therefore, they lead us to a better life. External piety and devotions, vocal prayers, vigils and fasts are good and needful but only as a frame for an intense interior life of humility, unceasing prayer and trust in God. If the latter are absent, the former are not of much use."[39] On mystical states Fr Michael said that they could be understood only by those who experienced them personally. "As a blind man," Fr Michael said, "cannot picture colors, so an earthly man is unable to picture wonders perceived in contemplation. These wonders are usually rewards for those who have obtained a spiritual crown. According to Staretz Ambrose of Optino, there are five crowns. The most glorious is given for the patient endurance of sorrows. The remaining four are given for virginity, monastic life, spiritual direction of others and sickness borne with resignation. To the five crowns correspond seven heavens. Five of them are reserved for those who follow the Lamb wherever he goes, that is, for the ascetics, mystics, and religious, while the other heavens are for the rest. . . . Mind you, all those crowns and heavens signify only various mystical and spiritual states. They are incommunicable. None but those who experienced them personally can understand them."[40]

During our third meeting we discussed the blessed valley of tears, daily celebration of the Liturgy, frequent Communion and the divine will. The staretz fully agreed with St Isaac the

38. Ibid., pp. 22-23.
39. Ibid., p. 24.
40. Ibid., p. 26.

Syrian that as long as one did not enter into the valley of tears he still served the world, that is, he still led a worldly life and worked for God only outwardly while his inward man remained sterile. Tears of repentance, according to St Isaac, are the signs of the awakening of that inner man. "I have known people," the staretz said, "who passed through this blessed valley of tears." St Isaac says truly that those who received the grace of tears find out that wandering thoughts during the time of prayer cease and their very nature is changed. Such contemplatives enter into the peace described in the Epistle to the Hebrews. When this peace is attained, their minds begin to contemplate the mysteries. The Holy Spirit begins to reveal to the mystic heavenly things. God comes to dwell in him."[41]

Fr Michael celebrated the Liturgy alone each day, just as Bishop Theophane the Recluse had done. "Nothing," he said, "makes a priest better and more spiritual than the daily celebration of the Holy Liturgy. But we must remember the saying of one great mystic. No one should celebrate or take Communion unless he does so with tears of repentance and joy."[42] The staretz recommended frequent Communion to the laity. The discussion on the divine will was most illuminating. "Nothing happens in this world," Fr Michael said to me, "apart from the will of God. By his will, for example, you left Russia for the West without knowing where you would go and why. God has settled you now in Oxford, in England, and you now write books and articles. Again by the will of God you came here to see me. Why, you do not know at present but you will understand in due course. The same thing happens to everybody, myself included."[43] The staretz told me then the story of his own ordination and also the story of a bishop.

The fourth talk was almost entirely devoted to mystical subjects. At that meeting Fr Michael handed me another leaflet. It not only answered my question but summed up all

41. Ibid., pp. 31-32.
42. Ibid., p. 32.
43. Ibid., p. 33.

our talks. The leaflet was entitled: "Attain peace of mind."
On the last day of his life, the leaflet stated, St Seraphim of
Sarov thrice said to a monk whom he loved: "Attain peace of
mind, Father." "What St Seraphim said to that monk I repeat
to you. While we have no peace of mind, we cannot see God.
We are able to understand Divine Providence looking to our
past, but we do not know what to do now and what to plan
for the future. If we have no inward peace, it means that we
are still divided in ourselves and blinded with passions, which
prevent us from seeing the world as it really is. But when we
attain an inward peace our passions are mastered and we see
clearly who we are and where we are going. It is impossible to
be a good servant of the Lord and to labor in his vineyard in
whatsoever capacity with any success, unless inner peace is
attained first. People value this peace above all else, but it is
obvious they cannot obtain it from those who do not have it
themselves. So many sermons, books and exercises produce
no effect because they are not born of inner peace, meditation and detachment. But when you attain inward peace
everything is all right because God is with you. Only in deep
inward peace can we see God and understand his will. All our
works, however secure and solid they might appear, are built
on shifting sands and will collapse, as the house on sand
about which we read in the Gospel, unless we attain serenity
of mind and know where to build and how to build."[44] Fr
Michael gave me then some personal counsels. His views on
silence, with which we finished our conversation, were taken
from St Isaac the Syrian. "When you put on one side every
ascetical exercise and on the other silence, you will soon find
out that the latter is the most important of all. People give us
many counsels but when we become familiar with silence, all
human counsels become superfluous as well as all our former
works. We will find that they all belong to the past and that
we approach perfection."[45] Fr Michael obviously wanted to
return to his solitude.

I attended on one occasion the Liturgy which he said alone

44. Ibid., p. 36.
45. Ibid., p. 38.

during the night. This was a true Liturgy of contemplation. The notion of time and space melted away. This was eternity. How long this Liturgy lasted, I cannot say. It seemed time stood still. A few hours later, I left Uusi Valamo and Northern Finland for quite a different world.

To describe the personality of Fr Michael I would use a description given to us by St Macarius the Great, an Egyptian mystic of the fourth century, which I have found in the *Dobrotolyubie* of Bishop Theophane the Recluse. "In him," St Macarius writes of the true mystic, "grace acts in such a way that his body and heart are in deep peace. His soul in its tremendous joy becomes like that of the innocent child. He judges no one, neither Greek nor Jew, neither sinner nor layman. This interior man looks on everyone equally. He rejoices with the entire world. His only desire is to honor and to love the Greek and the Jew. He is the son of the King because he trusts in the Son of God as his father. The door of the invisible world opens before him and he enters into many mansions. And once he enters these mansions, the doors of others open before him. If he entered a hundred mansions, the doors of another hundred would open. He is continually enriched. The more he is enriched, the more are the wonders revealed to him. To him, as to the son and heir, God entrusts that which cannot be apprehended by human nature or expressed by word." Such was Fr Michael. This is the true portrait of the Russian mystic, beginning with St Sergius of Radonezh, St Nilus of Sora, Paisius Velichkovsky, St Seraphim of Sarov and many others and ending with Fr Michael.

CONCLUSION

I HAVE TRIED TO PRESENT the Russian mystics to Western readers, and I hope I have succeeded to some degree. There is no similar book, not even in Russian. I have broken new ground. There are, of course, many defects, but, on the whole, I hope the picture is clear.

Russian mystics continue the Patristic tradition. Except St Demetrius of Rostov and St Tikhon Zadonsky, they remained quite unaffected either by Counter-Reformation mysticism or by that of Protestantism. Even these two Russian saints were affected by Western influences only very slightly. As one Cistercian abbot told me, after reading the talks with Fr Michael: "This is simply the mysticism of the Fathers." He is right.

Russian mystics lived and still live in the Patristic age. Their own tradition is a variation of the Byzantine. Their spiritual ancestors are Symeon the New Theologian and Gregory Palamas, Gregory of Sinai and Nicephoros the Monk. Russian mysticism is closely connected with Mount Athos, the cradle of the Hesychast tradition. But the first sources of Russian mysticism go far beyond Symeon the New Theologian or Palamas. St Isaac the Syrian, St John Climacus, Abbot Dorotheus and St Macarius the Great made a far greater impression on Russian mystics than Symeon or Gregory.

On the whole Russian mysticism can be regarded as a variety of that of Mount Athos. It is also based on the Prayer of Jesus and custody of thoughts. Russian monks were influenced by Mount Athos from the very beginning. The influence of the Holy Mountain asserted itself again in the fourteenth century, the age of St Sergius of Radonezh. In the fifteenth century St Nilus of Sora, the first Russian mystical writer, came along. His school, the Trans-Volga Elders, did not survive him for long. Their ideas were far too advanced for their age. Russian mysticism declined before the advancing formalism and ritualism of the Josephites.

The seventeenth century saw Russian mysticism at its lowest ebb. Yet at the close of the century we see St Demetrius of Rostov, who, however Latinized, belonged nonetheless to the Byzantine tradition. St Tikhon Zadonsky hardly could be pictured as a typical representative of Byzantine tradition but he certainly was not opposed to it. He lived in the eighteenth century, when a new revival of Russian mysticism took place. Originated by Paisius Velichkovsky on Mount Athos and in Rumania, it soon spread all over Russia, producing a rare constellation of Russian mystics in the nineteenth century. By his translation of *Philokalia* into Slavonic and through his numerous disciples, Paisius mightily influenced the monks of Russia. All the Russian mystics after Paisius may be regarded as his disciples in one way or another.

The Russian mystics of Mount Athos, Valaam, Optino, Glynsky, Svensky, and Roslavl all depend in the end on Paisius. St Seraphim of Sarov stands alone, as does George the Recluse. Bishop Ignatius Bryanchaninov and Bishop Theophane the Recluse, although neither direct nor indirect disciples of Paisius, nevertheless moved in the same world as he did. Some Russian mystics stressed one aspect of Christian faith and some another but this was largely due to their temperament. While St Demetrius of Rostov, St Tikhon Zadonsky, George the Recluse and Bishop Ignatius Bryanchanino stressed Calvary, repentance, the sadness of life, and dwelt on the dark night of the soul, St Seraphim of Sarov, the Startzy of Optino, Bishop Theophane the Recluse and Staretz Basil Kishkin stressed the Resurrection, forgiveness and the joy of life in God. They dwelt on the transfiguration of the soul.

The chief Russian mystical treatises are: *The Tradition of Sketic Life* of St Nilus of Sora; *On True Christianity* of St Tikhon Zadonsky; *The Way of Salvation* of Bishop Theophane the Recluse and the first volume of *Works* of Bishop Ignatius Bryanchaninov. The astonishingly profound mystical works, the anonymous *Tales of the Russian Pilgrim* and the *Talks of St Seraphim of Sarov with Motovilov* form a group apart. The other Russian mystical writings are chiefly diaries or letters. Theophane the Recluse and Bishop Ignatius, however, wrote voluminous treatises comparable to Western mystical works. The Russians are simpler, fresher and more straightforward. They are not overburdened with scholarly terms, mannerisms and obscurities. They do not consider meditation as prayer and, consequently, are free of the technicalities which make the reading of so many Western spiritual books so tiresome. In short Russian mystical treatises still preserve the freshness, simplicity and clearness of the writings of the first monastic fathers.

Although I have done my best to include as many Russian mystics as I could, some have been omitted for lack of space. I have selected mystics according to my estimation of their importance. The selection might have been different if the book were written by someone else.

I had the opportunity while writing this book to work in public and private libraries in Rome, Paris, London, Oxford, Athens, The Hague, Mount Athos, Valamo, and many other places. I am especially indebted to the libraries of the Pontifical Oriental Institute in Rome and of St Panteleimon's Monastery, Mount Athos. The first is probably the best library in Western Europe as far as Eastern Churches are concerned. Its Russian department is very rich and includes many books from the libraries of the Russian Synod, Home Office, Optino Monastery, and so forth. The second library, besides being rich in Russian ascetical and mystical books, also contains a large number of Russian manuscripts of great value.

The serious study of Russian mysticism has hardly begun. There is not even a critical edition of the *Tales of the Russian*

Pilgrim. The manuscripts which I found at St Panteleimon's still await publication. I did not look through the Valaam manuscripts. They may include some valuable matter as well.

It is very difficult to say anything about the future of Russian Orthodox mysticism. The present conditions in the Soviet Union and in the Russian diaspora do not generally favor the growth and development of monasteries, the natural cradles of mystics. Valaam and St Panteleimon's are starving for recruits and are reduced to a rapidly dying out older generation. In the Soviet Union monasteries certainly exist and are visited by great crowds of pilgrims. They also contain some mystics. It can be presumed that there are monks of high spirituality in the Laura of the Holy Trinity in Zagorsk, near Moscow, and in the Patriarchal Monastery in Odessa. We know, however, very little of them. The conditions in the Soviet Union do not permit the publication of religious reviews and books to any great extent. We do not know for how long monasteries will be allowed to exist there.

In the United States there is a Russian Monastery in Jordanville, New York, which produces some ecclesiastical publications where mystical and ascetical problems are discussed. This monastery, however, belongs to the Russian Church outside Russia, a group which does not recognize the Russian Patriarch. The *Messenger* of the Russian Exarchate in Western Europe, published in Paris, often prints good articles on mysticism in Russian and French. The *Messenger* has gathered quite a number of writers on mysticism, such as Professor V. Lossky, Archbishop Basil Krovoshein, Archimandrite Sophrony Sakharov and others. There is also a great interest in mysticism among Russian theologians and monks in the Soviet Union, as it is evidenced by articles in the *Journal* of the Patriarchate, printed in Moscow. It may well be that after a cold winter a new spring will come and with it a new revival of Russian mysticism.

GLOSSARY

Note: Transliterated Russian terms tend to be spelled in various ways. They are listed here as they are usually spelled in this book, although exceptions may be found according to the sources quoted.

Acedia—Etymologically it means a lack of care, of interest, negligence. In ascetical writings, following St John Cassian, it is taken as the sixth capital sin: spiritual torpor or boredom.

Antidoron—Bread, blessed but not consecrated, which is distributed in small pieces to those at the Liturgy who have not communicated. Originally only the remains of the Eucharistic loaves were used for this, and pieces were sent as goodwill tokens to those not present at the Liturgy.

Apophatic theology or spirituality—One that emphasizes the unknowability of God and the sinfulness of man.

Cherubikon—The hymn sung during the Great Entrance (*q. v.*). It symbolizes the entrance of all the saints and the righteous, honoring Christ who has sanctified them and given them the powers of the Cherubim. It also symbolizes the 'laying aside of all earthly cares'. It had its origin, according to the historian Quadrinus, in the reign of Justinian the Orthodox, who succeeded his uncle, Justinian the Great, in 565.

Chrysobulls—A golden bull or seal.

Dobrotolyubie—Literally, 'Love of Beauty'. The title given by Paisius Velichkovsky to his Slavonic translation of the *Philokalia* (*q.v.*). It contains only twenty-five of the thirty-six treatises of the *Philokalia*. It was first printed by Gabriel Petrov, the Metropolitan of St Petersburg, in 1793. It was translated into Russian by Bishop Theophane the Recluse (a rather free translation in five volumes) and published at St Panteleimon's Monastery, Mount Athos, in 1877.

Ektenia—Litanies. The word means supplication or fervent prayer that comes out of the heart, as the opening words of the litany imply: 'Let us all say with all our souls and with all our minds'.

Great Entrance—The procession after the Liturgy of the Word and in which the gifts are carried to the sanctuary for the Liturgy of the Eucharist.

Hesychasm—From *hesychia:* tranquillity, silence, quietness. A method of prayer which integrates a simple ejaculatory prayer, such as the Jesus Prayer, with bodily functions of breathing and heart beat. It was propagated on Mount Athos by the Sinaite (*q.v.*) and became a movement in the Church under the aegis of Gregory Palamas.

Hieromonk—A monk who has been ordained to the priesthood.

Hieroskhimnik—A skhimnik (*q.v.*) who has been ordained to the priesthood.

Idiorhythmic—Literally, one's own rhythm. Originally it was a synonym for self will. Later it came to describe a form of monastic life where each monk had his own rule of life and means of support. All the principal monasteries on Mount Athos at one time adopted this form of life, but some have now returned to the more traditional cenobitic way.

Ikon—An ikon is a sacred picture painted according to rather rigid traditional norms. The ikon occupies a prominent position in Orthodox life. In Russia ikons were found not only in the churches and monasteries but in every home. They would hang or rest on a shelf diagonally across a corner opposite the door, and a reverence would be made to them on entering and leaving the room.

Ikonostasis—The screen which sets the sanctuary off from the rest of the church. It is pierced by three doors: a central or royal door and two flanking doors. On either side of the royal doors, which are backed by a drapery, there are ikons of Christ and the Theotokos. The screen is covered with ikons according to traditional norms and the devotion of the particular church.

Josephites—The followers of Joseph of Volokolamsk who advocated a traditional and rather formalistic monastic observance, first in the face of the Non-possessors (*q.v.*) and then later in face of the liturgical reforms of Patriarch Nikon.

Kafisma—Literally, sitting (because the congregation may sit during it): the name given to the hymn sung at the end of the diverse sections of psalmody read at Matins.

Keleinik—A monk who is assigned to serve a bishop (who is a monk) and to celebrate the offices and liturgy with him.

Kellion—One of the simplest units of monastic organization: a 'cell' where monks live in small groups under a superior or spiritual father.

Lavra—Originally a monastery which followed the rule of St Anthony, later used simply to designate certain large monasteries. Besides Kiev, there were eight monasteries in Russia which bore this title and there is the Great Lavra on Athos.

Megaloschemos—A monk who has received the great

skhema (*q.v.*). This is the highest form of monastic profession. Commonly there are three degrees of monastic profession accepted in the East (although some of the ancients, especially Theodore the Studite opposed this division): rassophoros (*q.v.*), microschemos, and megaloschemos.

Metanias—Prostrations made in prayer, profound inclinations signifying a change of heart (*metanoia*), penitence, sorrow, reverence.

Non-possessors—Those monks who opposed the retention of large landed estates by monasteries. They had their origin as a distinct group in Russia with St Cyril and the founding of Belozersky Monastery. Their most notable partisan was St Nilus of Sora.

Old Ritualists—Those who did not accept the liturgical reforms brought about by Patriarch Nikon in the seventeenth century.

Onomolaters—Drawing their inspiration from the writings of Skhimnik Hilarion this group held that the Name of Jesus expressed the Divinity or was the Deity. They caused considerable division and disturbance on Athos and in Russia until they were condemned and compelled to leave the Holy Mountain in 1913. The movement rapidly died out.

Palamites—The followers of St Gregory Palamas who espoused his theological theories, especially that of uncreated energies.

Paramicroi—A lower class of monks found in idiorhythmic (*q.v.*) monasteries.

Paterikon—A menology or calendar of saints and holy men arranged for liturgical use giving a brief account of their lives and virtues. Each monastery could have its own.

Philokalia—A collection of patristic and hesychast writings concerning interior prayer and the monastic life, forming a masterly summary of Orthodox mystical and ascetical teaching. It was compiled by Metropolitan Macarius of Corinth and St Nicodemus Hagiorite and first published in Venice in 1782. It was translated into Slavonic under the title *Dobrotolyubie* (*q.v.*).

Podvig—A notable exploit. When applied to the spiritual life it refers to outstanding achievements in the life of prayer or ascetic exercises. The one who performs a podvig is called a *podvižnik*.

Podvories—A prioress.

Poustyna—Literally a desert, a place of retirement for prayer.

Prayer of Jesus—A brief ejaculatory prayer addressed to Jesus, drawn from Scripture, usually taking the form: 'Lord Jesus Christ, Son of God, have mercy on me, a sinner.' The practice of the Jesus Prayer was revived on Mount Athos in the fourteenth century by the Sinaite (*q.v.*) and has in recent times been greatly popularized through the *Tales of the Pilgrim*.

Proistamenoi—The ruling class of monks in the idiorhythmic (*q.v.*) monastery.

Psalmist—The psalmist in Russian parish churches is a layman, occasionally a man in minor orders, who acts as reader and choirmaster.

Raskol—The Great Russian Schism arising out of the liturgical reforms of Patriarch Nikon and leading to the beginning of Russian Nonconformism. See *Josephites*.

Rassophoros—The lowest level of Russian monasticism after the novitiate. The monk is tonsured but takes no vows.

Rossikon—The Monastery of St Panteleimon on Mount Athos.

The Sinaite—St Gregory of Sinai. He took the habit in the monastery on Mount Sinai around 1330. Later he went to Mount Athos and revived there the practice of contemplative life and interior prayer, especially the Prayer of Jesus.

Skete—A small monastic village where the monks live alone or in small groups and have a common church where they celebrate the Liturgy together. There is no limit to the size of a skete and some on Athos have had over six hundred members.

Skhema—The monastic habit. There are two kinds signifying the two higher degrees of the monastic life: the little skhema and the great or angelic skhema, which implies a stricter life of asceticism and prayer.

Skhimnik—A monk who has received the great skhema (*q.v.*).

Solea—In front of the inner sanctuary of the church a raised platform or step on which the singers stand and the faithful receive Holy Communion.

Starchestvo—A practice whereby the monk reveals to his staretz (*q.v.*) all his inner thoughts, intentions, and temptations, and receives his counsel. It is usually done daily, at least at the beginning of monastic life.

Staretz (pl. *startzy*)—A monk distinguished by his great piety, long experience of the spiritual life, and gift for guiding souls.

Štatny monastery—A monastery subsidized by the state, a practice begun under Catherine II (the Great) during the eighteenth century when the monasteries had been deprived of their estates. In actual practice it was usually a very meager allowance.

Stavrophoros—or *microschemos* is a lower degree of monastic profession, between that of the rassophoros and the megaloschemos (*q.v.*).

Stavrapigiac monastery—Originally a monastery founded by a patriarch and remaining under patriarchal authority, it later meant a monastery directly subject to the Holy Synod rather than to the local bishop.

The Tradition—*The Tradition of Sketic Life* written by St Nilus of Sora and commonly adopted in the East as the rule of life for sketes.

Trisagion—Or Thrice-holy Song, used in the Liturgy, is traditionally held to have been taught to Acacius in heaven in 434 and is found in the Acts of the Fourth Ecumenical Council, 451: 'Holy God, Holy Mighty, Holy Immortal One, have mercy on us.'

Trudniks—Monastic oblates.

Umilenie—A warm heart brought about in the man practicing interior prayer by a touch of the Holy Spirit.

Uverenie—The divine guidance of the heart.

Yurodivuie—A special type of Russian saint, the fool for Christ's sake. These men ridiculed the customs and manners of this world and left their fortunes, homes and families in order to live solely in the care of Divine Providence. It was a life of extreme poverty and austerity in the midst of humiliations.

Zapiskis—Notes or memoirs.

Zaštatny monastery—A monastery that did not receive a state subsidy, in contrast to a štatny monastery.

†

SELECT BIBLIOGRAPHY

Works in the English language appear in bold type.

Amman, A. *Storia della Chiesa Russa e dei paesi limitrofi.* Torino, 1948.

Behr-Siegel. *Priere et Sainteté dans L'Église Russe.* Paris, 1950.

Belyaev, J. *Razskazy iz russkoy istorii (Tales from Russian History).* 4 volumes. Moscow, 1866–72.

Bolshakoff, S. The Foreign Missions of the Russian Orthodox Church. London, 1943.

Brian-Chaninov. *L'Eglise Russe.* Paris, 1928.

Bulgakov, S. The Orthodox Church. London, 1933.

Danzas, J. The Russian Church. London, 1936.

Denisov, L. *Pravoslavnie Monastyri Rossijskoy Imperii (Orthodox Monasteries of the Russian Empire)* St Petersburg, 1910.

Dobroklonsky, A. *Rukovodstvo po istorii russkoy Tserkvi (Manual of Russian Church History)* Moscow, 1893.

Fedotov, G. The Russian Religious Mind. Cambridge, Mass., 1946.

—————— . **A Treasury of Russian Spirituality. New York, 1948.**

Florovsky, G. *Puti russkago bogosloviya (Ways of Russian Theology).* Paris, 1937.

Golubinsky, E. *Istoriya russkoy Tservki (History of the Russian Church).* Moscow, 1900–1901.

Gumilevsky, Archbishop Filaret. *Obzor Russkoy Dukhovnoy Literatury (Review of Russian Spiritual Literature)* 2 volumes. Kharkov, 1895.

Imperial Archeographic Commission, Acts. St Petersburg, 1841.

Istoriya Russkoy Ierarkhii (History of the Russian Hierarchy) 6 volumes. Moscow, 1807–15.

Klyuchevsky, V. A History of Russia. 5 volumes. London, 1911–13.

Kologrivov, I. *Essai sur la Saintete en Russie.* Bruges, 1953.
———— . *Istoriya S. S. S. R. do XIXth=go veka (History of the U.S.S.R. till the end of the XIXth Century.)* Moscow, 1945.

Leroy-Beaulieu, A. *The Empire of the Tsars and the Russians.* 3 vols. New York, 1893–96.

Lossky, V. *Essai sur la theologie mystique de l'Eglise d'Orient.* Paris, 1944. ET: *The Mystical Theology of the Orthodox Church.* Cambridge: Clarke, 1957.

Makary, Mitropolit (Bulgakov). *Istoriya Russkoy Tserkvi (History of the Russian Church).* 12 volumes. St Petersburg, 1883–1903.

Milyukov. P. *Outline of Russian Culture.* 3 vols. Philadelphia, 1942.
———— & Seignobos-Eisemann. *Histoire de Russie.* 3 vols. n.p., 1937.

Mirsky, D. *A History of Russian Literature.* **New York, 1927.**

Moine de l'Eglise d'Orient. *La Priere de Jesus.* Chevetogne, 1951.

Monk of the Eastern Church. *Orthodox Spirituality.* **London, 1945.**

Nikolsky, N. *Istoriya Russkoy Tserkvi (History of the Russian Church).* Moscow, 1930.

Pierling, P. *La Russie et la Saint Siege.* 3 vols. Paris, 1896–1901.

Platonov, S. *Geschichte Russlands vom Beginn bis zur Jetztzeit.* Leipzig, 1927.

Pravoslavnaya Bogoslovskaya Encyclopediya (Orthodox Theological Encyclopaedia). 7 volumes. St Petersburg, 1900–1907.

Pravoslavniya Obiteli Rossiiskoy Imperii (Orthodox Monasteries of the Russian Empire.) St Petersburg, n.d.

Rouet de Journel. *Monachisme et monasteres russes.* Paris, 1952.

Russkaya Istoricheskaya Biblioteka (Russian Historical Library) 34 volumes. St Petersburg, 1872–1926.

Russky Biografichesky Slovar (Russian Biographical Dictionary) 25 volumes. St Petersburg, 1896–1918.

Russky Entsiklopedichesky Slovar (Russian Encyclopedia) 41 Volumes. St Petersburg, 1890–1904.

Russkiya Letopisi, Polnoe Sobranie (Complete Collection of Russian Chronicles.) 24 volumes. St Petersburg.

Smolitsch, I. *Russisches Monchtum. Entstetung, Entwicklung und Wesen, 988–1917.* Wurzburg, 1953.

Sovietskaya Entsiklopediya (Bolshaya). Moscow—in progress.

Sumner, B. *Survey of Russian History.* New York, 1943.

Tolstoy, N. *Russkiya Svyatuini i Drevnosti (Russian Sanctuaries and Antiquities)* 3 Volumes. Moscow, 1861–66.

Tyszkiewicz, S. & Belpair, T. *Ecrits d'ascètes russes.* Namur, 1957.

Vernadsky, G. *Political and Diplomatic History of Russia.* Boston, 1936.

Zarin, P. *Asketism.* 2 volumes. St Petersburg, 1907.

Zenkovsky, V. *Istoriya Russkoy Filosofii (History of Russian Philosophy)* 2 volumes. Paris, 1948.

Zernov, N. *The Russians and their Church.* London, 1945.

Zhitiya Svyatuikh, 14 volumes. Russian Synod., 1903–1917.

Znamensky, P. *Uchebnoe Rukovodstvo po Istorii Russkoy Tserkvi (Manual of Russian Church History).* St Petersburg, 1904.

Zverinsky, V. *Material Dlya istoriko-topograficheskago izsledovaniya o pravoslavnuikh monastuiryakh v Rossiiskoy Imperii (Material for the historical topographic research on Orthodox Monasteries in the Russian Empire).* 3 volumes. St Petersburg, 1890–97.

CHAPTER ONE:
RUSSIAN MONASTERIES BEFORE THE FIFTEENTH CENTURY

Abramovich, D. *Izsledovanie o Kievo-Pecherskom Paterike kak istoriko-literaturnom pamyatnikom (Study of Kievo-Pechersky Paterikon as historico-literary monument).* St Petersburg, 1902.

Belyaev, I. *Istoriya Novgoroda Velikogo (History of Novgorod the Great).* Moscow, 1866.

Dvornik, F. *Les Slavs, Byzance et Rome au IXme siècle.* Paris, 1926.

288   *Select Bibliography*

————— , *The Making of Central and Eastern Europe.* London, 1949.

————— , *Preg. Sergii Radonezhsky.* Sergiev Posad, 1908.

Fedotov, G. *Svatuie Drevney Rusi (Saints of Ancient Russia).* Paris, 1931.

Goetz, L. *Das Kiever Höhlenkloster als Kulturzentrum der vormongolischen Zeit.* Passau, 1904.

Golubinsky, E. *Prepodobnui: Sergii Radonezhsky.* Sergiev Posad, 1892.

Grekov, B. *Kievskaya Rus (Kievian Russia).* Moscow, 1944.

Ikonnikov, V. *Opuit izsledovaniya o kulturnom znachenii Vizantii (Essay on the Cultural Importance of Byzantium).* Kiev, 1869.

Kadlubovsky. *Ocherki Zhitii Svyatuikh (Lives of the Saints).* Warsaw, 1902.

Kazansky, P. *Istoriya Russkago Monashestva do Osnovaniya Troitse-Sergievoy Lavrui (Story of Russian Monasticism to the Foundation of the Laura Troitse-Sergii).* Moscow, 1855.

Kievo-Pechersky Paterik. *Pamyatniki Russkoy Literatyrui.* Odessa, 1872.

Leib, B. *Rome, Kiev et Byzance a la fin du XI siècle (1088–1099).* Paris, 1924.

Leonid, Arkhim Kavelin. *Svyataya Rus (Holy Russia).* St Petersburg, 1891.

Nikon, I. *Zhitie Prep. Sergiya (Life of St Sergius).* Moscow, 1885.

Ostrogorsky, G. *History of the Byzantine State.* Oxford, 1956.

Pamyatniki Drevne-Russkoy Uchitelnoy Literaturui (Monuments of Ancient Russian Edifying Literature) 3 volumes. St Petersburg, 1894.

Priselkov, M. *Ocherki po tserkovno-politicheskoy istorii Kievskoy Rusi (Essays on the Ecclesiastical and Political History of Kievan Russia)* St Petersburg, 1913.

Taube, M. *Rome et la Russie avant l'invasion des Tartares.* Paris, 1947.

Vasiliev, A. *History of the Byzantine Empire, 324–1453.* Madison, 1952.

Yakovlev, N. *Kievskiya Religioznuiya Skazaniya (Kievan*

Religious Tales). Odessa, 1870.

Zernov, N. *St Sergius, Builder of Russia.* London, 1937.

CHAPTER TWO: ST NILUS OF SORA

Arkhangelsky, A. *Nil Sorsky i Vassian Patrikeev, ikh Literaturnuie Trudui i idei v drevney Rusi (Nilus Sorsky and Vassian Patrikeev, their literary works and ideas in ancient Russia).* St Petersburg, 1882.

Bulgakov, P. *Prepodobnui Josif Volokolamsky.* Moscow, 1865.

Kalestinov, N. *Veliky Staretz.* St Petersburg, 1907.

Kern, K. *Antropologiya Sv. Grigoriya Palamui.* Paris, 1950.

Kontsevich, I. *Styazhanie Svyatago Dukha v Putyakh Drevney Rusi (Acquisition of the Holy Spirit in Ancient Russia).* Paris, 1952.

Krivoshein, Basil. *The Ascetic and Theological Teaching of Gregory Palamas.* London, 1954.

Kudryavtsev, M. *Istoriya Monashestva Severo-vostochnoy Rossii (History of Russian Monasticism in North-East Russia).* Moscow, 1861.

Molchanov, Alexis, Bp. *Vizantiiskie Tserkovnuie Mistiki 14-go Veka (Byzantine Church Mystics in the Fourteenth Century).* Kazan, 1906.

Muraviev, A. *Russkaya Fifaida na Severe (Russian Northern Thebaide).* St Petersburg, 1855.

Nicholas Cabasilas. *Le Vie en Jesus.* Amay, 1932.

Prosvetitel, of St Joseph of Volokolamsk, Kazan, 1857.

Smirnov, S. *Kak sluzhili miru podvizhniki drevnei Rusi (How the Saints of Ancient Russia Served the World).* Sergiev Posad, 1903.

Sokolov, I. *Sostoyanie monashestva v Vizantiiskoy Tserkvi polovinui IX-go do XIII-go veka (State of Monastic Life in the Byzantine Church from the Middle of the Ninth till the Thirteenth Century).* Kazan, 1894.

Suirku, P. *Zhitie Grigoriya Sinaita (Life of Gregory Sinaita).* St Petersburg, 1909.

Uspensky, F. *Filosofskiya i bogoslovskiya dvizneoiya v XIV veke (Philosophical and Theological Movements in the Fourteenth Century).* Odessa, 1892.

————— , *Ocherki po istorii vizantiiskoy obrazovnanosti (Essay on Byzantine Culture).* Odessa, 1892.

CHAPTER THREE:
RUSSIAN MONASTICISM IN THE SIXTEENTH,
SEVENTEENTH, AND EIGHTEENTH CENTURIES

Andreev, V. *Raskoliego znachenie v narodnoy russkoy istorii (Schism and its Meaning in the History of the Russian People).* St Petersburg, 1870.

Avvakum, Archpriest. *Life.* London, 1926.

Barsov, T. V. *Sv. Synod v ego proshlom (Holy Synod in the Past).* Petersburg, 1896.

Bolshakoff, S. *Russian Nonconformity.* Philadelphia, 1950.

Buikovsky, J. K. *Istoriya Staroobryadchestva vsekh soglassi (History of All The Groups of the Old Ritualists),* Moscow, 1906.

Chechulin, N. *Goroda Moskovskago gosudarstva v XVI veke (Towns of the Muscovite State in the XVIth Century).* St Petersburg, 1889.

Chistovich. *Feufan Prokopovich i ego vremya (Theophane Prokopovich and His Age).* St Petersburg, 1888.

Chodynicki, K. *Kosciol Prawoslawny a Rzeczpospolita Polska 1370–1632 (The Orthodox Church in Poland from 1370 to 1632).* Warsaw, 1934.

Denisoff, E. *Maxime le Grec et l'Occident.* Paris-Louvain, 1943.

Denisov, S. *Vinograd Rossiisky (Russian Vineyard).* Moscow, 1906.

Diakonov, M. *Vlast Moskovskikh gosudarey (Power of Muscovite Sovereigns).* Moscow, 1889.

Dmitrievsky, A. *Bogosluzhenie v Russkoy Tserkvi v XVI veke (Divine Service in the Russian Church in the XVIth Century).* Kazan, 1884.

Doroshenko, D. *History of the Ukraine,* Edmonton, 1939.

Fedotov, G. *Sv. Filip, Mitropolit Moskovsky.* Paris, 1928.

Filipov. *Istoriya Vuigovskoy Staroobryadcheskoy Pustuini (Story of the Old Ritualist Vuig Monastery).* Moscow, 1862.

Select Bibliography   291

Golubev, S. *Kievsky mitropolit Petr Mogila i ego spodvizh-niki (Peter Mogila, Metropolitan of Kiev, and His Collaborators)*. Kiev, 1883.

Grass, K. *Die russischen Sekten*. Two volumes. Leipzig, 1907–1914.

Ikonnikov, V. *Maksim Grek*. Kiev, 1915.

Kapterev, N. *Kharakter otnoshenii Rossii k pravoslav-nomu vostoku v XVI i XVII stoletiyakh (Character of Relations between Russia and the Orthodox East in the XVIth and XVIIth Centuries)*. Moscow, 1885.

———— . *Patriarkh Nikon i Tsar Aleksey Mikhailovich (Patriarch Nikon and Tsar Alexis Michaelovich)*. 2 volumes. Sergiev Posad, 1909–1912.

Kharlampovich, K. *Malorossiiskoe vliyanie na Veliko Russkuyu Tserkovnuyu Zhisn*. Kazan, 1914.

Kudryavtsev, M. *Istoriya Pravoslavnago monashestva v Severo-vostochnoy Rossi do vremen prep. Sergiya Radonezhskago (Story of Russian Monasticism in North-East Russia since St Sergius of Radonezh)*. Moscow, 1861.

Lebedev, N. *Macary, Mitropolit Vserossiisky*. Moscow, 1877.

Malinin, V. *Staretz Eleazarova Monastuiry Filofei*. Kiev, 1901.

Maria [Odoevsky], Abbess. *Zapiski (Memoirs)*. Limited edition of fifty copies, Novgorod, 1912.

Morogov, P. *Feofan Prokopovich, kak pisatel (Theophane Prokopovich as a Writer)*. St Petersburg, 1880.

Nikolsky, N. *Kirillo-belozersky Monastuir*. St Petersburg, 1897.

Palmer, W. *The Patriarch Nikon*. London, 1871–76.

Pascal, P. *Avvakum et les débuts du Raskol*. Paris, 1938.

Pavlov, A. *Istorichesky Ocherk Sekulyarizatsii Tserkov-nuikh Zemel v Rossii (Historical Study of the Secularization of the Church Lands in Russia)*. n.p., 1871.

Perov, N. *Eparkhialnoe Upravlenie v Russkoy Tserkvi. (Dioscesan Administration in the Russian Church)*. Ryazan, 1882.

Pokrovsky, I. *Russkiya eparkhii v XVI–XVIII vekakh (Russian Dioceses from the XVIth to the XVIIIth Centuries)*. 2 volumes. Kazan, 1898–1913.

Runkevich, S. *Istoriya Russkoy Tserkvi v synodalny period (Study of the Russian Church in the Synodal Period)*. St Petersburg, 1900.

Shlyapkin. *Sv. Dimitry Rostovsky (1651–1708) i ego vremiya (St Demetrius of Rostov and his Time)*. St Petersburg, 1891.

Shmurlo, E. *Russkie katoliki kontsa XVII-go Veka (Russian Catholics at the End of the XVIIth Century)*. Belgrade, 1931.

Subbotin, N. *Materialui dlya istorii rakola (Materials for the History of the Schism)*. 9 volumes. Moscow, 1875–1895.

Titlinov, B. *Pravitelstvo Annui Ioannovnui i ego otnoshenie k Delam Pravoslavnoy tserkvi (The Government of the Empress Anne and its relation to the Affairs of the Orthodox Church)*. Vilno, 1905.

Tarasy [Kurganovsky]. *Perelom v Drevnerusskom Bogoslovii (Change in Old Russian Theology)*. Warsaw, 1927.

Zazykin, M. *Patriarkh Nikon*. 3 volumes. Warsaw, 1931–38.

Zernov, N. **Moscow: The Third Rome**. London, 1937.

Znamensky, I. *Polozhenie dukkhovenstva v tsarstvovanie Ekaterinui II i Pavla I (The Situration of the Clergy in the Reign of Catherine II and Paul I)*. Moscow, 1880.

CHAPTER IV:
ST TIKHON ZADONSKY

Arndt, J. *Vier Bücher vom wahren Christentum*. Hamburg, 1724–27.

Blagovidov, T. *Ober-prokururui sv. Synoda v 18 veke i v pervoy polovine 19 veka (High Procurators of the First half of the Nineteenth Century)*. Second edition. Kazan, 1899.

Gorodetzky, N. **The Humiliated Christ in Modern Russian Thought**. London, 1938.

——, **Saint Tikhon Zadonsky, Inspirer of Dostoevsky**. London, 1951.

Hall, Joseph. *The Art of Divine Meditation*. London, 1607.

————, *Meditations. Newly enlarged with ten vows.* London, 1609.

Poselyanin, E. *Ocherki iz istorii russkoy tserkovnoy i dukhovnoy zhizni v XVIII veke (Stories from the Russian Church and Spiritual Life of the Eighteenth Century).* St Petersburg, 1902.

Lebedev, A. *Svyatitel Tikhon Zadonsky i vseya Rossii chudotvoretz, ego zhizn, pisaniya i proslavlenie (St Tikon Zadonsky, Russian Miracle worker. His Life, Writings, and Canonization).* St Petersburg, 1865.

Popov, M. *Arseny Macejvich i ego Delo (Arseny Macejvich and his Work).* St Petersburg, 1912.

Runkevich, S. *Istoriya Aleksandro-Nevskoy Lavrui (1713–1913). (History of the Lavra of St Alexander Nevsky).* St Petersburg, 1913.

Tvoreniya izhe vo svyatuikh otza Nashego Tikhona Zadonskago. 6th edition. *(Works of St Tikhon Zadonsky)* 5 volumes. Moscow, 1898–1899.

Znamensky, P. *Dukhovnuie shkolui v Rossii do reformui 1808 goda (Clerical Schools in Russia till the Reform of 1808).* Kazan, 1881.

CHAPTER FIVE:
PAISIUS VELICHKOVSKY

Barsky-Grigorovich, V. *Puteschestviya po sv. Mestam Evropui, Azii i Afriki (Travels to the Holy Places of Europe, Asia, and Africa).* St Petersburg, 1788.

Chetverikov, S. *Moldavsky Staretz skhi-arkhimandrit Paisii Velichkovsky.* 2 volumes. Petseri, 1932.

Hausherr, I. *La methode d'oraison hésychaste.* Orientalia christiana, 36. Rome, 1927.

Lot-Borodine, M. *La doctrine de la deification dans l'église grecque jusqu'au XI siècle,* Revue de l'Histoire des Religions, 105–108 (1932–33).

Porfiry Uspensky, Bishop. *Istoriya Afona.* 4 volumes. Kiev–St Petersburg, 1877–92.

Sokolov, I. *Sv. Grigory Palama, Arkhiepiskop Fessaloniksky, ego trudui i uchenie ob isikhii (St Gregory Palamas, Archbishop of Thessaloniki, his Words and*

Doctrine on Hesychia). Moscow, 1913.

Vostorgnutuie Paisius. *Vostorgnutuie Klasui (Harvest).* Moscow, 1849.

Zhitie i pisaniya moldavaskago Startza Paisiya Velichkov-skago (The Life and Writings of the Moldavian Staretz Paisius Velichkovsky). Moscow, 1892.

CHAPTER VI:
RUSSIAN MONASTICISM IN THE NINETEENTH CENTURY

Arseniev, N. *Holy Moscow.* London, 1940.

Feofaniya [Gotovtseva], Abbess. *S pismami k Vuisochai-shim Osobam i Arkhm Feofanu (Letters to the Imperial Family and to Archimandrite Theophan).* St Petersburg, 1868.

Georgy Zatvornik. *Pisma v Boze pochivayushchago Zatvornika Zadonskago Bogoroditskago Monastuirya Georgiya s prisovokupleniem Kratkago izvestiya o zhizni ego (Letters of George the Recluse with an appendix containing his short life).* 2nd edition in two volumes. Moscow, 1844.

Poselyanin, E. *Russkie Podvizhniki XIX veka (Russian Ascetics of the Nineteenth Century).* St Petersburg, 1910.

Shakhova, E. *Pamyatnuiya Zapiski o zhizni igumenii Marii, osnovatelnitsui Spaso-Borodinskago Obshchezhitelna-go Monastuirya (Memoirs of the Life of the Abbess Mary, Foundress of the Spaso-Borodinsky Cenobitic Monastery).* St Petersburg, 1865.

Shilder, N. *Imperator Aleksandr I.* Four volumes. St Petersburg, 1904.

Skazanie o zhisni i podvigagakh startza Kievo-Pecherskoy Lavrui ieroskhimonakha Parfeniya (Relation of the Life and Words of Staretz Parthenius of the Lavra of Kievo-Pechersky). Kiev, 1898.

Tyszkiewicz, S. *Moralistes de Russie.* Rome, 1951.

Zapiski Igumenii Taisii, Nastoyatelnitsui Pervoklassnago Leushinskago Monastuirya (Notes of Taisiya, Abbess of Leushin). Petrograd, 1916.

Zhisneopisaniya Otechestvennuikh podvizhnikov blago-

chestiya 18 i 19 vekov (Lives of Russian Ascetics of the Eighteenth and Nineteenth Centuries) 14 volumes. Moscow, 1907–12.

Znosko, V. *Krista radi yurodivny Ieroskhimonakh Feofil, podvizhniki Prozorlivetz Kievo-Pecherskoy Lavrui (Megaloschemos Theophilus, Fool for Christ's Sake and Prophet of the Lavra of Kievo-Pechersky).* Kiev, 1906.

CHAPTER VII:
ST SERAFIM OF SAROV

Beausobre, J. *Flame in the Snow.* London, n.d.

Chichagov, L. *Letopis Serafimo-Diveevskago Monastuirya (Chronicle of Serafimo-Diveev Monastery).* Moscow, 1896.

Colloquio del grande santo russo Serafino di Sarov con N. A. Motovilov sulle mete della vita cristiana. Rome, 1944.

Denisov, L. *Zhitie prepodobnago otza nashego Serafima Sarovskago (Life of St Serafim of Sarov).* Moscow, 1904.

Dobbie-Bateman, A. *St Seraphim of Sarov.* London, 1936.

Iliin, V. *Prepodobnui Serafim Sarovsky.* Paris, 1930.

Nilus, S. *Svyatuinya pod spudom. Taina monasheskago dukha (Hidden Sanctuary. The Mystery of the Monastic Spirit).* Sergiev Posad, 1911.

Obshchitelnaya Sarovskaya Pustuin i Dostopamyatnuie inoki v nei podvizavshiesya (Cenobitic Sarov Monastery and its Memorable Monks) Moscow, 1884.

Petrov, G. *Prepodobnui Serafim Sarovsky.* Moscow, 1903.

Pisma Filareta Mitropolita Moskovskago i Kolomenskago k Vuisochaishim Osobam i Raznuim Drugim litsam (Letters of Filaret, Metropolitan of Moscow to August Persons, and Various Other People). Tver, 1888.

Poselyanin, E.. *Prepodobnui Serafim Sarovsky Chudotvoretz.* St Petersburg, 1903.

Serafimo-Diveevsky Obshchezhitelny Monastuir (Serafimo-

Diveev Cenobitic Monastery) Moscow, 1874.

Skazaniya o podvigakh zhizni startza Serafima (Relations of the Life and Deeds of Staretz Serafim). St Petersburg, 1849.

Svatui Serafim. Odessa, 1903.

Volzmsky, V. *V obiteli prepodobnago Serafima (In the Monastery of St Serafim)*. Moscow, 1914.

Yuriev, V. *Zhizn, podvigi, chudesa i otkruitie moschei prep. Serafima (Life, Works, Miracles, and Canonization of St Serafim)*. Moscow, 1904.

Zhitie i podvigi ieroskhimonakha Ioanna, osnovatelya i pervonachalnika Sarovskoy Pustuini (The Life and Works of John, Founder of Sarov Monastery). Murom, 1892.

CHAPTER VIII:
BISHOP IGNATIUS BRYANCHANINOV

Ignatius (Bryanchaninov), Bishop. *Sochineniya (Opera)*. Four volumes. St Petersburg, 1865–67.

————. *O molitve Iisusovoy (On the Prayer of Jesus)*. St Petersburg, 1867.

————. *Otechnik. Izbrannuiya izrecheniya svyatuikh inokov i povesti iz zhizni ikh (Paterikon. Selected Sayings of Holy Monks and Tales from their Lives)*. 4th edition. St Petersburg, 1903.

————. *On the Prayer of Jesus.* London, 1952.

Shilder, N. *Imperator Nikolai I*. Two volumes. St Petersburg, 1908.

Sokolov, L. *Episkop Ignaty Bryanchaninov. Ego zhizn, lichnost i moralnoasketicheskiya vozzreniya (Bishop Ignatius Bryanchaninov, His Life, Personality, and Ascetical Views)* Two volumes. Kiev, 1915.

Zhizneopisanie Episkopa Ignatiya Bryanchaninova sostavlennoe ego blishnimi i pisma Preosvyashchennago k blizkim emu litsam (The Life of Bishop Ignatius Bryanchaninov, composed by his close friends, and Letters of the Bishop to his Friends). St Petersburg, 1881.

CHAPTER IX:
STARETZ OF OPTINO

Adrian, Ieromonakh. *Rukovodstvo k Dukhovnoy zhizni startza Adriana (Guide to the Spiritual Life of Staretz Adrian)*. 2 vols. St Petersburg, 1861.

Agapit, Arkhimandrit. *Zhizneopisanie v Boze pochivshago Optinskago Startza ieroskhimonakha Ambrosiya (Life of Staretz Ambrose)*. 2 vols. Moscow, 1900.

Amvrosy (Grenkov). *Sobranie pisem optinskago startza Amvrosiya k monashestvyushchim (Letters of Staretz Ambrose to Religious)* 2 vols. Sergiev Posad, 1908–1909.

Antony (Putilov), Abbot. *Pisma k raznuim litsam Igumena Antoniya (Letters to Various Persons of Abbot Anthony)*. Moscow, 1869.

Beausobre, J. *Russian Letters of Direction, 1834–60: Macarius, Staretz of Uptino*. London, 1944.

Bolshakoff, S. *The Doctrine of the Unity of the Church in the Works of Khomyakov and Moebler*. London, 1946.

Chetverikov, S. *Zhizneopisanie optinskago startza, ieroskhimonakha Amvrosiya (Life of Staretz Ambrose)*. Kozelsk, 1912.

———. *Optina Pustuin (Optino Monastery)*. Paris, 1926.

Grigory, Arkhim. *Skazanie o zhizni optinskago startza otza ieroskhimonakha Amvrosiya (Life of Staretz Ambrose)*. Moscow, 1893.

Juvenaly, Arkhim. *Zhizneopisanie nastoyatelya Kozelskoy Vedenskoy Optnoy pustuini Arkhimandrita Moiseya (Life of Archimandrite Moses, Abbot of Optino)*. Moscow, 1882.

Kologrivof, I. *Constantino Leontjev, la sua vita e il suo pensiero*. Brescia, 1949.

Leonii, Arkhim (Kavelin). *Istoricheskoe Opisanie Kozelskoy Optinoy Pustuini (Historical Description of Optino Monastery)*. St Petersburg, 1862.

Leontiev, K. *Pravoslavnui nemetz Otetz Kliment Soderholm, ieromonakh Optinoy pustuini (Fr Clement Soderholm, monk of Optino)*. Warsaw, 1880.

Makary, Staretz. *Sobranie pisem blazhennuiya pamyati optinskago startza ieroskhimonakha Makariya K monashestvuiyuschchim (Letters of Staretz Macarius to Religious).* Moscow, 1862.

————. *Sobranie pisem blazhennuiya pamyati optinskago startza ieroskhimonakha Makariya (Letters of Staretz Macarius to Lay folk),* 2nd edition. Moscow, 1880.

————. *Pisma optinskago startza ieroskhimonakha Makariya k blagochestivoy Kristianke (Letters of Staretz Macarius to a Christian Lady).* Sergiev Posad, 1911.

Mochulsky, K. *Dukhovnui put Gogolya (The Spiritual Road of Gogol).* Paris, 1934.

————. *Dostoevsky.*

————. *Vladimir Soloviev.*

Ocherk Zhizni nastoyatelya Optinoy pustuini Arkhimandrita Isaakiya (Life of Isaac, Abbot of Optino). Moscow, 1899.

Orlovsky. *Pustuinniki Roslavlskikh Lesov (Hermits of the Forest of Roslavl).* Smolensk, 1904.

Pervy Veliky Staretz Optinsky, Ieroskhimonakh Leonid (First Great Staretz of Optino, Megaloschemos Leonid–Leo). Shamordino, 1917.

Skazanie o zhizni i podvigakh startza Optinoy pustuini, ieroskhimonakha Makariya (The Life of Staretz Macarius, by Archimandrite Leonid Kavelin*).* Moscow, 1861.

Smolitsch, I. *Leben und Lehre der Starzen.* Vienna, 1936.

Sumarokov. *Staretz Makary Optinsky.* Harbin, 1940.

Zhizn, Monakha i pustuinnozhitelya Vasiliska (Life of Vasilisk, monk and hermit). Moscow, 1849.

Zhitie i podvigi Boze pochivshago skhimonakha Zosimui, ego izrechenniya i izvlecheniya iz ego sochinenii (The Life and Sayings of Father Zosima). Moscow, 1889.

CHAPTER TEN:
BISHOP THEOPHAN THE RECLUSE

Briefe eines Starzen. Russische Frommigkeit. (Extracts from Letters on Christian Life of Theophan).

Tr. N. von Bubnov. Wiesbaden, 1947.

Dobrotolyubie. Theophane's Tr. of *Philokalia.* 6 vols. Moscow, 1884–1905.

English translation: *Dobrotolyubie of Theophane.* London: Faber and Faber.

Klyucharev, A. *Feofan Zatvornik.* Kazan, 1904.

Korsunsky, I. *Svyatitel Feofan Zatvornik i podvizhnik Vuishenskoy Pustuini (Bishop Theophane, Recluse and Ascetic of Vuisha Monastery).* Moscow, 1899.

Smirnov, P. *Zhizn i uchenie preosvyashchennago Feofana, vuishenskago zatvornika (The Life and Teaching of Bishop Theophane, Recluse of Vuisha).* Shatzk, 1905.

Theophane the Recluse. *Muisli na kazhdui den goda (Thought on Every Day of the Year).* Moscow, 1881.

————. *Tolkovanie pastuirskikh poslanii sv. Apostola Pavla (Commentary on the Pastoral Epistles of the Apostle Paul).* Moscow, 1882.

————. *Slova na Gospodskie, bogorodichnuie i torzhestvennuie dni (Sermons on the Festivals of the Lord, Our Lady, and others).* Moscow, 1883.

————. *Psalom 118 istolkovanny (Commentary on Psalm 119).* 2nd edn. Moscow, 1891.

————. *Chto est zhizn dukhovnaya i Kak na nee nastroitsya (What is Spiritual Life and how to begin it).* 3rd Edition. Odessa, 1891.

————. *Pisma k raznuim litsam u raznuikh predmetakh verui i zhizni (Letters to various Persons on Various Subjects of Faith and Life).* 2nd edn. Moscow, 1892.

————. *Tolkovanie poslaniya sv. Apostola Pavla k Ephesyanam (Commentary on the Epistle to the Ephesians).* 2nd edn. Moscow, 1893.

————. *Tolkovanie poslaniya sv. Apostola Pavla k Galatam (Commentary on the Epistle to the Galatians).* 2nd edn. Moscow, 1893.

————. *Tolkovanie poslanii sv. Apostola Pavla k Filipiitsam i Solunyanam I-ro II-go (Commentary on the Epistles to the Philippians and Thessalonians).* Moscow, 1895.

————. *Nachertanie khristianskago nravoucheniya (Christian Moral Teaching).* Moscow, 1895.

———. *Tolkovanie poslanii sv. Apostola Pavla kolossayam i k Filimony (Commentary on the Epistle to the Colossians and to Philemon)*. Moscow, 1899.

———. *Sobranie pisem (Collected Letters)*. 6 vols. n.p. 1898–99.

———. *O pravoslavii s predosterezheniyami ot pogreshnostei protiv nego (On Orthodoxy with a Warning about Sinning Against It)*. Moscow, 1902.

———. *Pisma o Dukhovnoy zhizni (Letters on the Spiritual Life)*. 4th ed. Moscow, 1903.

———. *Put ko spaseniyu (The Way to Salvation)*. 9th edn. Moscow, 1908.

———. *O pokayanii, prichaschenii sv. Khristovnikh tain i ispravlenii zhizni (On Repentence, Communion, and Correction of Life)*. 6th edn. Moscow, 1909.

———. *Tolkovanie pervago poslaniya sv. Apostola Pavla k Korinfyanam (Commentary on the First Epistle to the Corinthians)*. Sergiev Posad, 1913.

———. *Tolkovanie Vtorogo poslaniya sv. Apostola Pavla Korinfyanam (Commentary on the Second Epistle to the Corinthians)*. Sergiev Posad, 1913.

———. *Tolkovanie poslaniya sv. Apostola Pavla k Rimlyanam (Commentary on the Epistle to the Romans)*. Sergiev Posad, 1913.

CHAPTER XI:
RUSSIAN MONASTICISM IN THE TWENTIETH CENTURY

Anderson, P. *People, Church and State in Modern Russia*. New York, 1944.

Bolshakoff, S. *The Christian Church and the Soviet State*. London, 1943.

———. 'Le Metropolite Antoine de Kiev,' *Irénikon*. Sept. Oct. 1936.

———. 'Christian Unity. A Personal Study of A Great Problem.' *Voice of the Church*. Lisle, Illinois, 1941–44.

Curtiss, J. *State and Church in Russia, 1901–1907*. New York, 1940.

Fedotov, G. *The Russian Church Since the Revolution*. London, 1928.

Georgievsky, Evlogy, Mitropolit. *Put moei zhizni (The Way of My Life).* Paris, 1947.

Hecker, J. **Religion and Communism.** London, 1933.

Johansen, Alf. *Den Russiske Kirke i Dag.* Copenhagen, 1950.

Letopis Sv. *Andreevskago Skitana Afone, 1841–1863* (Chronicle of St Andrew, Skete on Mount Athos). Moscow, 1911.

Nikon, Rklytsky, Bishop. *Zhisneopisanie Blazhenneishago Antoniya Mitropolita Kievskago i Galitskago (The Life of Anthony Metropolitan of Kiev).* 2 vols. New York, 1956–57.

Palmieri, Aurelis. *La Chiesa Russa.* Florence, 1908.

Parfeny, Inok. *Skazanie o stranstvii i puteshestvii po Russii, Moldavii, Turtsii i Svyatoy Zemle (Tale of Wandering and Travelling in Russia, Moldavia, Turkey and the Holy Land).* 4 vols. Moscow, 1855.

Patriarkh Sergy i ego dukhovnoe nasledstvo (Patriarch Sergius and His Spiritual Inheritance). Moscow, 1947.

Russky Manestuir Sv. Velikomuchenika i Tselitelya Panteleimona na Svyatoy Gore Afonskoy (The Russian Monastery of St Panteleimon on Mount Athos). Moscow, 1886.

Strannik. **Otkrovennuie Razskazui Dukhovnomy otzu svoemu (Sincere Tales of a Pilgrim to his Spiritual Father).** 3rd edn. Kazan, 1884.

French translation by J. Gauvain. 'Récits d'un pèlerin russe,' Cahiers du Rhône 12. Neuchâtel, 1945.

English translation by R. M. French. *The Way of a Pilgrim.* London, 1943. (This translation also includes the so-called second part, which is absent in the original manuscript.)

Greek translation by Archimandrite Panteleimon Karanikola of Apostoliki Diakonia, Athens. (The same archimandrite cooperated in the new edition of the Philokalia at Athens, which is finely produced. The first edition of the Philokalia, which appeared in Venice in 1782, contains in its first part writings of the following Fathers and mystics: Anthony the Great, Isaiah, Evagrius, Cassian, Mark, Hesychius, John Damascene, Philemon, Theognost, Philotheus of

Sinai, Elias and Theophane. The second part includes writings of Peter of Damascus, Symeon Metaphraste, Symeon the New Theologian, Nicetas Stethatos, Theolepte, Nicephoros, Gregory Sinaita, Gregory Palamas, Callixte, and Ignatius Xanthopoulos, Callixte the Patriarch, Callixte Angelikoudes, Callixte Cataphygiotes, Symeon of Thessalonica, Mark of Ephesus, Maximus Kausocaliptis. Paisius, translating the Philokalia made little change, but Theophane the Recluse did a lot. He devoted a whole new volume to St Theodore Studiee, for example.)

Timashev, N. *Religion in Soviet Russia.* 1917-1942.
Zametki Poklonnika Svyatoy Gorui. (Notes of a Pilgrim to the Holy Mountain). Kiev, 1864.

CHAPTER XII:
RUSSIAN MYSTICS OF THE TWENTIETH CENTURY

Amand de Mendieta, E. *Le Presqu'ile des Calvyers.* Bruges, 1955.

Bolshakoff, S. *Contemporary Mystics, Vol. I. Father Michael, Recluse of Uusi valamo.* Oxford, 1956 (private, limited edition).

——. 'The Monastic Republic of Mount Athos.' *Social Justice Review.* St Louis, 1957.

Byron, Roberto. *Monte Athos, Paese governato du Dio.* Milan, 1952.

Dawkins, R. M. *The Monks of the Athos.* London, 1936.

Dölger, F. *Mönchsland Athos.* Munich, 1943.

Hasluck. *Athos and its Monasteries.* London, 1924.

Hilarion, Skhimonakh. *Na Gorakh Kavkaza (In the Mountains of the Caucasus).* 2nd edn. Batalpashinsk, 1910.

Muraviev, A. *Puteshestvie po svyatuim mestam russkim (Travels to Russian Holy Places).* St Petersburg, 1837.

Nikolai, Metropolite de Krutitci. *Sermons.* Paris, 1956.

Opisanie Valaamskago Monastuirya (Description of Valaam Monastery). St Petersburg, 1895.

Ostrov Valaam i tamoshny monastuir (Island of Valaam and the Monastery There). St Petersburg, 1852.

Sandberg, B. *Valamo*. Helsinki, 1936

Semenov-Tyan-Shansky, A. *Otetz Ioann Kronshtadtsky*. New York, 1955.

Sofrony, Ierom. *Staretz Siluan*. Paris, 1952.

Truitsky, S. *Ob imenaku Bozhiikh i imyabozhnikakh (On Divine Names and Onomolaters)*. St Petersburg, 1914.

Valaamsky Monastuir i ego podvizhniki (Valaam Monastery and its Ascetics). 3rd edn. St. Petersburg, 1903.

Valaamskoe Slovo o Valaamskom Monastuire (Valaam Word of Valaam Monastery). St Petersburg, 1871.

CISTERCIAN
PUBLICATIONS

Titles Listing

1977

THE CISTERCIAN FATHERS SERIES

THE WORKS OF BERNARD OF CLAIRVAUX

Treatises I (Apologia to Abbot William, On Precept and Dispensation) CF 1

On the Song of Songs I CF 4

On the Song of Songs II CF 7

Treatises II (The Steps of Humility, On Loving God) CF 13

Five Books on Consideration CF 37

THE WORKS OF WILLIAM OF ST THIERRY

On Contemplating God, Prayer, Meditations CF 3

Exposition on the Song of Songs CF 6

The Enigma of Faith CF 9

The Golden Epistle CF 12

THE WORKS OF AELRED OF RIEVAULX

Treatises I (On Jesus at the Age of Twelve, Rule for a Recluse, The Pastoral Prayer) CF 2

Spiritual Friendship CF 5

THE WORKS OF GUERRIC OF IGNY

Liturgical Sermons
two volumes CF 8, CF 32

OTHER WRITERS

The Letters of Adam of Perseigne CF 21

The Way of Love CF 16

John of Ford, *Sermons on The Song of Songs* CF 29

THE CISTERCIAN STUDIES SERIES

CISTERCIAN STUDIES

The Cistercian Spirit: A Symposium in Memory of Thomas Merton CS 3

The Eleventh-century Background of Citeaux by Bede Lackner CS 8

Studies in Medieval Cistercian History, edited Joseph F. O'Callahan CS 13

Contemplative Community edited M. Basil Pennington CS 21

Bernard of Clairvaux: Studies Presented to Dom Jean Leclercq CS 23

William of St Thierry: The Man and His Work by J. M. Dechanet CS 10

Thomas Merton: The Man and His Work by Dennis Q. McInerny CS 27

Cistercian Sign Language by Robert Barakat CS 11

Studies in Medieval Cistercian History, II ed. John R. Sommerfeldt CS 24

Bernard of Clairvaux and the Cistercian Spirit by Jean Leclercq CS 16

MONASTIC TEXTS AND STUDIES

The Climate of Monastic Prayer by Thomas Merton CS 1

Evagrius Ponticus: Praktikos and Chapters on Prayer CS 4

The Abbot in Monastic Tradition by Pierre Salmon CS 14

Why Monks? by Francois Vandenbroucke CS 17

Silence: Silence in the Rule of St Benedict by Ambrose Wathen CS 22

The Sayings of the Desert Fathers tr Benedicta Ward CS 59

One Yet Two: Monastic Tradition East and West CS 29

The Spirituality of Western Christendom ed. E. R. Elder CS 30

Russian Mystics by Sergius Bolshakoff CS 26

In Quest of The Absolute by Joseph Weber CS 51